More Than Just a Union

The Story of the NFFAWU

More Than Just a Union

The Story of the NFFAWU

Gordon Inglis

Jesperson Press
St. John's, Newfoundland
1985

Jesperson Press
26A Flavin Street
St. John's, Newfoundland

Cover & Text Design: Sheila Gillard Studio Ltd.
Typesetting: Jesperson Printing
Printed and Bound in Canada.

The publisher acknowledges the assistance of the *Cultural Affairs Division* of the Department of Culture, Recreation and Youth of the Government of Newfoundland and Labrador which has helped make this publication possible.

Appreciation is expressed to the *Canada Council* for its assistance in publishing this work.

Cataloguing in Publication Data

Inglis, Gordon.
More Than Just a Union

Bibliography: p.
Includes index.
ISBN 0-920502-60-1

1. Newfoundland Fishermen, Food and Allied Workers — History. I. Title.

HD6528.F652N48 1985 331.88'1392'09718 C85-099097-1

For Dorothy,
who also knows something about organizing.

Table of Contents

Preface

In the spring of 1970, the St. John's *Evening Telegram* carried an article entitled "Newfoundland in the Protest Age." Citizens of Cox's Cove, Hallstown, McIvers, Brown's Arm, the Blackhead Road and a dozen other places were out with placards, demanding the attention of their government to problems ranging from the closing of a hospital to dust from road construction falling on newly-washed clothes. The sources of their annoyance were immediate and specific, but their choice of means of expressing it was part of a much wider phenomenon affecting the entire Western world.

In Canada, it was the time of the FLQ and the October Crisis, of the Just Society and the Company of Young Canadians, of Women's Lib, student revolt, American war-resisters, and the movement for Native rights. In Newfoundland the swirling currents of challenge, experiment, and social innovation mingled with more local ones generated by two decades of rapid social change brought on by Confederation. It was the time of the Northern Regional Development Association and the Fogo Island Co-op, of the *Alternate Press*, the New Labrador Party, and the Mummer's Troupe. Of all the organizations born in the province in that turbulent era, perhaps none has had such a profound effect on its society as the Newfoundland Fishermen, Food, and Allied Workers' Union.

This book is an attempt to tell the story of the NFFAWU — or perhaps more accurately, *a* story, since other people will have different perspectives on the events described here, and some will feel that important pieces have been left out. In any case, the day-to-day happenings on which it is based are still going on; new chapters are being lived, and remain to be written.

It may well be asked why a social anthropologist should presume to take on such a task, one that seems more appropriate to an historian or a journalist. I was led to it by an interest in social change — in the forces that cause people to act and react in ways that alter the circumstances of their lives. The fishermen's union seemed to provide a neat case-study through which an important period in the life of Newfoundland society could be explored. Beyond all that, and academic considerations apart, it is a rattling good tale, full of real-life drama, and excitement, and humour.

The sources on which the pages that follow are based range from newspaper reports to government documents to interviews tape-recorded by journalists on the spot when things were happening. Mostly, however, I have made use of oral testimony by people who were directly involved in the events described, either as participants or observers. Wherever possible, I have tried to present the story as they told it, in their own words. In some cases I have attempted to represent not merely what they said to me, but how they said it — the flavour and rhythm of their speech. This is a bold and somewhat dangerous undertaking, for it is not easy to depict speech-patterns in print, and the author who tries to do it risks giving offence. I can only hope that the people I have quoted will not be offended: the eloquence and colour of what they told me deserves to be recorded, however inadequately, and the risk seems worth taking.

Although my original intention was an analysis of social change, I quickly found that the narrative kept taking precedence. The story demanded to be told, and I have tried to tell it. I have also, however, tried to set it in its many contexts. This has required comment not merely on matters social and cultural, where I can claim at least some competence, but also on the fishing industry where I can claim little or none. The Newfoundland fishery is a vastly complex organism; even the experts cannot agree on how it works or even what it is. To those readers who will find my discussion of it inadquate I offer no apology, but ask their forbearance. My purpose has been to tell the story of the fishermen's union, and I have trespassed on their preserves only when it could not be avoided.

One aspect of the story that will undoubtedly be widely noticed is the relative infrequency with which women are mentioned in its pages. This is not, I sincerely hope, an oversight on my part but rather an accurate reflection of the times. Although during the period covered women made up a rapidly-increasing proportion of the work-force in the processing plants and were even occasionally represented in the boats, and although many of them played a role at the local level in their union, they have hot played a commensurate role in its leadership. This situation is now changing, and in future accounts of the NFFAWU women will undoubtedly have a much more prominent place.

I am deeply indebted to many people for co-operation and assistance extended during the preparation of this book. I wish to offer my sincere thanks to the Social Sciences and Humanities Research Council of Canada, which provided a fellowship that supported part of the research; to Memorial University of Newfoundland for granting a sabbatical leave; to Tom Nemec of the University's anthropology department who generously made available his extensive files of newspaper clippings; to Lester Janes of Burgeo who kindly lent me a scrapbook of the Burgeo strike; to Dave Quinton of the CBC who made available a file of historic audio tapes; to Stratford Canning who made available written material and much helpful advice; to Peter Sinclair who provided information and encouragement; to the staff at Memorial's Centre for Newfoundland Studies and at the A.C. Hunter Library's Newfoundland Collection; to the staff and officers of the NFFAWU; to Anne Douglas and Marilyn Furlong who typed the manuscript with patience and skill; and to Angela Rebeiro of Jesperson Press, who saw it through the publication process.

Mostly, I wish to thank the men and women with no professional connection with the work, members of the NFFAWU and others, who took time out from their own busy lives to talk to me and provide the material on which the book is mainly based: Rev. Charles Abraham, Anne Alexander, Raoul Anderson, James K. Bell, Frank Benoit, Philip Benoit, Frank Benn, Harvey Best, Charles Borsk, Rev. Joe Burke, Kevin Carroll, Richard Cashin, Rosann Cashin, Frank Chafe, George Coley, Kevin Condon, Ed Finn, Austin Green, Leslie Harris, Anne Hart, Les Janes, Ed Johnson, Lester Kean, Berch Lake, Harold Lake, Spencer Lake, Ray Larkin, George Lavers, Elliott Leyton, Fred Locking, Dan MacDonald, Jim MacDonald, Earle McCurdy, Rev. Des. McGrath, Pat Marchak, Ed Maynard, Neil Murray, John Myles, Levi George Norris, Ralph O'Keefe, Woodrow Philpott, Dave Quinton, Dan Seymour, Max Short, Bill Short, Gordon Slade, Robert Spence, Roger Stirling, Cyril Strong, Gilles Theriault, Pearl Warren, William Warren, Lawrence Willnough and Tom Wise.

To reduce distraction for the reader, numerals indicating footnotes have not been included in the text. Information on the sources quoted or otherwise referred to is given page-by-page in a section entitled "Notes and References" beginning on page 301.

Chapter 1

The Great Northern Peninsula of Newfoundland stretches northward from the main body of the island like a pointing finger. At its base the deep fjords and timbered slopes of Gros Morne provide spectacular scenery reminiscent of Norway or British Columbia: to the north the Long Range Mountains move inland and the St. Barbe coast lies low and gravelly, constantly swept by westerly winds that blow across the choppy waters or the winter ice of the Gulf of St. Lawrence. It is a landscape of sand dunes, gravel banks, rocks tortuously carved by wind and ocean, and sparse, tough vegetation that leans inland, away from the sea.

Until 1904, this was part of the French Shore, where fishing rights had been guaranteed to France by the Treaty of Paris in 1763 and the settlement rights of Newfoundlanders restricted. Through the first half of the twentieth century it remained a nearly-forgotten corner, matched in remoteness and isolation only by the coast of Labrador and characterized mainly by its deficiencies. In the early 1960s, a road was pushed through but it was rugged and often impassable. The sixty-odd tiny settlements strung out over two hundred miles from Sally's Cove to St. Anthony ranged in size from five or six hundred people down to little clusters of three or four houses with fifteen or twenty inhabitants; most of them were on the provincial government's list for resettlement into what were euphemistically called "growth centres." There was no municipal or regional government. The coast received no television; radio reception was poor and spotty. There were no banking facilities, no access to daily newspapers, no libraries, no recreation facilities. There were virtually no water and sewer systems, and many settlements had no electricity. One- and two-room schools were housed in trailers and jerry-built temporary classrooms: in some of them thirty or forty children used a single toilet that could be flushed only once a day because of an inadequate septic system, and in at least one of them the hall floors were often inches deep in snow that sifted through cracks around the door.

In spite of its disadvantages, however, the area was not stagnant. By the 1960s a new generation had grown up—young people in their twenties and thirties who, despite the isolation and poor services, were better educated and held wider aspirations than their parents. Many had been away studying or working or with the armed services, and came back with new ideas. In 1967, with the assistance of Father Murphy, the parish priest, and the Extension Service of Memorial University, they formed the Northern Regional Development Association, a self-help organization that began to press for better services and improvement in economic conditions. The Association's self-imposed task was to convince both federal and provincial governments and private industry of the possibilities for development. All along the coast the fishery had great potential, but the fishermen needed better facilities for boats and gear, and a better means of marketing their catch. About mid-way up the peninsula was a cluster of towns within a few miles of each other that could become the hub of the area's development—Hawkes Bay for lumbering and pulpwood, and Port Saunders and Port au Choix as centres of the fishery. The Association grew rapidly in size and influence, and within a year was a force to be reckoned with.

In the summer of 1968, a new priest arrived in Port Saunders in a battered Volkswagen, accompanied by a large Newfoundland dog. The Reverend Desmond McGrath was six feet two, burly, broad-shouldered, and, at thirty-three, already balding. The dog, Tam, was shaggy and black, weighed almost as much as his master and, according to some unsympathetic observers, was usually in need of a bath. Both were destined to make their mark on the St. Barbe Coast.

Taking over the parish was a new experience for Father McGrath. He had grown up in the industrial town of Corner Brook, gone to university in Nova Scotia, studied theology in Toronto, and spent his first seven years as a priest back in Corner Brook at the Cathedral Parish. He had visited the Northwest Coast and other rural areas of Newfoundland, but only for short periods. Now, he found himself in sole charge of a parish consisting of a 150 miles of primitive coastline and equally primitive road, responsible for the spiritual guidance of about one third of its seven or eight thousand inhabitants. He had long believed that the Church could not minister to peoples' souls without taking account of the total condition of their lives, and he made it his first concern to learn how his new charges lived.

Soon the tall priest, the little car, and the big black dog were familiar sights from one end of Holy Family Parish to the other. Looking back thirteen years later, a Port au Choix man remembered: "I believe Father Des had a cup of tea in every house on this coast. Didn't matter if they were R.C. or Church of England, or anything else. And he was welcome, too, wherever he went." And another: "Yes, sir, he'd come wherever people was—down to the wharf, aboard of our boats . . . He's the first priest—first clergyman of any denomination—that I ever seen in a bar. He'd come right in, sit down with you and have a drink."

"The dog was right sociable, too," grins another. "I daresay half the dogs on the Northern Peninsula today is descended from him."

Father McGrath learned quickly, and much of what he learned was disquieting. Educational facilities were improving, but they were still far behind: the children of one small community in the parish did not go to school at all during his first winter because no teachers could be found for its shabby little two-room school. It was a time of change. People were leaving some of the smaller communities for the "growth centres" at Port Saunders and Port au Choix, but those centres were ill-prepared to receive them. Peoples' expectations were rising, but opportunities were not keeping pace. Unemployment was high, and incomes low.

Father McGrath threw himself into the life of the parish. On Sundays he travelled 150 miles to celebrate three masses. He coached a hockey team. He supported the Northern Regional Development Association. When a group of archaeologists from Memorial University in St. John's discovered some ancient Indian remains at Port au Choix, he worked with a citizens' group to convince the Provincial Department of Education to construct a small museum on the site, refusing to allow the remains to be moved until the museum was promised. This was his first direct experience of local organization in confrontation with established institutions, and it gave him a sense of the power of collective action. The museum remains a popular tourist attraction.

More and more, the young priest found his attention focused on the fishery as the key to many of the area's problems. The resource was rich; large trawlers from mainland Canada, the United States, and across the Atlantic were reaping a valuable harvest from the Gulf of St.

Lawrence. Apart from a bit of lumbering, most of the employment in the area was in the inshore fishery, and the fishermen impressed him. "They were real go-getters," he says. "They started fishing as soon as they could in the spring, and they fished until the ice stopped them. In March they were out after seals . . . It was obvious that they had tremendous potential." They had demonstrated that potential by their willingness to try new methods and new gear. Many had moved up from the open trap-boat to longliners, vessels of thirty-five to forty feet, with a crew of three or four. With the encouragement of the Port au Choix processing plant owned by Fishery Products Ltd., some of the longliner skippers were experimenting with dragging for scallops, a new and promising fishery in the area. They were good fishermen, they worked hard and, as long as fish prices remained adequate, they could make a reasonable living. A newspaper article of the time estimated that in the new scallop fishery a crewman could make as much as four thousand dollars a year.

Going to sea with the fishermen, Father McGrath also learned other sides of the story. The hours were long and the work was hard, uncomfortable, and dangerous. That "reasonable living", if calculated on an hourly basis, was woefully small return. Most of the longliners were fishing with gill-nets, long strips of mesh like fences or tennis-nets, left anchored to the bottom to trap the fish by the gills when they try to swim through. More and more frequently, when the fishermen returned to haul up their nets, they would find only a loose buoy or nothing at all—the nets were being torn up and dragged away by big steel trawlers. This was one of the many manifestations of the generally chaotic state of the fishery. On the Grand Banks, one hundred and more miles off the Newfoundland coast, huge factory trawlers of a dozen nations were competing for the resource—full-scale floating factories that catch the fish, process and package it, and even convert the offal to fish meal. The Russians had hospital ships, vessels for transport and servicing—a complete industry afloat. In the face of this sort of competition, smaller and less efficient trawlers—Canadian, American, French, Portugese—moved into the Gulf of St. Lawrence, and there they competed with the inshore fishermen of the St. Barbe coast. In the autumn of 1969, a newspaper report said that out of forty-five longliners based in Port au Choix, only four were still fishing. The rest had lost so much gear to the draggers that they could not continue.

One of the main things Father McGrath learned about the fishermen was that they were relatively powerless within the multi-million dollar industry of which they were the foundation. They were not employees; they were, as their forefathers had been for generations, independent producers like the small farmers of the Canadian west. They bought their own boats, nets, and gear—often on credit advanced by the fish companies—and sold their product, in theory at least, to the highest bidder. In practice they were at the mercy of the fish companies. The companies set the prices, and the only effective choice a fisherman had was whether he would go fishing or not. If he fished, he could accept what the company offered and sell his catch, or dump it and earn nothing. There was little collective action; each fisherman dealt individually with the buyer. Stories of arbitrary and high-handed treatment by the buyers are legion, and often it is the petty things that are remembered rather than the more extreme examples. Port au Choix fishermen tell with wry humour of a buyer in the mid-1960s who had a "heavy hand on the weights":

> You see, we'd load the fish onto a scale that was balanced by weights. He'd wait until she was just about balanced—maybe only a pound or two more would balance her. Then he'd take a big fish—twelve or fourteen pound—and he'd heave it on and grab the weights to stop them goin' up, and he'd say, 'Okay, boys, take her away!'
>
> We was only gettin' a few cents a pound at that time, but a few pounds here and a few pounds there, it would add up. That's the way they served us—any way they wanted to.

In the summer of 1969, the United Maritime Fishermen (UMF), a co-operative based in Nova Scotia, was buying lobster in Port au Choix for trucking back to the mainland. Scallops are another product with a high price-to-volume ratio, and the UMF representatives began to buy those, too, offering the fishermen a slightly higher price than the local plant. The local plant promptly raised its own prices, and a minor price war ensued. At the outset, the fishermen were getting seventy-five cents a pound for shucked scallops; within a week or so they were getting ninety-five. When the lobster season was over the Nova Scotian buyers went home, and on the following day the local fish plant went back to paying seventy-five cents a pound. It was a powerful lesson in the economics of monopoly.

As a student at St. Francis Xavier University in the 1950s, Father McGrath had absorbed the principles of the Antigonish Movement, founded in the 1920s by Fathers Moses Coady and "Jimmy" Tompkins among the impoverished fishermen of northeast Nova Scotia. Now, faced with the problems of the fishermen of his own parish, he talked to them of co-operatives. "He's a great man for convincing you," says one of the fishermen. "He talked us blind about co-ops. He could see we needed some kind of organization, and he kept after us."

The fishermen appreciated his efforts, but they were not enthusiastic. "We'd had a co-op before, you see. All our fathers was into it. It went broke . . . people lost money . . . it was always an argument . . . some people thought others was getting more out of it than they should . . . There was no way in the world that fishermen in Port au Choix was going to get involved in a co-op."

At the same time, the Northern Regional Development Association and Extension workers from Memorial University were also talking organization. One of the Extension workers, Harvey Best, recalls leaving a copy of a union constitution with one of the fishermen. A great many ideas were in the air in the autumn of 1969 when Father McGrath got involved in one of his usual discussions with longliner skippers Gene Gould, Ralph O'Keefe, and Robert Spence aboard Spence's boat in Port au Choix. The fishermen had been discussing their problems among themselves, and one of them—they are not sure now which it was—told Father McGrath the conclusion he had reached: what they needed was not a co-op, but a union.

There was, in fact, an organization in existence that was sometimes referred to as a fishermen's union—the Newfoundland Federation of

Fishermen (NFF), started in the 1950s by Premier J.R. Smallwood—but it had never provided the kind of representation that the three longliner skippers had in mind. Since the fishermen were not employees the Federation could not bargain directly with the fish companies for prices or working conditions: it acted primarily as a lobby group. In 1969, dissatisfaction with the Federation was widespread among the fishermen: only about four thousand were members out of a potential seventeen thousand or more. Some of them had tried to push the organization toward a more militant stance and some, when that failed, had taken direct action outside it.

When they spoke of a union, the three Port au Choix men were undoubtedly thinking of events of the previous year, which had been a particularly bad one for the chronically troubled east coast fishery. Markets for both salt and fresh fish had tumbled. The federal government had provided 2.5 million dollars to buy up part of the companies' unsold inventory of salt fish and promised a scheme to support the incomes of fishermen selling to freezing plants, but at the height of the 1968 season the fishermen were being offered prices substantially below those of the previous year. While governments, companies, and the Federation of Fishermen argued, small groups of fishermen in two widely-separated locations—Hants Harbour in Trinity Bay, and Port au Choix—independently decided to tie up their boats in protest. At Port au Choix, fifty longliners and fifty smaller vessels joined the strike.

The tie-up undoubtedly played a part in forcing the hand of government and companies to see that fishermen got prices close to the average of the previous three years, and it represented the sort of direct action that Gould, Spence, and O'Keefe had in mind when they spoke to Father McGrath of a union. A spokesman for the Hants Harbour fishermen had been thinking the same way, and had said so to reporters covering their tie-up, but the Port au Choix men were not contemplating a large, province-wide organization. As one of them remembers, "we were thinking it would be just Port au Choix and Port Saunders and any of the others on the coast that might want to join." The more they talked, the more animated they became. None of them knew exactly what a union of fishermen would look like, but the idea of a democratic organization promoting the fishermen's collective interests was tremendously exciting. At the same time, the fishermen were intimidated: they had no idea how to organize such a thing. "If you want it, and are willing to stick with it," Father McGrath told them, "I'll do everything I can to help you get it going." They left the informal meeting determined to spread the idea to everyone who would listen.

There was a good deal of resistance. "Lots of people were scared of the idea," one of the founding members says. "We were scared of co-ops, and most people were scared of unions. We didn't know anything about them." But a growing little core of fishermen were talking to their neighbours and friends, echoing Father McGrath's urging: "At least we can look into it. It can't do us any harm to find out." By November, enough fishermen were interested, and a meeting was held in the school at Port au Choix. Sixty-nine men attended. They discussed their grievances and their needs, and elected a steering committee to pursue the inquiry and take the first steps toward formal organization.

Now that the process had begun, the fishermen were excited. They wanted action, and they wanted it in time for the beginning of the season in the spring of 1970. For the steering committee, the job turned out to be more difficult than they had imagined. A union, they found, was a complicated organization, and the legal implications were terrifying. "I knew that if we got something going we'd have legal problems in the spring," says Father McGrath "If we were going to get anywhere—and stay out of jail—we needed some advice. I thought about the lawyers I knew, and which of them might grasp the importance of what we were trying to do." He thought of a classmate and friend from his university days, Richard Cashin. To many, it would have seemed an unlikely choice.

Grandson of Sir Michael Cashin, once Prime Minister of Newfoundland; nephew of Major Peter Cashin, who led the anti-Confederate forces in 1948; and son of a wealthy businessman; Richard Cashin seemed the very prototype of the St. John's Establishment. In 1962, twenty-five years old and barely finished law school, he was elected to the House of Commons for St. John's West, and held the seat until 1968. In 1969 he was beginning, without any great enthusiasm, to practice law in St. John's when he happened to fall in with a group of fishermen who wanted to sue the Electric Reduction Company (ERCO) at Long Harbour for polluting the water and the fish of Placentia Bay with phosphorous. Cashin took the case and, in the course of winning a substantial settlement, learned some of the same lessons that McGrath was learning on the St. Barbe coast. The two had seen each other only once since they were classmates at St. Francis Xavier, but each was vaguely aware of what the other was doing.

They disagree about just how they got together in 1969. As Cashin remembers it, he had been hearing about the Northern Regional Development Association, and wrote to his ex-classmate for more information, but received no answer. McGrath does not recall receiving the letter. He says he called Cashin that autumn and invited him to come out to the west coast for a visit, though he did not tell him exactly what he had in mind, and Cashin demurred. Both agree, however, on what happened next. In February of 1970, McGrath telephoned Cashin and asked him to come out. Mid-winter is a poor time to travel in western Newfoundland, and 1970 was a bad year. Cashin, with a comfortable home and improving law practice in the city, said that he would come, but in the spring. After some arguing back and forth in the jocular, bantering manner of old university friends, McGrath played his trump card: "What would you think of organizing a fishermen's union?" Within a week, Cashin arrived at the priest's house in Port Saunders. "We talked all night," McGrath says, "and when daylight came we made breakfast and went out to talk to fishermen."

Ideas about the proposed organization were still rudimentary. Back in St. John's, Cashin examined legislation on the fishery, on labour, and on co-operatives. He studied the legal structure of unions and co-ops. He wrote to Vancouver for a copy of the constitution of British Columbia's United Fishermen and Allied Workers Union (UFAWU), an action that was to take on ironic significance a few months later. Initially so reluctant to visit the Northern Peninsula in winter, he was soon back there discussing organization in kitchens over endless cups of tea. He and Father McGrath visited co-operatives in the Maritime provinces, and they went back to St. Francis Xavier University to discuss their ideas with the professors who had taught them about the

Antigonish Movement ten years before.

On April 25, about two hundred fishermen met in Port au Choix and formed themselves into a union, adopting a constitution that Cashin had drawn up on the model of the fishermen's union in British Columbia. Most of the members were from Port au Choix and Port Saunders; there were also local committees at Bartlett's Harbour, forty miles to the north, and at Anchor Point, forty miles beyond that. It was planned to establish such committees in any community along the coast with more than twenty fishermen, and it was estimated that the potential membership might be six hundred.

There was little in the stated aims of the new organization to differentiate it from the Federation of Fishermen. The new union was intended

> . . . to promote economic interests of fishermen; to work with and promote other organizations . . . working for the betterment of fishermen; to work with other organizations to present a strong united voice of fishermen; to develop, in conjunction with the Northern Regional Development Association, a comprehensive fishery development plan for the region and to make arrangements for the purchasing of fuel, gear, and other goods on a collective basis.

George Lavers of Port Saunders was elected president, and Fintan Gould of Port au Choix secretary. In keeping with its intended regional scope, it was to be called the Northern Fishermen's Union (NFU).

The event passed with little fanfare; the St. John's *Evening Telegram* did not get around to reporting it until four days later, and the report made no mention of either Father McGrath or Richard Cashin. Of course, the attention of the media was fully occupied with other matters. Premier Smallwood, after surviving an internal threat to his leadership of the Liberal Party during the previous autumn, was coming under increasingly heavy fire from a Conservative opposition that grew visibly in confidence every day. The newspapers were understandably preoccupied with the spectacle of the old campaigner, the "only living Father of Confederation," fighting for his political life as he responded to complex charges about the brewery in Stephenville and the rental of space for provincial liquor stores. Besides, as the Northern Fishermen's Union was being born, the Progressive Conservatives were holding *their* leadership convention, and electing a scion of a wealthy fish merchant family, Frank Moores, as their leader.

Still, the activities of Cashin and McGrath on the Northern Peninsula had not passed unnoticed, and the gossip networks of St. John's were full of rumour and speculation. On the day after the *Telegram*'s report of the founding of the Northern Fishermen's Union, the Newfoundland Federation of Fishermen announced that it had applied, several days previously, to be recognized as "the bargaining agent and official representative of all Newfoundland fishermen" in its dealings with the Fish Trades Association, the organization of fish processors. It also announced its intention to press the government for changes in the Labour Relations Act that would allow "the necessary protection for fishermen provided for other workers" under the Act.

A few days after the founding meeting of the NFU, Cashin was on Fogo Island in the northeast, acting as a resource person for the Extension Division of Memorial University, which was assisting the islanders to form what was to become a highly successful co-operative. He had been invited because of his work with the Placentia Bay fishermen; his presence had nothing to do with the Port au Choix union. Newspaper reporters, however, found this difficult to believe. A brief article in *The Evening Telegram* stated bluntly that Cashin was in Fogo "helping to form a fishermen's union." The article went on:

> However, Mr. Cashin says he is not instrumental in the move to help fishermen organize themselves into a union.
>
> 'I've been involved with other people and I've been asked by certain individuals and groups to help,' he said.
>
> But he said he was not in a position to state who the 'individuals' or 'groups' were.

The reporter's probing and Cashin's reticence reflect the situation at the time. It was clear that something important was going on, but no one was quite sure what it was—including the people in the middle of it.

During the previous winter, while representing the Placentia Bay fishermen against ERCO, Cashin had met Fred Noble and Les Andrews, two of the few remaining Labrador skippers from the Bonavista region. On the way back from Fogo Island, he dropped in to visit them, and discovered that a small organization of Bonavista Bay fishermen were planning a trip to St. John's. The previous year's fishery on the Labrador had been a disaster, and the schoonermen were going to appeal to the government for assistance. Cashin helped prepare their brief, and accompanied them in their meeting with the premier. He was impressed with their performance. "It was quite a loud, noisy meeting. They were very outspoken. They had none of the subservience and deference I'd noticed in some of the other fishermen I'd dealt with." The delegation managed to win a programme of assistance to fishermen suffering the effects of the bad season.

Meanwhile, back on the west coast, the Northern Fishermen's Union was getting down to work. In a move strongly prophetic of what was to come, it had already created a second division by signing up most of the workers in the Port au Choix processing plant. Its first real task, however, was to negotiate on behalf of the fishermen with the owners of the plant, Fishery Products Ltd. If it was going to do that, the company had first to recognize its existence. Recognition of a union as bargaining agent for a group of workers can come about in one of two ways: the company may simply accept the union and enter into negotiations with it, or the union may apply to the provincial Labour Relations Board to be legally certified; if the application is successful, the company is required by law to negotiate with the union. Companies may give voluntary recognition for various reasons. They may, for example, feel that certification is inevitable, and wish to avoid the annoyance of legal hearings. Sometimes it is a "sweetheart deal", where a company accepts one union in order to keep out another that may be more militant, or makes an arrangement with the union leadership, trading voluntary recognition for painless contract negotiations.

In the legal certification procedure, the union must be able to demonstrate that the workers concerned are eligible in law for union membership, and that more than fifty per cent of them are paid-up members of the union. If this can be done successfully, the government will order a certification vote, and if a majority of the workers vote in favour the company is compelled to recognize the union whether it wants to or not.

The Northern Fishermen's Union had no choice. They could not apply to the government for certification because fishermen were not legally eligible for union membership. According to the law, they were not employees, but rather independent operators; the Labour Relations Act did not apply to them. The only way they could negotiate with the Fishery Products plant was if the company voluntarily agreed to the negotiations. Accordingly, the new union's executive sent off a letter to the company asking for a meeting. The company replied that they might be willing to meet, but gave no date.

Some of the reasons why a company might voluntarily deal with a union have been outlined. There is, however, another. A union that is strong and united can sometimes make things so difficult for an intransigent company that the company would rather negotiate than put up with the annoyance and loss of business. That is more or less what had happened in British Columbia: there, the United Fishermen and Allied Workers—the union whose constitution had provided the model for the Port au Choix group—had waged a strenuous campaign of boycotts, strikes, tie-ups, pickets, demonstrations, and less genteel tactics, eventually forcing not only voluntary recognition from the major fish companies, but also a special waiver of legislation that allowed the union to be the legal bargaining agent for BC fishermen.

The choices open to the fishermen of Port au Choix were narrow to begin with, and they were growing narrower. As the weeks went by and no date was set for a meeting, they began to contemplate their first strike. They were nervous but committed, and so was their parish priest. One of them recalls a conversation with Father McGrath:

> I says to him, 'Well, Father, if I goes to jail, at least you can bail me out.' 'No,' he says, 'I won't.' 'What?' I says. 'If I goes to jail you won't bail me out? Why not?' 'Because I'll be in there with you,' he says . . . . And he would've been, too.

As is usual in such circumstances, emotions ran high. On another occasion some of the fishermen were giving vent to their frustrations, talking of punched noses and broken heads. One of them remembers Father McGrath putting things in perspective:

> 'Well, boy,' he says, 'if you takes off your jacket and gets into a fight, you'd better be damn' sure you're right. Because,' he says, 'if you takes off your jacket, I'm takin' off mine. And if I gets into a fight I want to be damn' sure I'm on the right side.'

The union sent a telegram to the company, asking for a meeting on June 4; the season was already under way—if the union was to accomplish anything in 1970, discussions had to begin soon. They got no reply, and a strike was planned for June 10. On that day, the fishermen would tie up their boats and picket. The little union's other division, the fish-plant workers, would go to work as usual at eight a.m., and at nine they would walk off the job in sympathy with the fishermen.

On the day before, a new church at Bird Cove was being consecrated, and a CBC television team from Corner Brook came in to cover the event. After it was over, the reporter asked the parish priest if there were any other stories they might cover while they were there. Father McGrath could only say that he was sure there *would* be; he suggested that the t.v. crew stay overnight. When the plant-workers walked out of the fish plant the next morning, they walked onto the screens of television sets across Newfoundland. By that evening a meeting between the company and the union was scheduled for the following week.

During the organizing of the union and the days leading up to the strike, Father McGrath's discussions with fishermen had been widely talked about, and they had not gone unnoticed by the company. Clearly, they had paid particular attention to one of his lines of argument. He had not lost his interest in co-operatives, and over and over again he had assured the fishermen that they had nothing to fear from Fishery Products. If they can't run a fish business properly, and pay a decent price to fishermen, he insisted, *we can.* Just how they would manage to be in a position to do so he had not thought out, but the conviction with which he repeated the assertion made some people think he had something up his sleeve. The meeting was finally held in a school the Roman Catholic School Board was renting from the United Church. Both sides were nervous. The company opened their side of the negotiations with a firm statement: "Let's get one thing clear at the outset: you're not going to get this plant!"

The idea that the company had taken them so seriously was immensely heartening to the union team, but they quickly learned that their battle was just beginning. The company's position was simple. The plant workers were free to organize under the provisions of the Labour Relations Act; workers in three other Fishery Products plants were represented by unions, and, the company said, they got along quite well. Further, the company would deal with the NFU in the same way that they would deal with locals of the Federation of Fishermen—that is, they would be willing to meet with them and discuss problems, but no more. They would not recognize the Northern Fishermen's Union as a bargaining agent. The union's carefully prepared proposals for price agreements, grievance procedures, and so on were firmly rejected. The talks were lengthy and sometimes heated, but the company was not going to budge.

The fishermen of Port au Choix were learning some further lessons about power. They might be able to pry some concessions out of Fishery Products, but that was not what they had formed their union for. They had envisaged a fundamental change in their relationship with the company, but the company had no intention of going along. They appealed for help to the MP and the MHA for the area, but it was clear that they needed a broader base of support.

One of the problems of the old Federation of Fishermen was its shortage of funds. Dues were only two dollars a year, and it depended for most of its budget on an annual grant from the provincial government. Conscious of this, members of the Northern Fishermen's Union set for themselves the surprisingly high dues of five dollars a *week* during the fishing season. Payment was voluntary, but there was no difficulty collecting; the main problem was that during the fishing season union members had little time to devote to the administrative details of the organization. Once, when Father McGrath had not visited the little community of Anchor Point for a few weeks, a member of the local committee came to him with over a thousand dollars in back dues and an expression of concern that the collection should not be forgotten. The union hired Ed Broaders, a local school teacher, to set up its administration on a more business-like basis, and organization continued on the coast. But the rallying of support from outside the region required another strategy, and that task fell to McGrath and Cashin.

They did not have to search for the opportunity. Fishermen all across the province were keenly interested in what was happening at Port au Choix, and anxious to learn more. One of the groups particularly interested was the Bonavista North Fishermen's Association, the group that had so impressed Cashin during their meeting with Premier Smallwood a few weeks before. When the Bonavista Bay Development Association offered to hold a meeting in their area so fishermen could learn more about what was happening on the west coast, Cashin and McGrath quickly agreed to come. It was a strange meeting, full of ironies and pregnant with possibilities only dimly realized by the participants.

By North American standards, Newfoundland is a small place, and from the outside its people and ways of life seem—and, under the influence of modern communications are becoming—homogeneous. But it is also by North American standards an old society; until the middle of this century it remained a separate country and it retains until today internal structures and differentiations on a more European scale. Accent and attitude vary from bay to bay, and even from village to village; the characteristics of people from different bays or peninsulas are discussed as though they represented different ethnic groups—as, indeed, to some extent they do.

Different areas are identified with different religious denominations—here Anglican, there Catholic, or Salvationist, or United Church—and the sectarian divisions have been built into the society's institutions. Even what is termed for convenience the Newfoundland fishery is not one fishery but many, with a myriad of local and regional variations. In spite of its small size, Newfoundland is a society as diverse and complex as many much larger.

The diversity was amply reflected at the Bonavista North meeting. The audience included men who owned large, expensive vessels which travelled hundreds of miles to fish, and others who fished only a few miles from their home communities from small open boats. The staunchly Protestant crowd of working men was addressed by the Catholic lawyer from St. John's and the Catholic priest from Corner Brook in a hall belonging to the Loyal Orange Lodge.

Cashin and McGrath spoke of the beginnings of the NFU and laid out the challenge of organization. Whatever their differences, they said, fishermen across Newfoundland faced similar problems; together they could change their condition. It was not an easy audience—the Bonavista Bay men listened impassively and the visitors could not tell what sort of impression they were making. When the speeches were finished, one after another, fishermen stood and spoke in response. Older men first, then younger, they told of their own experiences of injustice and hardship, of failures and victories in the past, and of the need for a real union of fishermen. To Cashin and McGrath it was a baffling performance, and it was not until much later that they realized that what they had been witnessing was a ritual rooted in the religious background of the area—like a Methodist or Salvationist congregation, the fishermen were confirming the "sermons" with personal testimony. But there was no mistaking what they had to say. On the way home in McGrath's Volkswagen the two friends alternated between elation and terror, for it was clear that they had on their hands the beginning of a province-wide organization.

That meeting was the first of many. The two friends travelled the province, speaking in musty halls, schoolrooms, and church basements. They worked out their speeches in the car and then, in the heat of oratory, stole each other's material. Sometimes they would argue for two hundred miles, interrupt the argument to address a meeting, and then continue it for most of the night in someone's kitchen or on the road home. They played roles, asking each other the questions they might expect from reporters or anticipating arguments they might expect from fish company negotiators. For a time, they lived in fear that some enterprising reporter would ask how they proposed to establish a price for fish, because they had no idea of the answer. But the question was not asked and they continued to sign up fishermen in the Northern Fishermen's Union.

It was a ramshackle organization. In Port au Choix it had two locals, an executive, and a paid secretary; in the rest of the province, it consisted simply of fishermen who had signed a card. There were no new locals. The original members on the northwest coast continued to pay their dues, but most of the others did not—there was no means of collecting. Apart from the plant workers at Port au Choix, it was a union of inshore fishermen and even if it were able to organize dues-paying locals, it could not legally bargain for its members or provide them with normal union services. In the summer of 1970, Newfoundland fishermen were not so much joining a union as supporting an idea. It was an idea they all shared, but it rested for the moment on two men arguing in a car.

At the end of July, the Newfoundland Federation of Labour was holding its annual convention in Corner Brook. The Northern Fishermen's Union was not part of the Federation, but Father McGrath asked to be allowed to speak to the delegates. An objection came from Fred Locking, Newfoundland representative of the Amalgamated Meat Cutters and Butcher Workmen of America. A few years before, the Canadian Labour Congress had given his union jurisdiction for organizing in the fishing industry; that being so, he argued, there was no room for another fishery union. The objection was overruled and McGrath gave his speech. Among other things, he told the meeting that if the Northern Fishermen's Union, which now claimed a membership of over fifteen hundred, was to become part of the Federation of Labour, the Federation would never again be able to hold its convention in a hall of that size—they would need a lot more room. The delegates responded with a unanimous endorsement of the NFU's efforts and its campaign to have fishermen included under the provisions of the Labour Relations Act. One of the other speakers at the convention was the newly-elected leader of the provincial Progressive Conservative Party, Frank Moores.

McGrath's speech and Locking's objection brought to a head a question that had been simmering below the surface during the hectic months of organizing. What was to be the future of the Northern Fishermen's Union? Would it remain independent? Would it amalgamate with some larger group? At the time a bitter and protracted labour battle was going on in Nova Scotia, where the UFAWU of British Columbia had organized trawlermen in the Strait of Canso; the Nova Scotia fish companies had refused to recognize the union, and the trawlermen had been on strike since March. They had their own clerical backing, most notably from the Reverend Ron Parsons, an Anglican clergyman and a Newfoundlander, who was walking the picket lines with the strikers. Parsons had heard about Port au Choix, and had appealed to the Newfoundlanders for support. Just a week before the Federation of Labour convention, the president of the NFU had sent a telegram to the president of the BC union stating:

> We sympathize with and encourage your work in Nova Scotia. We are facing similar problems here in Newfoundland. Fishermen must organize and be recognized in fishermen's unions. Please inform if we can be of any help to your union.

The UFAWU and the new Newfoundland union had much in common. The BC union had provided the model for the NFU's constitution. Many of the striking Canso fishermen were Newfoundlanders who had moved to the mainland; one of the strike-bound companies in Nova Scotia had plants in Newfoundland. Several times during that hectic summer, Cashin and McGrath had discussed the possibility of merging their new organization with the BC union.

The same thought had occurred to others, to whom it was less welcome: among these were officials of the Canadian Labour Congress (CLC). The UFAWU had received a great deal of support for its organizing drive from other unions in eastern Canada, but it was not popular with the central organization of Canadian labour. It had been expelled in 1952 by the CLC's predecessor, the Trades and Labour Congress during a period when the Canadian labour establishment, with the assistance of the federal government, was purging radical and national unions in favour of unions that were less politically-oriented and "international"—which meant American unions with Canadian branches. The UFAWU was still excluded. The CLC had given jurisdiction for the fishing industry to the Amalgamated Meat Cutters and Butcher Workmen, a powerful international centred in Chicago, and that union was beginning an organizing drive in Newfoundland. The strike in Nova Scotia was already causing the CLC a good deal of trouble, and an alliance between the UFAWU and the NFU would add to their problems. CLC representatives and the Executive of the Newfoundland Federation of Labour arranged for a meeting between the executive of the NFU and representatives of the Meat Cutters.

Neither side was enthusiastic. Fred Locking of the Meat Cutters was new to Newfoundland. He had come in 1968 to take over the organizing of the province's fish-plant workers, and resented the intrusion of the NFU. The Meat Cutters had their organizing plan worked out—first the plant workers, then the trawlermen. The inshore fishermen they were less certain about—perhaps they might come later, or perhaps they would be better off with a co-operative. A life-long union man who had begun his career at the age of fifteen in a Yorkshire machine-shop, Locking was suspicious of the involvement of a priest and a lawyer with an independent income.

For their part, the men of the NFU were not impressed with the organizing plans of the Meat Cutters. They were inshore fishermen, and they wanted a union structure in the fishery in which their interests could not be played off against the interests of plant-workers.

Ed Johnson, the CLC Regional Representative, was impressed by the fishermen of the NFU and by Father McGrath. "They knew what they wanted," he says, "and Father McGrath was an excellent negotiator. He could see the problems, but he wouldn't give way on the main objective." It was agreed that the two unions would co-operate and assist one another, with the Meat Cutters continuing the organization of fish plants and trawlermen, and the NFU organizing inshore fishermen. A second meeting was set for September at the Meat Cutters' Canadian headquarters in Toronto.

The NFU fishermen went back to their boats with a lot to think about, and, back on the road, McGrath and Cashin went over the arguments again and again. The UFAWU had the sort of union in BC that they would like to see in Newfoundland. A comprehensive fisheries union established on both coasts would be a powerful instrument for achieving fishermen's goals, especially since BC firms had moved into the east coast fishery and BC herring seiners, having virtually wiped out the resource on the Pacific coast, had moved east by way of the Panama Canal and were whittling away at the herring shoals of the Atlantic.

On the other hand, the UFAWU's exclusion from the CLC was a serious drawback—only a few months before, a petition by the BC union to rejoin the national body, in spite of strong support by the British Columbia Federation of Labour and a number of other unions, had been turned down. In Nova Scotia, there were ominous signs that the combined forces of government, fish companies, and the CLC were going to break the BC union's strike and their east coast organizing effort. If the Newfoundlanders were to throw in their lot with the UFAWU, they could find themselves isolated, four thousand miles from the centre of their union's strength, and without the sympathy of the most powerful elements of the labour movement. And although they do not talk much about it now, Cashin and McGrath were alarmed by the BC union's reputation for being communist-led. They decided that if they could get the terms they wanted, they would opt for the Meat Cutters.

In Port au Choix the NFU's secretary went back to teaching school and the union scored a coup by hiring Ed Maynard, secretary of the Northern Regional Development Association (NRDA). Maynard was a native of the area who had been away in the army for a time and had returned to work as a microwave technician for CN Telegraph. Besides his work for the development association, he and his wife operated a small confectionery store and take-out, which led a newspaper columnist to observe that the union was being led by "the three traditional enemies of the fishermen" a priest, a lawyer, and a businessman. It would have been hard to find anyone at the time who would believe that within two years Maynard would be the provincial Minister of Labour.

Early in September McGrath and Cashin were in Toronto laying out their terms for a merger. They wanted a comprehensive union, including plant workers, inshore fishermen, and trawlermen. They wanted top priority for a campaign to get collective bargaining rights for fishermen, and they wanted financial support for organizing. In return they promised a union with ten thousand members. The international's Canadian executive were impressed, and a tentative agreement was reached, subject to ratification by the head office in Chicago.

Shortly after, with Cashin back in St. John's and McGrath in his parish house at Port Saunders, the call came. Could they be at an executive meeting of the Meat Cutters in Chicago at 2:00 p.m. the following day? "They didn't seem to have any idea how far away we were," says McGrath. Hurriedly, the two friends agreed to meet in Montreal, McGrath barrelling down the gravel road to Deer Lake in the pre-dawn darkness. They picked up a lucky connection, and were in Chicago by noon. McGrath had left dressed for the chilly October winds that blow across the Gulf of St. Lawrence, and found himself sweating into his clerical collar in Chicago's twenty-five degree heat. With the president and vice-president of the Canadian branch, they were ushered into the mahogany-panelled boardroom of the union that had been spawned in festering Kansas City slaughterhouses at the turn of the century, and now represented more than six hundred thousand food workers across North America. The meeting was brief and to the point. A quick description of the situation in Newfoundland; a few questions. How many members? In two or three years, they said, ten thousand. The Newfoundlanders retired to an ante-room to await the decision.

The Amalgamated Meat Cutters' secretary-treasurer and unchallenged boss since the 1940s was Patrick E. Gorman, a tough, hard-bitten veteran of fifty years in the union. McGrath had heard of him as a well-known supporter of Catholic causes; he also knew that his wife had recently died. While waiting, McGrath wrote out a card for Gorman, offering condolences and promising a mass in Port au Choix in memory of his wife. It was a typical gesture, and although Cashin twitted him later about using his priestly office to influence the negotiations, McGrath knew it could have no effect on the decision that was being made behind the mahogany door. Later, he heard that when Gorman found the card he blew his nose, wiped his eyes, and said, "Well boys, I know we made the right decision." By that time, the two Newfoundlanders were in a taxi on their way back to O'Hare airport with a commitment for a merger of their little union with the giant international.

Back in Montreal, they picked up a flight home, an overnight EPA milk-run touching down at airports through the Maritimes. Early next morning in Stephenville, McGrath happened to meet William Callahan, the provincial Minister of Resources, who was setting out on a helicopter trip to the Northern Peninsula. McGrath accepted a lift; he could always get somebody to drive his car home. An hour later a group of Port Saunders children gaped in astonishment at the unaccustomed sight of a helicopter flapping in for a landing above their town. One of them, in high excitement, described the event for his mother, and when she asked the obvious adult question, "Who was on it?" the child replied in anti-climax, "Oh, 'twas only Father McGrath."

In a little over twenty-four hours, McGrath had been to Chicago and returned with a commitment of an immediate transfer of fifty thousand dollars for organizing the fishermen of Newfoundland, and the promise of more if it was needed.

A few weeks later, the members of the Northern Fishermen's Union and three locals of the Meat Cutters in the fish plants in Trepassey, Port Union, and Harbour Breton ratified a new charter, and the Newfoundland Fishermen, Food, and Allied Workers' Union (NFFAWU) was born. Locking was to administer the funds from the parent union and with the staff he had recruited before the merger to continue organizing fish plants. Cashin and McGrath were to go back on the road, organizing fishermen. By November the NFFAWU published the first *Union Forum*, a quarterly newsletter, produced so hurriedly that on the cover the name of the new union was recorded incorrectly. Plans were laid for a convention to be held the following spring that would ratify the new structure.

The first publication put up a brave front, but the NFFAWU was a decidedly precarious venture. Although Locking had given up active opposition to the merger, he was still privately unconvinced that it was a good idea. The Port au Choix group and the others who had joined the NFU had set out to form a fishermen's union, but now found themselves part of a much more comprehensive structure: only three plant locals had signed up to get the combined union started, but the international had eight or nine others that were expected to come in. If they all did so, the NFFAWU would have as its core about two thousand dues-paying plant workers bargaining under the Labour Relations Act, and the fishermen had a number of hurdles to jump before they could match the plant-workers in organization. Even among the plant-workers, there was a wide diversity: some of the locals had been in existence for a long time, having been formed on their own initiative as much as twenty years earlier; others were relatively new and had little experience of union activity. No one was quite sure how all this was to be brought together into an effective structure.

At the centre stood an oddly-assorted triumvirate: one professional union organizer whose main experience was in meat-packing plants in the Prairies, one idealistic parish priest, and one wealthy young lawyer-politician whose motives were increasingly being subjected to public question.

A lot of people were looking on: fishermen with growing interest; fish companies with reserve, and advocates of social change with high excitement. Many of the watchers had high hopes, but even the most enthusiastic could hardly have predicted that they were watching a union that within a dozen years would represent virtually all the fishery workers in Newfoundland and be moving into Nova Scotia.

Chapter 2

The rapid advance of the NFFAWU over the next few years would have been remarkable in any industry, but in the context of Canada's Atlantic fishery it was almost miraculous. At the beginning, editorial writers predicted that the union could not work: as it grew, each new difficulty or set-back was taken as an indication that it was about to collapse. The reasons for both the union's success and the editorialists' predictions of its failure are deeply rooted in Newfoundland's history as a fishing nation.

It was fish that brought Europeans to Newfoundland in the first place, it was fish that dictated the pattern of their settlement, and it was the catching, drying, and trading of fish that laid down the forms and structures of their society. At first, the fish traders did not want people to settle in Newfoundland at all, preferring to control a seasonal fishery from home ports in England. Some settlement took place anyway, and as conditions of market and competition changed, it became advantageous to have a fishery based in Newfoundland. The population grew. By the middle of the nineteenth century, Newfoundland was a self-sufficient unit within the British Empire, having its own responsible government and an apparently secure position as the world's largest exporter of dried salt codfish, a product very highly regarded on the European market: in the previous century Giacomo Casanova had apparently fuelled his amorous engines at least partly with what he called "good, sticky salt cod from Newfoundland." The colony's people were scattered around six thousand miles of rugged coastline in over a thousand settlements which ranged in size from a few families to a few hundred. Control of trade, finance, and government was centred in the capital city of St. John's, and the vast interior of the island was virtually uninhabited.

According to Newfoundland's premier economic historian, the late David Alexander, this traditional fishing economy reached a peak in the 1880s and, in good years at least, provided for the people of the country a living standard comparable to that of working people elsewhere in the Western world. It was almost exclusively a cod fishery; even up to the present, for many older Newfoundlanders "fish" means "cod" and other species are called by name. It was also a sort of cottage industry. The early fishing operations had been carried on by merchant companies who brought out employees and indentured labourers, but it was soon recognized to be more advantageous to the traders if the fishing families looked after their own upkeep, catching fish "independently" and trading it to the company. By the nineteenth century, most of the fish caught in Newfoundland waters were taken by men sailing or rowing out from their home settlements in small, open boats. Their catch was processed—split, salted, and tended while drying in wind and sun—by the entire household.

A somewhat higher level of capitalization existed in the Banks and Labrador fisheries. From centres mainly—though not exclusively—along the northeast coast, schooner operators would carry fishing crews and even families "down north" to the Labrador coast for the summer season, where they would prosecute the fishery either as "stationers" from shore camps or as "floaters" from the schooners themselves. Mainly—but again not exclusively—along the south coast, operators of banking schooners would carry men and dories to the great cod-rich shallows of the Grand Banks a hundred miles and more away from shore: with the schooner as a floating base, the dorymen would range out, two to a boat, bringing in the fish on hook and line.

Except for a small section of the southwest coast, it was very much a seasonal occupation, pursued in the few short months of summer and early autumn. In the northern fishery, this meant that each season represented a single voyage, from home port to the Labrador coast and back with the catch. This has left its mark in the vocabulary of the people: even now, when a Newfoundland fisherman refers to "the voyage" he does not mean a trip to the fishing grounds, but rather the whole season's operation.

The fishermen and their families grew most of their own vegetables; cut their own fuel and lumber; built houses and boats; killed seals; kept poultry, small livestock, and sometimes even a cow or two; hunted, trapped, and in general pursued an intricate seasonal round of work to maintain themselves. For the necessities they could not produce and the rare luxuries they could afford they depended upon the merchant, who outfitted them with gear and supplies in the spring, bought their fish in the autumn, and sold them their supplies for winter. In this "truck" or barter system, most fishermen and their families rarely saw cash from one year's end to the next: their fortunes and misfortunes were represented by entries in the merchant's ledger. Many of the outharbour merchants were themselves in a similar debt-and-credit relationship with larger mercantile houses in St. John's. At the peak, in the late 1800s, ninety per cent of the male work force was occupied in the fishery.

Aware that the industry could not expand indefinitely, the Newfoundland government pursued a policy of development very similar to Canada's—a heavily-subsidized railway was built across the island and inducements were offered to encourage agriculture and manufacturing. These efforts were not notably successful. The climate and the soil make agriculture very much a marginal enterprise, and the domestic market for manufactured goods was too small to keep many factories going. Like the honest working girl of Victorian melodrama driven by grim necessity to sell her favours in the streets—though undoubtedly without the same consciousness of wrongdoing—Newfoundland began to advertise her charms to international capital. By land-grants, tax concessions, monopolies, and subsidies of all kinds, the government attempted to entice international developers to the island: all they asked in return was jobs and the promise of growth—and occasionally some financial assistance for the politicians. It is a strategy familiar enough from recent history all over Atlantic Canada, and it was no more successful a hundred years ago than it has been lately. All of the enterprises sponsored in this way cost the government money, but only a very few were successful enough to survive, and fewer still successful enough to add to the productive capacity of the country.

During the first half of this century, while population increased, the traditional fishery steadily declined. Worldwide changes in food processing and distribution meant that salt codfish came more and more to be a product most in demand among the very people least able to pay for it, in countries where financial conditions were least stable, and even there it began to face stiff competition from high-quality fish from

Scandinavia and other places. The large industrial enterprises that survived, like the pulp and paper mills at Grand Falls and Corner Brook and the Bell Island iron mines, were not sufficient to take up the slack, and thousands of Newfoundlanders did what citizens of small and struggling countries have had to do throughout the modern era—they emigrated. By the middle of the 1930s, there was one native of Newfoundland abroad for every six at home, and the largest concentration of Newfoundlanders outside of St. John's was to be found in Massachusetts. The government slid deeper and deeper into debt and political confusion. In 1934, it reached a point of collapse. Independent government was suspended, and the administration was taken over by a Commission appointed from London.

The Great Depression of the 1930s was hard everywhere, but it was cruelly hard in Newfoundland, where *per capita* incomes were half of what they were in Canada, and the dole, if one could get it, was six cents a day. The Second World War brought some economic relief, with jobs for as many as twenty thousand Newfoundlanders in the building of American military bases, but did nothing to solve the basic economic problems. After the war, it was largely the promise of improved incomes and services that convinced a bare majority of Newfoundlanders to vote for confederation with Canada in 1949.

An immediate improvement in cash incomes in the depressed rural areas came with Canadian old-age pensions and family allowance, but the problems of providing productive employment remained. Under Premier J.R. Smallwood, the new provincial government tried the same set of policies pursued by their predecessors in the colonial government at the turn of the century. With Ottawa's assistance, they built roads, water and sewer systems, hospitals, and schools, and extended electric power lines. They attempted to encourage the development of manufacturing for the domestic market, but with no more success than before. And, inevitably, they used subsidies, grants, and give-aways to entice multinational capital to the province.

The focus was on industrialization, and through it all the fishery was given little emphasis: Smallwood now denies it, but he is still popularly believed to have told the inshore fishermen to "burn their boats" and that there would be "two jobs for every man." The fishermen did not entirely follow this advice, but those who could do so moved in and out of the fishery as employment prospects waxed and waned in other sectors. After twenty years in Canada, Newfoundland in 1969 could still be described as a dual economy. On one side was a small "modern" sector represented primarily by construction and the resource extraction industries of pulp and paper and mining. On the other side was the large, depressed "traditional" sector of the inshore fishery, where changes had come slowly and reluctantly, and basic techniques were much as they had been for generations. For the whole province, the *per capita* income was still only slightly more than half of Canada's, and the inshore small-boat fishery was regarded by most people as something to escape from when conditions allowed; an occupation of last resort, pursued when other possibilities were closed.

As might be expected, labour organization followed the faltering path of industrialization. The first workers' organizations in Newfoundland were formed among tradesmen in maritime occupations, such as shipwrights, followed later by other trades such as coopers and masons. They were modelled after early British labour organizations; most were called "protective associations" and incorporated some of the functions of fraternal societies, like sickness benefits and burial insurance. With the opening of large internationally-funded industry at the turn of the century came branches of large international unions based in the United States and Canada, first in the railway and later in the pulp and paper plants and the mines.

On the whole, the labour movement in Newfoundland lacked any strong political orientation, and the radical ideologies associated with labour organization elsewhere were almost entirely absent. There were a number of attempts from the late 1800s to form a central federation of unions, and in 1919 one such body ran labour candidates in a general election, but such direct political action was unusual. One reason that has been advanced for the lack of labour radicalism is the relative stability and isolation of the population. In Canada and the United States, burgeoning industrialization in the second half of the nineteenth century attracted waves of immigrants who brought with them new political ideas from Britain and Europe. In Newfoundland, major immigration was over by the early 1800s. When the new industries started, they employed mostly native Newfoundlanders whose families had come from the English west country or Ireland generations before. And, because of Newfoundland's political separateness and geographical isolation, there was relatively little direct contact with labour movements elsewhere.

One Newfoundlander who did have direct experience of foreign labour movements was Joseph R. Smallwood. In the 1920s he was in New York working as a reporter for socialist newspapers and spending his spare time as a speaker for the Socialist and Progressive Parties. In 1925 he returned to Newfoundland as an organizer for the International Brotherhood of Pulp, Sulphite and Paper Mill Workers of America. He doubled the union's membership in a few months, founded a Federation of Labour with himself as president, and then set out to walk nearly six hundred miles along the railway, organizing track labourers. That federation did not last long either, and soon Smallwood was in Britain, haunting Labour Party meetings.

In the Depression years, union membership in Newfoundland declined drastically. In 1937 a small group of activists formed a Trades and Labour Council and embarked on an organizing campaign. The core of the Council came from the internationals, but it welcomed independent Newfoundland unions: indeed, it took special pains to avoid any suggestion of foreign influence or alien political ideology. In 1938, its executive members signed an oath attesting that

> . . . neither A.F.of L., nor C.I.O., nor any other group, either directly or indirectly, is behind the Newfoundland movement financially or otherwise. Neither is the movement prompted from abroad in any shape or form . . .
>
> And finally, we swear that the officers and members

> . . . are utterly and unreservedly opposed to the tenets of communism and fascism or any similar isms, and forthrightly declare ourselves adherents of democratic principles and unalterable believers in the Christian foundation of civilization and unswervably loyal to our King and Country.

Such an extravagant oath might be expected in a society where radical ideologies represented a real threat to established order. In Newfoundland, however, no such threat existed. The oath seems, rather, to be no more than a manifestation of the general effort by labour to avoid any taint of extremism, illegality, or foreign ideology.

This attitude has been explained as being the product of a strong cultural conservatism and respect for authority. Richard Gwyn refers to Newfoundlanders' "deep-rooted horror of law-breaking," and he quotes A.P. Herbert, who called them "the most law-abiding people on earth." It is one of the peculiarities of the place that such generalizations can retain the ring of truth in spite of the fact that Newfoundlanders have been able throughout their history to condone—or at least to accept—the most outrageous skulduggery and outright corruption from their politicians, and have as a people earned no small reputation for cheerful disregard of regulations, whether pertaining to hunting or fishing, the importation and manufacture of alcohol, or the requirements of the Unemployment Insurance Commission.

A partial explanation of the contradiction may be found in the nature of the society and its historical distinction between individual and institutional spheres of action. Unlike many immigrants to North America, the first Newfoundlanders did not come as refugees escaping oppression: settlement was brought about by the expansion of an operating mercantile system of employers and workers, exploiters and exploited, oppressors and oppressed. When the employees became "independent" fishermen, they remained at the bottom of the pyramid, held there by the iron rules of a one-product economy. For generations, thousands of their descendants maintained an orderly way of life in tiny villages where authority—in the form of magistrates, police, and even clergy—was only an occasional presence. They developed a system based on individual effort, kinship, and personal loyalty. At the same time, utterly dependent for survival on the structures of the larger society outside, they retained an over-arching allegiance to the abstractions of Church and State. It may be that in this contradiction lies some of the secret of J.R. Smallwood's success. He was able to represent the abstract authority of established order, and, at the same time, to be "Joey", the self-styled "little fellow from Gambo", talking man-to-man, doing favours for his friends, and winking at the rules.

The labour organizing drive went on during the war years with considerable success. When Donald McDonald, then regional director for the Canadian Congress of Labour (CCL), visited Newfoundland in 1947 he wrote that "It was my first impression that St. John's . . . was perhaps the most highly organized city that I have ever visited . . . The same holds true of Grand Falls, Corner Brook, Bell Island, and Deer Lake." At the time, the proportion of organized workers was higher than in Canada.

Outside of the pulp and paper industry, mining, and the railway, however, most of the unions were small independents, directly chartered by what was now the Newfoundland Federation of Labour (NFL), and not affiliated with large internationals. They were, on the whole, neither very militant nor very powerful. Among the leadership, however, was a small core of socialist thinkers. When, in 1946, a National Convention was to be elected to decide the political future of Newfoundland, they attempted to form a labour party out of the Federation of Labour, and very nearly succeeded. When the elections were held, a number of union leaders ran, and of the forty-five members elected, six had labour affiliations.

Once Confederation became a fact in 1949 and Smallwood became premier, he promptly set up a Labour Advisory Committee that was almost entirely composed of union men, and he largely accepted their recommendations. His government quickly passed a series of Acts pertaining to labour relations, trade unions, minimum wages, and workers' compensation, giving Newfoundland some of the most progressive labour legislation in the country. For nearly a decade after, unions in the province enjoyed very cordial relations with the government, but Smallwood's style of leadership and the nature of Canadian union organization made a confrontation inevitable.

When Newfoundland became a province of Canada, the Newfoundland Federation of Labour became a branch of the Trades and Labour Congress, the Canadian equivalent of the American Federation of Labour. At the time, the TLC was in competition with another national labour body, the Canadian Congress of Labour. The policy of the TLC was to merge small local unions into the large U.S.-based internationals. Some efforts were made in this direction, but in practice the traditional openness of the Newfoundland Federation to small independent unions continued. When the TLC and the CCL merged on a national level in 1956 to form the present Canadian Labour Congress (CLC), however, the pressure became greater. One focus of it was in the logging industry that supplied the paper mills, where three rather weak independent unions represented about twelve thousand loggers who worked under appallingly primitive conditions for pitifully small rates of pay. There was some disagreement among the loggers about which union to join, and the International Woodworkers of America (IWA), with the blessing of the CLC, moved in and began organizing.

The IWA organizers were tough, competent professionals, and they moved quickly. By 1959, the union represented the great majority of the loggers and was into a head-on confrontation with the pulp and paper companies. It was a new kind of labour struggle for Newfoundland, marked by outbursts of violence and sabotage, and having none of the conciliatory mutual understandings that management and government had come to expect. The IWA was out to win against the companies; in the process it was gaining the allegiance of a significant body of workers, and the union's organizers made no secret of their political association with the CCF party elsewhere in Canada. Smallwood could not long ignore such a direct challenge to his rule. Launching a savage verbal attack on the leaders of the union, he established a government-sponsored Brotherhood of Woods Workers and set out to break the IWA.

The old, easy alliance between government and labour was over. Smallwood called a special session of the House of Assembly and pushed through a bill decertifying the IWA. To drive the point home the legislature also passed a series of harshly punitive measures giving the government power to decertify and disband unions almost at will. The province that was once admired and envied by labour movements elsewhere for having some of the most progressive labour legislation was now denounced for having some of the worst, and in Newfoundland the only organized voice of opposition was the Federation of Labour.

It was a difficult time to be carrying that banner. In the United States, Robert Kennedy was launching his campaign against corruption and gangsterism in the American labour movement, and the doings of such luminaries as Jimmy Hoffa and Hal Banks were recalled and widely publicized. The oratorical skills Smallwood had developed while promoting organized labour he now used to attack it, representing the IWA and international unionism as the leading edge of an invasion that would bring Mafia thuggery and terrorism to Newfoundland. The Federation's leadership fought back as best they could. They formed a political party intended to incorporate labour and non-union sympathizers—called the Newfoundland Democratic Party, anticipating the formation of the national New Democratic Party (NDP) by a year—but their efforts were of little avail. Smallwood appealed to the general public's traditional respect for order and fear of pernicious influences from abroad, and he largely succeeded in keeping the people's allegiance.

In 1960 he made overtures to the Federation of Labour that precipitated a split in its ranks. The Federation recovered and carried on its opposition, but the struggle had lost it membership and influence. Smallwood continued to warn against labour involvement in political action. He urged unions to break away from the Federation and the Canadian Labour Congress, and encouraged individual labour leaders to deal with him directly rather than through the usual channels. For seven years he refused to accept the Federation's annual brief to the government.

When the NFU was being formed in 1969 the labour movement was beginning to recover and several unions were developing a more militant stance, but relations between labour and government were still far from cordial.

For all its local peculiarities, labour organization in Newfoundland was shaped by the same forces that produced labour movements in the rest of the industrial world: the social grouping of workers in common work-places, and their recognition of mutual interests *vis a vis* employers. It was not until after the Second World War that the fishery began to develop the first of these characteristics to any marked extent. The fishery was different from other industries, but fishermen had common interests, too, and at the beginning of this century they produced one of the most remarkable social movements in labour history.

There had been sporadic efforts at organization before. In 1832 fishermen of Carbonear and Harbour Grace rebelled against the debt-and-credit system that ruled their lives and demanded a different mode of dealing with the merchants. In the absence of the governor, the movement was put down in spirited fashion by the colony's chief justice with threats of imprisonment, whipping, and transportation to what were then even less-desirable parts of the Empire.

In the 1840s there were strikes among the fishermen who travelled to St. John's in hope of getting places on the sealing vessels that left for the ice each spring. These did not lead to any lasting organization, but occurred sporadically for many years as more or less spontaneous protests against a harshly exploitative system that required the men to pay "berth money" to the ship-owners merely for a place aboard, and up to thirty-three per cent interest on the value of any supplies advanced them for the voyage.

A less combative type of organization was formed in the 1860s by an Anglican clergyman in Trinity Bay. The Reverend George Gardner had been part of the social upliftment movement in England, and on coming to Newfoundland formed the Heart's Content Fishermen's Society, a fraternal organization offering sickness and death benefits and dedicated to moral betterment. It was later reorganized as the Society of United Fishermen, a Mason-like lodge with secret rituals and religious symbolism based on the fishery. A similar lodge, the Star of the Sea, was organized among Catholic fishermen in Placentia. The halls of both organizations are still to be seen in outport communities.

None of these organizations, however, had any effect on the fundamental structure of the fishery or the place of fishermen within it. And it was a bitterly hard system. At the beginning of the season, the fisherman went to the local merchant for equipment and supplies to carry himself and his family through the summer, and in the fall he turned over to the merchant his production of salt codfish. If the season was good, he might wipe out the spring debt and be able to purchase supplies to see the family through the winter—even, on occasion, to receive a few dollars in cash. If the season was bad—if the fish were scarce or the weather for drying them poor—he might not make enough to cover his existing debt, and would have to appeal for more credit for winter supplies. It was this round of indebtedness that drove fishermen to trek the lonely miles to St. John's in early spring and barter for a chance to suffer the privation and risk of the seal hunt.

The merchants stood to make a profit at each step: on the goods supplied to his customers, and on the sale of the fish for the export market. In anticipation of bad seasons and bad debts, he set the price of his goods exorbitantly high; in anticipation of bad overseas markets, he set the price of the fish he took from the fishermen punishingly low. When the fish were graded for quality and price, the job was done by a culler who, although ostensibly independent, was an employee of the merchant.

The outport merchant, in his turn, was bound by debt and credit to one of the large firms in St. John's, from which he got the food and salt and twine that he retailed to the fishermen, and to which he shipped the fish. He could not afford much compassion. Too much credit extended to his fishermen neighbours could drive him under. There was no negotiating over fish prices—they were set by the export companies, who scrambled each year for the overseas markets, cutting each other's throats and profits in the process.

One observer of the 1930s saw the system as a notable example "of very great interest to the student of theoretical economics." The Newfoundland fishery, he said,

> . . . is almost unique as an industry in that the class which owns the capital employed in it has managed, somehow or other, to throw the whole risks, or very nearly the whole risks, which capital normally takes and on which it bases its abstract claim for reward, onto the shoulders of the working classes. Moreover, it is a striking example of an industry in which the real capitalist has gone very far towards making profit the first charge on the proceeds of the sale of a manufactured article, taking precedence even of a bare subsistence for the primary producer.

This iniquitous economic system supported, and was supported by, a political system that contained its own share of iniquity. There was no municipal or regional government outside of St. John's; for each district, the sole representative of the people was the Member of the House of Assembly. The electorate was thinly scattered in a thousand tiny hamlets, many of which were isolated by ice and bad weather for half the year, and most of the people were prevented by lack of education and their position in the class structure from running for office. The middle class was tiny and concentrated in St. John's and a few other centres. As a result, government was left to a handful of lawyers and professionals who, with a few notable exceptions, used it as a means of enriching themselves and their friends. An appointed Legislative Council, corresponding to the House of Lords or the Canadian Senate, was usually filled with successful merchants.

In 1933 a Royal Commission consisting of a British Labour peer and two Canadian bankers, appointed from London to enquire into Newfoundland's chaotic affairs, described the workings of the political system as "a continuing process of greed, graft, and corruption which has left few classes of the community untouched by its insidious influences."

In equally vivid language they went on to describe a vast web of patronage that caused honest people to shun politics and tainted anyone who was forced to deal with it. It was this report that led to the suspension of responsible government.

The Commissioners probably exaggerated the relative depravity of Newfoundland politics: certainly, the sort of skulduggery they described was not unknown in many other jurisdictions of their time—and has not been unknown since. Thomas Lodge, one of the civil servants who took over the administration of the government, suggests that they had succumbed to a " . . . temptation which appears to be common to writers on Newfoundland affairs, to paint a picture with an over-emphatic brush." However, if the Newfoundland system was no worse than many others of the day, it was certainly no better, and Lodge goes on to acknowledge that it was, indeed, "disfigured by a series of acts of jobbery, corruption and dishonesty."

The twin evils of the credit system in the fishery and the spoils system in government produced many villains and few heroes—and at least one man who for many people was an outstanding combination of both.

William Ford Coaker was born in 1871 on the South Side of St. John's. At the age of eleven, like many other boys of his class, he was working on the waterfront, fetching and carrying in the warehouses of Job's, one of the big fish-exporting firms. At thirteen he led a strike among the boys, demanding wage parity with a neighbouring fish company, and won. His ability must have been recognized, for by the time he was sixteen he was engaged to manage a company store at Pike's Arm, near Twillingate on the Northeast coast, for the summer season. He continued this for four years, returning to St. John's for the winters, where he worked in the daytime and studied at night as a "private scholar" under William Lloyd, who was later, with Coaker's support, to be prime minister. When he was twenty, he bought out the store, and set himself up as an outport merchant.

Like many other small businessmen, Coaker lost everything in 1894, when the Newfoundland banks collapsed. He took to farming, using—and developing—his legendary massive physical strength in clearing land, and exercising his penchant for organization by setting up a night school and an Orange Lodge among his outport neighbours. As one of the few with more than a smattering of education—and more importantly as a supporter of the Liberal Party—he spent his winters in government jobs, as a telegraph operator and chairman of the local Roads Board. In accordance with established practice, he lost these appointments when the Conservatives were elected in 1897; when the Liberals came back to power in 1900, he became a telegrapher again, and a postmaster, and a sub-collector of Customs. He formed a union of telegraph operators and put out its newspaper.

All the while, Coaker was reading, and thinking, and studying the lives of the people around him. Finally, in the fall of 1908, after another season in which fish prices had dropped drastically, he took the product of his thoughts to the public. In two successive evenings at the Orange Hall in Herring Neck, he outlined his plan for an organization that would free the fishermen from their dependence on the merchants. Of the 250 or so who attended, nineteen signed up as the first members of the Fishermen's Protective Union (FPU) and adopted the elaborate constitution Coaker had drafted.

During the winter he travelled about the area recruiting, and by the spring had formed thirty locals. Members paid twenty-five cents—no small commitment for people whose total cash income for a year might amount to only a few dollars. Part of the fee stayed with the local Council, part supported a District Council in each electoral district, and ten cents went to a Supreme Council. To the modern eye, the FPU seems a curious, hybrid organization. It had the trappings of a fraternal order, with sashes, ceremonial regalia, and secret rituals; but where other lodges preached the virtues of humility and submission to authority, the FPU had a militant, cutting edge. Its members, exploited and denigrated for generations, proudly adopted the working fisherman's dark blue guernsey as a uniform. They wore union badges, and their newspaper, the *Fishermen's Advocate*, carried a motto that must have caused some twinges of alarm among the merchants: *suum cuisque* — to each his own.

The union's first target was the credit system. To break the stranglehold of the merchants, fishermen had to be able to buy and sell for cash at fair prices. At the beginning, local councils of the FPU merely pooled orders from their members; the goods were bought in St. John's and retailed at cost plus handling charges. Soon branch stores were opened. The Union Trading Company was formed, and fishermen used the money they saved under the new system to buy its shares. By 1919, it had over four thousand shareholders and a capital investment of a quarter of a million dollars. It operated forty cash stores, and did over three million dollars worth of business in the year. The original shares had earned eighty-eight per cent in interest.

And that was only part of it. Coaker used the profits to float new companies, moving from success to success in vivid demonstration of the power of wealth that could be generated in the fishery. The Union Export Company became a major exporter, shipping salt fish to Portugal, Spain, Italy, Greece, Brazil, and the West Indies. On the Bonavista Peninsula, a model community arose. At its height, Port Union had fish plants, warehouses, a seal oil plant, a ship-building yard, a woodworking factory, a machine shop, a cooperage, a soft-drink bottling plant, a movie theatre, a church, fifty tenement houses for employees, and a Congress Hall for the Supreme Council of the Union. The Union Electric Light and Power Company made the Bonavista area one of the few rural districts to be supplied with electricity, and in Port Union itself powered such futuristic innovations as modern mechanical fish-dryers and even elevators in the factories. In St. John's the Union publishing company printed both a daily and a weekly newspaper.

Coaker himself became a secular messiah. His visits to the isolated outports of the FPU domain were triumphal processions. He came ashore from the union yacht to the bellow of salutes fired from ancient sealing guns. He passed beneath triumphal arches of boughs decorated with union mottoes. Women spread his path with mats, laboriously hooked over long winter evenings with messages of welcome, and union halls echoed with song. In the labour movement in Britain and North America, union songs often made ironic use of tunes and phrases from hymns, but in the songs of the FPU there was no consciousness of parody:

We are coming Mr. Coaker, men from
  Green Bay's Rocky Shore
Men who stand the snow-white billows
  down on stormy Labrador;
We are ready and a-waiting, strong and solid,
  firm and bold,
To be led by you like Moses led
  the Israelites of old.
We are with the fight for freedom,
  and union is our song,
We are coming, Mr. Coaker,
  and we're forty thousand strong.

We are coming, Mr. Coaker,
  from the east, west, north, and south,
You have called us and we're coming
  to put our foes to rout;
We'll be brothers and all free men,
  and we'll rightify each wrong
We are coming, Mr. Coaker,
  and we're forty thousand strong!

The "forty thousand" is usually described as an exaggeration, since the peak of membership was never more than half that number. However, since most fishermen members represented a household operation of catching and processing, perhaps the larger figure has its own claim to accuracy. Whatever the numbers, the quasi-religious fervour was completely genuine.

Every facet of Newfoundland life was influenced by religion, including—and especially—politics. Coaker, himself an Anglican, intended from the outset that the FPU would be non-denominational, and at the outset it was. The first councils were formed in Anglican and Methodist districts of the northeast, but as soon as word of them spread, two were quickly formed in the heavily Catholic area south of St. John's. Religious leaders were wary. The Anglicans of the Society of United Fishermen warned their members off, and the Roman Catholic Archbishop in St. John's used the fact that membership required a secret oath to forbid Catholics from joining. The Protestant clergy did not have the same authority over their parishioners, however, and the movement continued to grow in Protestant districts. Coaker arranged for a declaration to be substituted for the oath, and the union did manage to keep members in a few isolated Catholic pockets of the northeast, but it could not overcome the opposition of the archbishop in the south. The union never surmounted this sectarian disability.

From the beginning, Coaker was aware that the union would also have to tackle the political side of the system. He told members that the Union party would "act exactly as the Labour Party in England—support the government that will do the utmost for the masses." However, in keeping with the conservative sentiments of the people, he added that, while the Labour Party was "not of an imperialistic tone," the Union party would stand strong for the Empire. The platform called for sweeping reforms. Besides a reorganized and rejuvenated fishery, there would be free and compulsory education, non-denominational schools, old-age pensions, minimum wage legislation, improved health care, conflict of interest regulations, and much more—a range of measures that would result in nothing less than the complete restructuring of Newfoundland society.

In 1913, the FPU formed an alliance with the Liberals, of which Coaker grumbled, "If we were able to fight Morris [leader of the governing conservative Peoples Party] and had the learning to run a government . . . we would not trouble to make terms with any party . . . ." Eight of the nine FPU candidates were elected, including Coaker himself, and sat on the Opposition benches with seven Liberals. In the House, and through the FPU newspapers and his regular circular letters to the local councils, Coaker exposed government mismanagement and corruption, attacking the "long-coated chaps"—the lawyers and politicians—and the Board of Trade, which he called the "merchants' union". He went to the ice with the sealers to observe conditions for himself, and managed to get bills passed instituting reforms in sealing and logging for the "sons of toil" who voted for his party.

Toward the end of the war of 1914-18, a National Government of both parties was formed, and Coaker sat as a minister. After the war he formed an alliance with Sir Richard Squires in a Liberal Reform Party, and when Squires became prime minister of what was now the Dominion of Newfoundland, Coaker became his deputy and minister of fisheries. He attempted to implement some of the FPU's long-planned fishery reforms, but a combination of his own heavy-handed methods, the post-war depression, and strong resistance from the fish exporters rendered his efforts unworkable. Fishery reform had been the keystone of FPU policy; when it failed the union seemed to lose its ideological core and Coaker lost some of the force that had propelled him. He did not lose his enthusiasm for grand schemes: he played a major role in securing Newfoundland's second big pulp and paper operation; but somewhere in the political labyrinth the flame of his reformer's zeal flickered and died.

Although at the beginning the FPU incorporated strong co-operative principles, the extensive operations it had developed had become not much more than a collection of limited companies, which Coaker ran, according to one historical authority, "autocratically and increasingly in accordance with mercantile principles." The FPU was no longer "strong and solid, firm and bold," pursuing freedom for the toiling masses: it was a commercial empire over which the members had little more control than they had over traditional private companies. Even now, some elderly men who were part of the early movement complain bitterly that they were never even able to get their initial investment back.

Coaker himself became wealthy. He accepted a knighthood in 1923, and with the rest of the Unionists was absolved of wrong-doing in an investigation of government corruption, but his days as the "northern Moses" were over. Some of the same people who had sung so lustily "We are coming, Mr. Coaker . . . " now sang a wryly humorous ballad in which Coaker dies and goes to hell where he tries to take over the administration. When an election is held, the damned souls vote for the devil over Coaker, apparently as the lesser of two evils. The Union Trading Company, set up to free the fishermen from bondage to the merchants, became one of the largest credit dealers on the island. In 1911 Coaker had bravely promised, "The Union cash stores will sell for cash, and it won't be many years before the credit system will disappear." In 1927, his instructions to store managers were blunt and succinct "never take [fish] if you have to pay cash for it."

Coaker retired to an estate in Jamaica in 1932, and died in Boston in 1937. The FPU commercial empire gradually disintegrated, though the Union Trading Company continued to operate until the late 1970s. In Port Union, Coaker's house and a few substantial buildings still stand, recalling times of both hope and disillusionment. There are no plaques or signs to guide the curious visitor, but above and behind the town, on a low, wind-swept hill, the occasional unsuspecting tourist comes upon an extraordinary private cemetery where the man himself lies buried in a style far grander than any other of Newfoundland's historical personages. A wall of concrete and decorative brick steps up the hill, enclosing a broad expanse of carefully-tended lawn. Wrought-iron gates lead through an arched entry to a neatly gravelled path that mounts the hill to the base of wide stone stairs. At the top of the stairs, the hill is crowned with a concrete platform, forty feet square, commanding a view in all directions. In the middle of the platform stands a marble sarcophagus surmounted by a formal bronze bust, larger than life-size, depicting a fleshy, balding man in late middle age. Oddly, it faces away from the town and the harbour; the blank bronze eyes gaze impassively inland over the sparse, weedy growth and gravel slopes outside the cemetery wall.

One of Coaker's most fervent admirers was J.R. Smallwood. It was a natural affinity: both men were outsiders to the established political system, both had a boundless energy for organizing, a gift for inspirational oratory, a penchant for grandiose schemes, and a vision of greatness for Newfoundland. In 1927, long before his own political star began to rise, Smallwood published an effusive biography in which he declared his conviction that Coaker would be "regarded by all as the greatest Newfoundlander since John Cabot." When he became premier, Smallwood had his own try at creating an organization of fishermen.

In 1951, on the day after the second anniversary of Newfoundland's entry into Confederation, a week-long fishermen's convention was held in the Gaiety Theatre in St. John's. It was a gala event, carried off in true Smallwood style. Two hundred fishermen, elected as delegates in their own electoral districts and including three Inuit from Labrador, converged on St. John's by coastal boat, train, and airplane. They made a grand auto tour of the city, pausing outside of Government House where the lieutenant governor, in full regalia, read them an address of welcome. At the theatre, they were addressed by Smallwood himself, the Leader of the Opposition, J.G. Higgins, and Monsignor Moses Coady, the old clerical hero of the co-operative movement in Nova Scotia.

The speeches all stressed that this was a momentous and historic occasion, and so it was: the first time that fishermen from all parts of Newfoundland had come together to discuss their common problems. They had plenty to discuss. Traditionally, Newfoundland's fish had been sold in Europe, the Caribbean, and South America for sterling, which was converted to dollars in London. In the economic confusion of post-war reconstruction, the conversion became more difficult, and few customers were willing to part with dollars for fish. With Confederation, Newfoundland also inherited Canada's problems with export and dollar conversion. In 1951 the Newfoundland fish exporting corporation was still struggling to get rid of the previous year's fish, and prices had dropped thirty-three per cent from the 1949 level. In some cases, Newfoundland fishermen were receiving half the price that their counterparts in Nova Scotia were getting. One delegate, who claimed to be the first man to have invested a dollar in Coaker's FPU, observed that a successful fisherman might expect to produce fifty quintals of fish in a season; at ten dollars a quintal, he could make five hundred dollars. He went on to say that, at that rate, it would take fifty years to earn twenty-five thousand—an amount that some people made in a year.

The convention provided little in the way of immediate solutions. Smallwood predicted a shift to fresh-frozen fish production, and said that in the next ten years ten thousand men would have to be taken out of the fishery and provided with other jobs. The main message was that the fishermen themselves must build an effective organization. The structure that he proposed looked very much like Coaker's FPU: local unions, regional federations, and an all-Newfoundland convention—a "fishermen's parliament" potentially representing twenty-eight thousand working fishermen. When a delegate said that the new organization must be "free of politics" he was roundly cheered: memories of Coaker remained strong.

The convention adopted a constitution and formed the Newfoundland Federation of Fishermen (NFF). Smallwood sent the delegates home with a rousing appeal for unity:

> The men of the south are no different from the men of the north; the west is the same as the east . . . during the past week men of all areas have been together and they know they are all the same . . . Through your united efforts, if it is God's will, Newfoundland will be a freer, happier, better place for the producers of this province . . .

A few days later in the House of Assembly, the leader of the opposition accused the premier of using the fishermen for political propaganda, noting that although he had been invited to address their convention no other opposition members had been involved, even those from fishing districts. Mr. Higgins was attacked in turn by Harold Horwood, later to be best known as a novelist, but then a young Smallwood lieutenant and fiery union organizer, who derided the fish merchants as "scum of the earth" and "conscienceless crooks," and triumphantly stated that the Federation of Fishermen was a manifestation of a new era—"the age of the common man."

In the years that followed, it became clear that the leader of the opposition had probably been closer to the mark than Horwood. The Federation did, for a time, reach a membership of ten thousand. With the assistance of the provincial government it lobbied for extension of unemployment insurance benefits to fishermen, managed to secure discounts from suppliers on fishing equipment, and pursued other reforms, but it did not confront the fundamental issue—the relationship between fishermen and fish companies. It had been born into the sticky web of Newfoundland politics and in spite of the efforts of a number of able members was never able to fight its way out.

It could have been created only by government: at the time no other agency had the resources for organization on such a scale. Since fishermen's incomes were low, membership dues had to be low—a dollar a year at first, and later two dollars. Most of the Federation's budget, therefore, came from an annual grant from the government. Smallwood bolstered the fishermen's pride and at the same time placated other taxpayers by saying that this was "the fishermen's own money," being, he claimed, interest on a fund established from a tax levied on saltfish exports during the war by the Commission Government. In the later 1950s, however, when an offer came from the Canadian Labour Congress for affiliation, the government made it clear that acceptance would mean withdrawal of the annual subsidy, and the CLC's offer was rejected. It may have been the fishermen's own money, but Smallwood's government held the purse-strings.

From the beginning, the Federation was in a classic double-bind. The only way to be independent of government would be to increase membership dues to twenty or thirty times their original level. In order to justify such dues, however, the organization would have to provide more direct services, but the most obvious of these, collective bargaining for fish prices, was ruled out by the provincial Labour Relations Act.

The founding convention of the NFF was chaired by Max Lane, a Clarenville magistrate who had been hand-picked by Smallwood for the job. He became the Federation's secretary-general, and remained a Smallwood man. Although the convention had been adamantly against political involvement by the Federation, the constitution was soon modified and Lane became a Liberal MHA. In 1959 Smallwood used him to head the ephemeral Brotherhood of Woods Workers that was created to break the IWA strike, and later rewarded him with a cabinet post.

In spite of its shortcomings, the Federation was an important step in the development of organization in the Newfoundland fishery. It was the first association to bring fishermen from all areas and religious denominations together, and it gave many of them a taste of what a real fishermen's organization could be like. Some of its most active local officers provided a core of experienced leadership for the NFFAWU when it was formed in 1970.

One who stuck by the Federation was Patrick J. Antle, a delegate to the original convention from the Burin Peninsula. Antle succeeded Lane as secretary-general, and devoted his career to an effort to make the organization work. He became its president in 1971, as Cashin and McGrath were beginning their sweep, and fought a tenacious rear-guard action to keep the Federation alive. He never accepted the notion of a union that would encompass plant workers, trawlermen, and inshore fishermen, and he was suspicious of the motives of McGrath and Cashin—he once mischievously suggested that they would have signed up the Sisters of Mercy if they could get them to pay dues. Under the pressure of competition, Antle used his position as president of the Federation to press for reforms, but the effort came too late. Smallwood, who had not let go of the Federation in its early and hopeful days, abandoned it to its fate and took no responsibility for its downfall. In a film interview in 1970 he said that he had wanted the fishermen to be "the most powerful body of voters in the province".

> I could invite them to form the Federation, and I could say that if you form this Federation we will match what ever you collect . . . we could do all that, but, I said, It's you that must have the power. It's you that must have the control. If they haven't, this could only be their fault. No one else's.

Even as he spoke, fishermen on the Northern Peninsula were preparing to correct that fault.

The fishermen at the 1951 convention that formed the NFF were primarily interested in the problems of the salt fish industry. From the turn of the century onward there had been some degree of diversification in the fishery: in a few places around the island lobster and salmon were canned, herring were salted for export, and salmon and halibut were shipped chilled or frozen, but until after the Second World War salt cod remained the mainstay. Beginning just before the war and accelerating after Confederation there was a shift toward the establishment of fresh fish freezing plants geared to the U.S. market and, in some areas, the use of large deep-sea trawlers to supply them. The larger of these plants provided some of the conditions for the development of conventional union organization—a regular, hourly-paid work force sharing common conditions and locations of work and a common relationship with an employer—and some small local unions began to be formed, centred on the processing plants.

The industrial conditions were not, however, clear-cut. At first there was no very sharp distinction among those who worked in the processing plants, those who caught fish from their own boats and sold to the plants, and those who crewed the offshore trawlers. The same man might do any of these, shifting from one to the other as opportunity allowed, and also possibly producing some salt fish for the traditional market. In any case, the communities were small and close-knit; members of the same family could be engaged in any aspect of the fishery.

One of the first local unions generated under the new industrial conditions, formed in the town of Burin in 1947, reflects this transitional stage in the development of the industry. It was called the Fishermen's and Workmen's Protective Union, and its early minute-books show it engaged in a broad range of activities: discussing wages and working conditions with plant management, providing sickness benefits for members, discussing prices for fresh fish with plant buyers and for salt fish with merchants, arranging for the co-operative purchase of household fuel and fishing supplies, and commenting on the prices of consumer goods.

The provincial Labour Relations Act of 1950 made a clear legal distinction between employees working for a set wage and others such as inshore fishermen, who were regarded as independent operators, and trawler hands who received pay based on a share of the catch and were regarded as "co-venturers" with the company that owned the vessel. Only the workers in the processing plants were allowed full collective bargaining rights, and the small locals came to be more clearly organizations of plant workers.

There were not many of them. The work force in most plants was small, the work was seasonal, and the turn-over of employees was high, all of which made organization difficult. Employers resisted. In the Bonavista area some of the strongest resistance came, ironically, from the FPU: in the 1950s it still claimed fifteen hundred members, and in some places it applied, with the collaboration of employers, for certification as bargaining agent for groups of workers. The Labour Relations Board, however, did not recognize the FPU as a valid union.

If the workers in a plant did succeed in organizing, there was no central union for them to join. At first the locals were directly chartered by the Newfoundland Federation of Labour, later by the American Federation of Labour, and, after 1956, by the Canadian Labour Congress. None of these bodies had the resources to provide extensive support, and much depended upon local leadership. In some cases, unions formed but were unable to maintain themselves against continued pressure from the employers.

Cyril Strong, who was provincial representative for the American Federation of Labour after 1949 and later for the Canadian Labour Congress, tells of one example on the southwest coast:

> I went down there and held a meeting. It was just a small plant—maybe twenty or thirty workers. I talked to them, and when I was done a fellow gets up and he says, 'Skipper, we'd love to have a union, but we've got no boss.' I says, 'What do you mean, no boss?' Well, it turned out that there was nobody there with an education above grade three or four. Nobody in the plant who could handle the paper work.
>
> Later on I got a call from there. A fellow had come back to town—he'd been overseas in the war and he'd been working some place away—well, he'd come back to town

> and was working in the plant. And he had some education. So they had their boss.
>
> He accepted the job as president of the local, so we got certified, and we got an agreement. It even had a union security clause in it—a closed shop.
>
> Before a year was out, he got promoted to foreman. They had some disagreement and he resigned as president, and the local just dissolved.
>
> I had some job explaining to the A Fof L why I was sending back a charter with a closed shop clause in it. Try explaining that to somebody down in the States! Here's a union with an agreement, a security clause, and money in the bank, and I'm sending back the charter!
>
> Most of the money they had went to the school there. I don't know if that was exactly legal, but the school needed it, and the union couldn't use it.

The five or six independent fish plant unions that did survive had few resources, and could not afford to take a very militant stance, but nonetheless they managed to make slow progress toward better pay and working conditions. In 1967, the Canadian Labour Congress embarked on a programme to incorporate the independent unions into large internationals, and a series of changes followed in rapid succession, involving what will undoubtedly be for the reader a bewildering sequence of names.

The CLC began by giving jurisdiction in the fishing industry to the United Packinghouse Workers of American (UPWA), which was made up mainly of workers in meat-packing plants, but included some leather and tannery workers. A representative of the UPWA came to Newfoundland and began to try to incorporate the fish plant unions. Shortly after, in 1968, the UPWA was absorbed into the Amalgamated Meat-Cutters and Butcher Workmen (AMCBW) whose members were largely in the retail section of the meat industry. It was under these auspices that Fred Locking came to Newfoundland as international representative, to complete the incorporation of the independent locals and to organize new ones. Shortly after that, the Canadian division of the Amalgamated Meat-Cutters and Butcher Workmen adopted the name of Canadian Food and Allied Workers (CFAWU), with head offices in Toronto, but this was a change in name only: it remained a regional division of the AMCBW.

This, then, was the situation when McGrath and Cashin began working with the fishermen of Port au Choix to form the Northern Fishermen's Union. About a hundred fish plants were operating in the province. Of these, thirty-four were fresh fish freezing operations: the rest were small collecting plants or were engaged in packing and shipping salt fish. Eight of the freezing plants and three of the others had operating unions. These were mostly in the larger plants and their collective agreements covered about seventeen hundred workers—approximately a third of the total fish plant work-force of about five thousand men and women.

A Royal Commission on labour legislation reported that up until 1969 the collective bargaining process had not been working well in the plants. Contract negotiations frequently ended in conciliation, and strikes were usually spontaneous protests against working conditions rather than a carefully used weapon in the bargaining process. Wages were considerably below Canadian averages for the fish-processing industry, and most fish plant workers earned less than such traditionally low-paid workers as shop clerks. Fred Locking, as international representative of the CFAWU, the Canadian division of the Amalgamated Meat-Cutters, was engaged in trying to pull the fish plant locals together and to organize more.

The fish plants were supplied by about nineteen thousand fishermen. About a thousand of these were in a special category: they were crewmen on large company-owned trawlers that fished the offshore banks, and were paid by the companies on the basis of a share of the catch. The rest were classed as inshore fishermen, but within that category there was a wide range in the sort of boats and gear used. The vast majority fished from small open boats within a few hours travel from their home ports. Approximately four hundred of them owned longliners, the larger covered vessels of thirty-five or forty feet in length that could travel greater distances to fish, and carried crews of three or four. None of the fishermen—including the trawlermen—were covered by the provincial Labour Relations Act. About four thousand belonged to the Newfoundland Federation of Fishermen.

It was the inshore fishermen, with a strong lead from the longliner skippers, who set out in 1969 to form the NFU with the help of McGrath and Cashin. By the fall of 1970 they had become part of an international union along with about two thousand plant workers, and were embarked on a campaign to change the whole relationship between fishermen and fish companies. The commentators and editorial writers who were looking on can, perhaps, be forgiven for predicting failure: they looked back over a long and bitter history. McGrath represented a crusading zeal for social reform and Cashin a shrewd political sense, both of which reminded people, inevitably, of the two sides of Sir William Coaker. The possibility that the NFFAWU would lose its way in the barren tangle of Newfoundland's political economy was very real.

On the other hand, there were new factors in the equation. The wage-earning fish plant workers were a new and growing force: they and the fishermen together could form a powerful alliance. The NFFAWU was backed by a massive international union, and had the blessing of the Canadian labour establishment. And all across Newfoundland, new forces of social change were at work. The Newfoundland fishery had interesting times ahead.

Chapter 3

The history of hardship and struggle outlined in the last chapter is unique only in its details: across Canada and throughout the industrialized world, working people have come through their own versions of it. But by the 1970s, for many of them that history had become remote and distant—something that had happened to other people a long time ago. In the small, stable fishing communities of Newfoundland, however, it was still happening, and the past was close, both in time and in the consciousness of the people. As wives and mothers they had "made" the fish that built Port Union and hooked the rugs that were so hopefully laid in William Coaker's path. As fathers and sons they had carried their fish to the merchants and received in return only the bare necessities for another year of hard work. If they had not been present themselves, every man in every harbour had heard first-hand accounts of Smallwood's Fishermen's Convention in the Gaiety Theatre. When Cashin and McGrath talked of union in the fishing communities, this was their audience.

Even before the merger and the creation of the NFFAWU, the two amateur organizers had begun to attract key recruits: men who knew—and had lived—the history and were eager for change. They were a strange and sometimes difficult assortment, different in temperament, habits, ideas, religion, and dialect. They had in common their experience of the Newfoundland fishery, and an ability to translate that experience into thoughts and words. Most important, they were working fishermen who had earned the respect of their fellows.

There was Lester Kean from Badgers Quay in Bonavista Bay, who had made his first trip to the Labrador fishery with his father at the age of eight, and went back every summer for the next twenty-eight years. As the Labrador fishery was failing in the early 1960s, he built himself a longliner, and began fishing with gill-nets fifty or sixty miles off Newfoundland's northeast corner. He and some others like him were in the process of forming their own organization, the Bonavista North Fishermen's Assocation, of which Kean was president, when they attended the meeting addressed by Cashin and McGrath in the Centreville Orange Hall. Lester Kean was one of the first to stand up after the guests had finished, and he began from that night to organize for the new union. He brought to the task a style that seems to be rooted in his Salvation Army upbringing—an enthusiasm tempered with moderation, uncompromising on what is right, but tolerant of human frailty.

There was Woodrow Philpott, from the tiny Pentacostal settlement of Cottles Island, not far from Twillingate in Notre Dame Bay. An ambitious and hard-driving young fisherman of thirty-five, Philpott had been in the boat for nearly twenty years when he heard of the stirrings of the new union on the radio, and telephoned to invite McGrath to come and speak. Without such sponsorship a Catholic priest would have had a hard time getting a hearing in the area but Philpott became the ambassador, and once the ice was broken the union message spread. On one occasion he organized a meeting for McGrath in the very hall where Coaker had launched the FPU sixty years before. A direct and forceful speaker, Philpott was unimpressed by rank or position, and deferred to no one. The other union men came to call him "Pastor" Philpott, partly because of his religious background but also partly in jest: though he has since reformed, he was at the time a hard-drinking rowdyman, who could be charming, logically persuasive, and bullyingly argumentative by turns.

There was Levi George Norris of Bay de Verde who, though not yet fifty, had spent nearly forty years on the water. He had gone in the boat with his father and grandfather at the age of eight, and grown up with a deep sense of the injustice of what he calls the "put-in and take-out system" of the traditional fishery. "Men fished all their lives," he says, "and got nothin', only gear and groceries.

> I remembers a time I went with my father takin' some fish to the merchant. It was all top quality fish—Madeira, we called it then. The culler, he started takin' up the fish and pullin' it abroad and smelling it, and then he'd throw it down. Said it was all West Indie—that's the poorest grade of all.
>
> So I was naggin' at the old man, and he was naggin' at the culler. Then the culler, he says to the old man, 'You come in to my office here,' and he took him into he's

> office. 'Look here,' he says, 'You let me do as I likes with your fish, and say what I likes about it. Maybe I'll call it West Indie, but I'll give you top price on your receipt. I've got to get so much West Indie, and if you just keeps quiet, I'll get it off the other boys.'
>
> That was the way it was. The only way my father could get the proper price for his fish was if somebody else got robbed. And even at that, it was no kind of pay for the work a fisherman did.

By the 1960s, Norris had worked himself up to a longliner, and was among the top fishermen in Bay de Verde, a community with an excellent reputation in the fishery. He was a member of the Federation of Fishermen, but took little interest in its activities. "I knew we needed a proper union," he says, "and so did the others. If somebody had come up with a union ten years earlier, we'd have been into it." Norris had heard about the activity on the St. Barbe Coast, and when Richard Cashin called to see if he would organize a meeting in his area, he was quick to agree. "That was the end of the Federation in Bay de Verde," he says. "From then on, everybody was for the union." The rest of the fishermen in his area were not so easy to convince, however, and Norris worked for the NFFAWU for four more years before gaining a sufficient majority for certification.

There was Kevin Condon from Calvert on the Southern Shore of the Avalon Peninsula, about eighty kilometres from St. John's, a wiry, weatherbeaten, soft-spoken man in his mid-fifties who had fished for a living since the age of twelve. In a quiet, determined way, Condon had bucked the system all his life, and more than one plant on the Southern Shore had refused to take his fish because he was a "troublemaker." He joined Smallwood's Federation of Fishermen early and became its vice-president. When the UFAWU in British Columbia was hitting the headlines he proposed that the Federation invite its controversial leader, Homer Stevens, to come to Newfoundland and discuss affiliation, but his proposal was overruled. Besides his work with the Federation, Condon appealed to the larger public in a series of letters to the editors of the St. John's newspapers, in which he set out clearly and vividly the problems of the fishermen. During the crisis year of 1968, as an executive member of the Federation, he wrote a letter exposing a betrayal by the fish companies: in the previous year, he said, they had promised to introduce a "check-off" system, refusing to buy fish from anyone who was not a Federation member, but they did not follow through. The only way to put an end to the "disgraceful situation" of the fishery, Condon argued, was by forming a strong uion of fishermen—something that the Federation, in his opinion, had not achieved.

When Richard Cashin approached him with the idea of the Northern Fishermen's Union, Condon tried again. As vice-president of the Federation, he called a special meeting of the executive and suggested that they join forces with the new organization. Again he was overruled, but this time Condon had an alternative. He resigned from the NFF and began to organize for the NFU.

His example brought in other members of the NFF, including Bill Short, president of the Pouch Cove local, a big, bluff fellow in his late thirties who shared with the others a family tradition in the fishery, the respect of his fellow fishermen, and a gift for colourful, persuasive talk. "If Bill couldn't persuade you," one of his colleagues says, "he'd talk you to death." Short had also inherited the resentment and frustration of generations:

> Our family had a good reputation as fishermen. None better. And yet we ended up with nothing. My grandfather fished on the Labrador all his life, and when he was seventy-three or -four, all he got was twelve dollars a quarter—not a month, a *quarter*—for poor relief. And to get that he had to wait for somebody to die.

He tells of his father, who would sometimes talk the fish buyer into giving him an extra quarter of a cent a pound, and then leak the information to others so they could demand equal treatment. Short had worked on the Great Lakes, where he was a member of the Seaman's International Union; he had crewed aboard trawlers on Newfoundland's south coast in what he calls "some of the most inhuman working conditions in any civilized country"; and when the union was being organized he was operating a longliner out of Harbour Grace. "I was right suspicious of Richard Cashin," he says:

> Here he was, a rich St. John's lawyer. What was he doing with a union? But when I seen men like Kevin Condon, and Woodrow Philpott, and Lester Kean, and Levi George Norris, and Father McGrath—well, I figured there had to be something to it.

Short was not alone in his suspicion of Cashin: this was an obstacle that each recruit in turn had to face for himself and, if he was to organize for the union, find a way of overcoming in others. It was part of a basic dilemma that had plagued fishermen all along. In spite of their intimate knowledge of their own sphere of the industry, they were always at a disadvantage when dealing with representatives of fish companies or governments. They needed someone who could talk to managers and politicians in their own terms, but such a person belonged, almost by definition, to a class with interests in opposition to their own or, like Coaker, was likely to be adopted into it.

The original members on the St. Barbe Coast had been won over partly by the trust that McGrath had built up, and partly by their own observations. "We didn't know what to make of Richard at first," one of them says,

> but Father Des brought him in, so we figured he must be all right. After a while, we didn't need Father Des to tell us. I've never seen anybody work the way them two done: and there was nothin' in it for them—they weren't getting anything out of it for themselves. That's what convinced people. After three months they had the support of every fisherman in Port au Choix.

> There used to be all that stuff in the papers about Richard wantin' to go back into politics—that bothered some people at the start of it, but after a while it didn't. Seeing the way he worked for us and stood by us like he done, nobody would hold it against him supposin' he did go into politics. They'd support him. I knows I would. He's after showin' us what he can do, and whose side he's on.

As organizing continued, the trust that they placed in Cashin and McGrath communicated itself to others.

For many of those who enlisted in the NFU and were gradually overcoming their reservations about Cashin, the merger with the plantworkers' international presented another dilemma. Especially in the northeast, the memory of the loggers' strike of 1959 was still strong. Some blamed the International Woodworkers of America and distrusted any international link; others were afraid that if they allied themselves with an outside union Smallwood would move against the fishermen as he had against the loggers. On the other hand, they were undertaking a massive organizing task. Although many fishermen had demonstrated their willingness to join the NFU and pay fees, they could hardly be expected to continue for long if the organization did not soon begin to show tangible results in the form of growing membership, progress toward bargaining rights, and better fish prices—and that was going to require money. Cashin and McGrath were working for nothing, and most of the men mentioned above were making organizing trips at their own expense. Warily, and with misgivings, the fishermen accepted the merger with the international.

With the money from the Chicago headquarters, the organizing campaign moved into high gear. There were two immediate objectives: to sign up as many inshore fishermen as possible, and to exert pressure on the government to allow them collective bargaining rights. The latter would require action at both the federal and provincial levels. Since the fishermen were regarded as independent operators, an attempt to band together and meet with fish processors to establish a price for their product would be prohibited by the federal Combines Act. It would be necessary for the application of the Act to be waived, but this was not a serious obstacle: the precedent had been set ten years earlier when the Act had been waived for British Columbia fishermen, and there was every reason to expect that the government would do the same for the Newfoundlanders once an effective union was in place. However, there would also have to be a change in provincial legislation, and that change would have to be made against the opposition of the fish companies and much of the business community. The union began a petition and letter campaign, but the serious pressure would come when they could show a strong representation in the many electoral districts where fishermen and their families voted.

Cashin and McGrath redoubled their efforts, criss-crossing the province by car, boat, and airplane. New organizers were hired, and experienced representatives came down from the Canadian headquarters in Toronto. The campaign to organize plant workers also continued, but Cashin and McGrath concentrated on signing up groups of fishermen in each of the traditional fishing areas, organizing them into committees that would send delegates to the founding convention to be held in the spring. The new union was gaining momentum—and an ever-increasing amount of attention from the news media.

By December of 1970, only three months after the formal announcement of the formation of the NFFAWU, twenty inshore fishermen, delegates from groups all across the province, met in the Battery Motel in St. John's with Cashin, McGrath, and Locking to plan further strategy and set up a steering committee that would act as an executive for the fishermen's section of the union until formal elections could take place at the convention. Over the next five months, in a series of meetings that were often turbulent and sometimes hilarious, the steering committee would establish the basis of Newfoundland's first fishermen's union.

Its members were the working fishermen who had taken the early lead in their own districts—Kevin Condon, Levi George Norris, Lester Kean, Woodrow Philpott, and Ralph O'Keefe, who had sat with his parish priest aboard the longliner in Port au Choix when the germ of the union began. All were strong personalities, and besides having to learn how to build a union they had to learn to understand and get along with each other. "We had some wild old meetings," one of them remembers:

> We'd argue and shout and pound the table. Some would want this, and somebody else would want that . . . Who was going to be eligible to join the union? Who was a *bona fide* fisherman? How was we going to set prices?

> But we learned. We'd screech and bawl at each other, and then somebody'd make a joke and we'd all be laughin'. And somehow we'd come to an agreement.
>
> Those were some of the best times of my life, those meetings.

All this mutual learning and testing included Richard Cashin, the man whose legal knowledge and political experience they were counting on to put their message across. "Richard didn't know very much about the fishery at the start of it, and that's the truth," one of the committee members says:

> he knew about the legal part—he knew about the government end of it, but he didn't know nothin' about our end of 'er. But, my son, he could learn! I've never seen anybody could learn things quicker or better than Richard Cashin.
>
> See, we knew our end of it—what was wrong and what we wanted—but we couldn't put it together. He'd take it all in and he'd put it all together the way we wanted it.

"And he was tough," another one of the group remembers. "We wasn't easy on him.

> But you couldn't put him down. He'd always come back for more. You could say anything to him. On times, I think he'd do it on purpose—stir us up a bit so we'd go at him, and he'd learn from that. So did we.
>
> One time we was goin' at him, all of us—I forgets what it was about now—and he jumps up from the table and says, 'If that's the way its' going to be, I'd just as soon jump out that window!'
>
> So somebody—I believes it was Kevin—says, 'Go ahead and jump, boy. We'll get along just as good without you.' And somebody else says, 'Here, take my key. My room's on the second floor—you can jump out there.' We all got a good laugh out of that.

The arguments and disagreements and the learning went on behind closed doors. The public—and the government—saw only a growing social movement as signatures on the union petition mounted toward the ten thousand mark. Early in January of 1971, Premier Smallwood announced that his government would introduce legislation to allow collective bargaining for fishermen during the new session of the House of Assembly. He also established a committee headed by the minister of fisheries to travel to Iceland and Norway to examine the structure of the fishery in those countries. Significantly, the committee included Pat Antle of the NFF and Richard Cashin as the nominee of the NFFAWU. Cashin returned from the trip with glowing reports of the position of fishermen in the Scandinavian industry, and the newspapers began to speculate freely that Newfoundland would soon have a new method of establishing fish prices, based on the Norwegian model. At the end of March, Smallwood established a Select Committee of the House to receive representations from interested parties and recommend legislation on the matter of collective bargaining for fishermen.

As the union's organizational net spread out it made one unusual catch that was to prove a stroke of fishermen's luck. Newfoundland members of the Retail Clerks' union had been having difficulty with their international headquarters, and the union's international representative, Ray Greening, had resigned his position and worked for several months without pay for the dissident locals, trying to establish an improved organization. At thirty-three, Greening was already a veteran: he had spent nearly sixteen years working for Canada Packers, and for many of those years had held office in his union local. Among those who took an interest in the Retail Clerks' problems was Charlie Borsk, a Toronto-based organizer for the CFAWU. Although he was in Newfoundland to assist in organizing fishermen and fishplants he, like Fred Locking, had a long association with the old Packinghouse Workers' Union, and thus with Ray Greening's ex-employer, Canada Packers. Borsk, among others, suggested that Greening would be a valuable addition to the NFFAWU. Greening took the job and brought with him the Canada Packers local and several locals of retail clerks, who formed an odd little extra in the rapidly-forming fish workers' organization.

He quickly became a model organizer, adding several new plants to the union's roster, and later became one of its most respected officers.

Media coverage of the union's activities drew attention to a fact that was already well known in the fishing harbours: its successes were at the expense—and threatened the continued existence—of the Newfoundland Federation of Fishermen. If the NFF had been a union, the NFFAWU would have been guilty of "raiding" and subject to punitive action by other labour organizations, but since the NFF was by its own definition an association of independent operators, anti-raiding regulations did not apply. Detractors of the Federation and its general secretary, Pat Antle, suggested that this was the reason that Antle had asked for recognition as bargaining agent for fishermen a year earlier, when the NFU was forming: if the bid had been successful, the charge of raiding might have slowed, or even prevented, the union's growth. As it was, although it was rarely stated in so many words, the two organizations were locked in a struggle that could have only one survivor. The government, in the form of J.R. Smallwood, watched but did not openly take sides, and the union pressed its advantage at every opportunity. Since its inception in 1951, the Federation had been allowed free office space in a government-owned building in downtown St. John's: the NFFAWU demanded equal treatment and was given a suite of offices in the same building.

A culmination of sorts was expected in April, when both the Federation and the union were scheduled to hold conventions—the union's first and the Federation's twentieth. Although the two events were, of course, completely independent, the news media—and fishermen around the province—would inevitably draw comparisons. As the convention dates approached, Pat Antle told the press that he felt that "politics played a part" in the formation of the new union, but he declined to elaborate. He expressed doubt that fishermen would gain any advantage from membership in a "sprawling union" like the NFFAWU with its national and international links. Antle also suggested that if the Federation did not approve an increase in fees, he would consider resigning. Richard Cashin said that Antle had forfeited any claim to representing the fishermen by opposing the check-off system before the House

Select Committee on bargaining rights. Antle said that bargaining should be open to any organization the fishermen of a given area should choose—union, federation, co-operative, or any other body.

The Federation convention came first, in the middle of the month, and the extent of the damage inflicted by the union became apparent: only twenty-three delegates attended. Henry Taylor, the retiring president, washed his hands of the matter, commenting that, "If fishermen are not interested enough to attend a meeting, then I cannot contact them. I refuse to knock on doors." In a backhanded swipe at Cashin he added, "I am not a politician." Antle, however, was not ready to give up. The Federation's executive was rearranged, and he became its president-manager. Fees were raised to ten dollars a year, and plans laid to hire an organizer. In a speech to delegates Antle left no doubt of his sentiments regarding unions, stating that in the USA, and to some extent in Canada, "a large segment of the working class are in far more danger of exploitation from big, greedy unions than they are from big, greedy business establishments that the unions were originally formed to protect them from."

Premier Smallwood addressed the small gathering, and told them that they must not clash with the NFFAWU—that open conflict between the two could destroy them both. The warning was no more than pious sentiment, for the Federation was already fighting a hopeless rearguard action. Two years later, its membership had dropped below a thousand, the government withdrew its funding, and Smallwood's "great organization of fishermen" faded into history.

The union convention, by contrast, was both a triumphant celebration and a skilfully staged propaganda event. It was held on the anniversary of the founding meeting of the Northern Fishermen's Union, not in a rural schoolroom this time, but in the Hotel Newfoundland in St. John's, in rooms more accustomed to Rotary Club luncheons and meetings of the association of fish processors. Ninety-three delegates attended and played host to representatives of the parent CFAWU, down for the event from Ontario, and officers of the Federation of Labour. The gala banquet was attended by the minister of fisheries, the leader of the opposition, representatives of the major religious denominations, and the premier himself, who was to give the after-dinner speech. According to some accounts, the convention cost twenty-five thousand dollars.

Proceedings got under way with speeches from visiting CFAWU and CLC officials. The delegates were coaxed into a ragged rendition of "Solidarity Forever", but the singing was less than spirited: many were not familiar with the song, and were uncertain about what it might mean. Their uncertainty may well have been increased when, following the hymn to working class unity, a representative of the CFAWU gave a speech in which he lambasted the UFAWU of British Columbia, which had been part of the inspiration for the original constitution of the NFU a year before. In the intervening twelve months, the CFAWU had raided the UFAWU's struggling local in Nova Scotia and put an end to the BC union's attempt to expand to the east coast.

With the formalities out of the way, they got down to the real business. The structure in the proposed constitution was explained. Seven fish plant locals had now agreed to be part of the NFFAWU: these, with others that would be organized, would constitute an Industrial Section. The fishermen would all belong to one local, and constitute a Fishermen's Section. The entire union would be governed by a provincial council made up of five delegates from each section and a president and secretary-treasurer elected from the delegates at large.

As debate on the constitution began, a note of dissension was raised, foreshadowing events to come. Chesley Beck, a plant organizer from the Burin Peninsula who had been recruited by Fred Locking before McGrath and Cashin came on the scene, stood up and questioned whether the plant workers really wanted to become involved in a joint union with the fishermen. When one of the Ontario officials tried to respond, Beck brushed his reply aside, saying that only the plant workers could answer. A vote was held, and the delegates unanimously accepted the new arrangements.

Outside the meetings, the delegates planned, partied, and argued in a dozen different accents, while journalists searched for inside stories—or attempted to generate them. At a late-night gathering in Father McGrath's hotel room, a prominent St. John's newspaperman asked him if he was happy to have brought "Mafia unionism" to Newfoundland, and the big priest picked him up by the scruff of the neck and threw him bodily out of the room.

The constitution and the resolutions were important business, but the event everyone was waiting for was the banquet and Premier Smallwood's speech. This was a different audience from the Federation's twenty-three delegates. He would not be able to avoid talking about collective bargaining for fishermen. Richard Cashin gave him a fulsome introduction, but made abundantly clear what the convention wanted the Premier to say. Mr. Smallwood, Cashin said, had the opportunity to pass a "Magna Carta" for fishermen:

> I have heard the Premier express fear that at some time the province of Newfoundland could fall into the wrong hands. Once legislation is passed giving collective bargaining rights to fishermen, he need never fear that again. The power will be where it belongs—in the hands of the people!

The Premier began with an historical lecture on his own involvement with fishermen's organizations—the FPU, his Bonavista co-operative, the NFF. He repeated the warning he had given the Federation—the province could not afford two fishermen's unions fighting one another. They must go their own ways, and the one that did the best job would survive. In five years' time, he predicted, one or the other would be gone.

If any of his audience's attention was wandering by this time, it was brought sharply back as the premier turned to the central issue of bargaining rights. He described the work of the House Committee, and said that legislation would be passed—provided the committee made its recommendations in time. This had a somewhat less positive tone than his promise of a few months before that the law would definitely be passed in the current session, and the delegates stirred uneasily. Their unease increased as he continued. The committee, he said, would recommend "*some kind* of collective bargaining legislation." But, he told them, "don't put too much confidence in getting that law passed."

As questioning murmurs arose from the assembly, the premier

launched into an explanation that taxed the reportorial powers of both journalists and the representatives of Memorial University's Extension Service, who were providing a record of the proceedings. If the law was too strong, he suggested, it could threaten the very existence of the union.

> . . . if it has enough sharp teeth in it, [if it is] able to bite, if it's that kind of law, the fishermen would say, 'Oh well, we don't need a union, we've got the law.'

Then, while delegates knit their brows, Smallwood pulled another oratorical rabbit from the hat:

> If the union is strong enough to persuade the government to bring that law into the House of Assembly; if the union is strong enough to persuade the House of Assembly to pass that law; if they're that strong, that's just fine. But if the law is passed and takes the place of the union, the law will not have the strength of the union behind it, and it would be no time before the law would become a dead letter.

Many of the delegates were now thoroughly confused. What was the premier telling them? Were they to have collective bargaining or not? Was he suggesting that if they got it, it would do them no good? While they puzzled, Smallwood slipped back into the role of labour organizer, urging them to make their union a strong one:

> It is life and death importance that you keep the organization strong; to make it bigger than it is; to make it stronger than it is; that it become a very, very powerful union.

What they were to do with their power was not made very clear, but there was one thing they were not to do—they were not to become greedy—to become a "dollar-grabbing organization." The premier made no direct reference to the union's international link, but was there a touch of warning—a faint echo of the IWA battle—in his statement that the Union "must be a patriotic body of Newfoundlanders fighting to uplift our province"? And was there a hint of menace in his observation that it could "have some hard sledding ahead"? It might, he said, "have come ahead a little too fast . . . found it just a little too easy . . . have not had enough opposition yet." When he finished, the applause was scattered and tentative.

Father McGrath thanked Mr. Smallwood for his remarks, observing that he was sure they would "be considered." On one matter, however, he wanted to assure the premier that "If anybody has the idea that something is being handed to them . . . we have only begun to fight." His final words were drowned in cheers and table-pounding.

As the premier was making his way out of the hall, his path was suddenly blocked by the looming, square-shouldered, square-jawed figure of Woodrow Philpott, who backed him into a row of chairs and angrily demanded to know whether or not bargaining legislation was to be passed. Smallwood started to reply that the matter was in the hands of the committee, but Philpott brushed the explanation aside. "You control that committee," he said. "We are not going to put up with promises any more. We want that law." Nervous bystanders moved to intervene and the premier, visibly startled by the confrontation, slipped away. The next day, at an emergency session, the delegates established a committee to call upon the premier to demand clarification of his remarks, and passed a resolution endorsing strikes and other emergency public action to be taken if bargaining legislation were not passed.

During the period leading up to the convention, there had been speculation about what would become of the co-founders of the NFU, both of whom had been acting in temporary, unpaid positions. McGrath had made it clear that he would be returning to parish work on the west coast and would be available to the union as needed in an advisory capacity, but nothing had been said of Richard Cashin. He had originally been billed as the organization's legal advisor but had quickly become its primary spokesman, and he had done a good job of it: at turning a phrase and catching a headline he had few equals in the province—or outside of it. Fishermen delegates, at least, had learned to trust his ability to translate their concerns into the language of practical politics. In late-night bull-sessions, and pushed by the organizers from Toronto, the idea took hold: why not let him continue to do it? Cashin, for his part, was considering his options. His financial condition was reasonably secure, but during his year of work with the union his income had been several thousand dollars less than his expenses. He could probably make a satisfactory career as a lawyer, and his political credentials, even after his falling-out with Smallwood, were well established. On the other hand, the past year had been one of the most exciting and satisfying of his life. During the convention, he paid his fees and joined the union he had helped to form.

On the final day, positions on the executive were filled. Alex Brown of Marystown became vice-president and head of the industrial section, and Woodrow Philpott filled the same office for the fishermen's side. Kevin Condon was nominated for secretary-treasurer, demurred because he did not have the necessary book-keeping skills, and was voted into office with assurances of expert help. The Executive Committees of the two sections were filled with plant workers and fishermen from every bay and peninsula, from Bonavista to Isle aux Morts, from St. Anthony to Pouch Cove. Elected to the paid, full-time position of president of the whole thing was Richard Cashin, descendant of fish merchants, city-bred lawyer, and sometime Liberal politician.

Chapter 4

With the excitement of the convention over and the delegates back in their boats and fish plants, a new phase of the work began. Adopting a constitution and electing officers merely established a framework. Now came the job of building it into an effective organization that could carry through on the promise of basic change in the power structure of the Newfoundland fishery. The union had to maintain the momentum gained in the organizing campaign, it had to begin to show tangible results for its members, and it had to keep abreast of events that were rapidly unfolding.

Premier Smallwood, possibly taking account of the mood of the fishermen, invited Richard Cashin to draft new legislation to allow them collective bargaining, but Cashin refused. Not only was he far too busy as president of the union, he could also see a hook buried in the otherwise tempting offer. Although the news media had been heralding a Norwegian-style system of setting fish prices, Cashin felt sure that this was not possible. The structures of the two societies were far too unlike, and to bring about such a radical change would require much more than a single piece of labour legislation. Any new law would be a compromise at best, and he was afraid that the union's ability to fight for further changes would be weakened if he took part in drafting it.

The government did not rise to the challenge either. Regulations to govern collective bargaining for fishermen were not published until October, and then they incorporated parts of the existing law which covered bargaining in more conventional industries. A plethora of complication arose. The Labour Relations Act, designed to regulate organizing campaigns in shops and factories, required that a union applying for certification must show valid memberships signed within the three months prior to the application. The fishermen who had joined the NFFAWU had done so over the period of a year, so new membership cards had to be collected. Then there was a problem of delineating areas for collective bargaining and check-off of dues, and the Labour Relations Board had to study the application of the law in these new and unusual circumstances. As a result, thousands of fishermen remained only nominally union members, not yet covered by contracts and paying dues, while the summer wore on and the most productive period of the inshore fishery passed by.

On the industrial side, the effort to organize plant workers was challenged head-on by one of the toughest, most intractable fish merchants in the province, and only a little over a month after its founding convention the union became engaged in a bitter strike that dragged on through the rest of the year, stretching its financial and human resources to the limit.

The international headquarters of the Amalgamated Meat Cutters and Butcher Workmen in Chicago grew increasingly alarmed as Newfoundland continued to absorb money without showing the promised increases in dues-paying membership. The original grant of fifty thousand dollars had been spent in six months; another fifty was allocated, and then another. In one way at least a union is like a business enterprise: money expended in new organization is expected to bring in a return. More may have to be put out to protect an investment already made, but eventually the books have to be made to balance and bad investments have to be written off. The Toronto central office of the CFAWU was bombarded by a series of increasingly anxious letters from the international's Secretary Treasurer, Patrick Gorman, who was clearly beginning to wish he had never heard of Newfoundland, and the Toronto office forwarded copies to St. John's with urgent queries of their own. "This can't go on forever," Gorman wrote when the expenditure was nearing three hundred thousand dollars. "We will have to get down to earth on this thing."

That, of course, was exactly what the Newfoundlanders were trying to do. The task fell on a very small group of people, most of whom were amateurs. Some of the newly-elected executive had no union experience, and what the others had was at the fish plant local level. Much the same was true of the handful of business agents. Most had local experience but had only recently been recruited as full-time functionaries, and Cashin, of course, was a newcomer to it all. Apart from visiting organizers from the CFAWU in Toronto, only Fred Locking and Ray Greening were career union men.

Underlying Gorman's growing anxiety were some questions that were also being asked with varying degrees of interest by the fish processors, government officials, journalists, and general public who were watching events in Newfoundland: just what sort of an organization was the NFFAWU? There had been doubts from the beginning whether the small-boat fishermen, as independent producers, could be properly organized into a union. There were even greater doubts whether their interests could be accommodated in the same organization with wage-earning plant workers. Was the union no more than a temporary display of discontent? And what of the leadership? The romantic tale of an outport priest organizing fishermen with the help of his ex-classmate made good news copy, but did it have any depth? Could Richard Cashin hold the organization together for the long haul? More important, did he want to, or did he have other plans? Could it be that the fishermen were being led down the garden path again by an opportunist who would sell them out when it suited his own political interests?

Skepticism about Cashin's motives had been widespread from the beginning. The first report in the St. John's *Evening Telegram* to mention his association with the Northern Fishermen's Union, back in May of 1970, asked rhetorically, "Is the move by Mr. Cashin an apparent attempt to gain political advantage in the province in preparation for his return to politics?" A year later, after Cashin was elected president, an associate editor of the same newspaper posed and answered the question this way: "Is he a politician on the make? No one really knows the answer to that one." Ray Guy, an enormously popular St. John's columnist, hinted broadly that the whole undertaking was an elaborate confidence trick. After a sly reference to the Cashin family's background as fish merchants, he went on:

> . . . now we see young Dicky and his clerical squire entering the lists on the other side, fearlessly declaring that the accursed oppressors of the poor, downtrodden fishermen should be gutted, head on.
>
> This is noble work and long, but not entirely without recompense both financial and political. There's more than one way to skin a happy peasant.

This focus on Cashin is understandable, considering his previous political career, but it also raises a fundamental question: in the interpretation of social events, how much importance should be given to the role of particular individuals? In the romantic imagination, individuals predominate, moulding and shaping history on an heroic scale. The social sciences provide a corrective, interpreting events as the product of social forces that operate in some senses independently of individual people, but even the most detached of scientific observers cannot escape the nagging question: would things have happened as they did if the players had been different? Or, more pointedly, without specific individuals would certain events have happened at all?

The questions are unanswerable, of course, but they are asked all the same, by laymen as well as professionals. Kevin Condon, after more than twenty years with the union and the Federation of Fishermen, has thought about the problem for a long time, and concludes that a fishermen's union was inevitable: "It had to come," he says. "We needed it and we was ready for it. If it hadn't come one way it would have come another." But he is equally firm about the role of individuals: "If it hadn't been for Richard, and Father Des, and Ray Greening, we wouldn't have got it when we did. And it wouldn't be the same union we've got now."

Woodrow Philpott, perhaps influenced by the fact that he is himself a ship's captain, answers the question with a nautical metaphor:

> On a boat, you can have the best crowd of men in the world, but you won't go nowhere without a good skipper. By the same token, you can have the best kind of skipper and he won't go nowhere without a good crew. The union's had both—a good skipper and a good crew.

Such observations as these, along with simple curiosity, justify a closer look at the people who played the key roles in the development of the NFFAWU—that, and the fact that within a year of its founding, a conflict in its leadership nearly tore the union apart.

Popular leaders must, by definition, answer some need of the people who choose them. At the beginning of the NFU the fishermen of Port au Choix needed—or, perhaps more accurately, *wanted* — someone who could handle the intricacies and protocols of a formal organization. But not just anyone would do. There were several more requirements, unspoken and quite possibly not even consciously recognized by the men themselves.

In Newfoundland the lines between social classes and between city and country are marked more clearly than anywhere else in English-speaking Canada by differences in accent and style of speech. These differences are often summarized by rural or working people as attributable to "education" or its lack, an equation that is not entirely accurate but has a measure of validity, since speakers of regional and class dialects tend to shed them—or at least modify them—when they move up the educational ladder. Living in a world where the power structures and mass communications media speak in the voices of middle-class St. John's, central Canada, Great Britain, and the United States, speakers of regional dialects, although they may be powerfully articulate in their own idiom, can be inhibited by a wider audience—especially if it includes people they conceive to be "educated". This does not prevent them, however, from being shrewd judges of how well someone else handles the language of officialdom, and choosing leaders on that basis.

Second, traditional outport society, while accepting the social distinctions that marked off a teacher, clergyman, or doctor from the ordinary folk, had—and still has—a strong egalitarian streak. A person who too eagerly seeks, or too readily accepts, a position of authority can be subject to sharp criticism. For this reason outsiders—incoming teachers or clergy or medical personnel—often find themselves pushed into leading roles in the local development association or municipal council. Since they already have a distinct social status, their election does not elevate them. Since they are not embedded in the community network of kinship and friendship, their being chosen cannot be the occasion of jealousy, and if things go wrong they may be blamed without undue disruption of community relations.

Third—and this is probably another aspect of the egalitarian sentiment—if leaders are chosen from among people who already enjoy high social status, Newfoundlanders like them to be able to display something of the "common touch." They may be vain, pompous, arrogant, or high-handed; they may slip from time to time into most of the Seven Deadly Sins; but all will be forgiven if they can show occasionally that at heart they are really pretty much like everybody else.

Finally, for highly-visible roles of popular leadership, Newfoundlanders have a weakness for colourful and—within limits—flamboyant personalities. It is almost as though, resenting the necessity of having leaders at all, they feel that if they must have someone in authority he or she should be in some respects "larger than life"—a personality drawn in strokes sufficiently broad to make the whole thing worthwhile.

McGrath, and then he and Cashin together, met the requirements. At the outset they provided the authority of education and social position, which not only lent weight to what might otherwise have been dismissed as merely a local group of disgruntled fishermen, but also helped the fishermen to develop confidence in their own cause. One of the union's founders recalls an incident from the early days of the NFU in Port au Choix:

> We wasn't used to all this union stuff at first, and we wasn't always too sure of ourselves. Sometimes it was hard for us to speak up.
>
> I remembers one time when Father Des put out a press release. He used some words—what was it now? 'bureaucratic incompetence'—that was it.
>
> I got a phone call from some newspaper fella, and he asked me what did we mean by it. I suppose he wanted examples, or something. Well, I thought I knew what it meant, but I wasn't too sure of myself, so I said I'd call him back. Father Des was away some place, so there I

> was phonin' all over trying to get hold to him and ask him what did we mean by 'bureaucratic incompetence'.
>
> I could have given lots of examples, only I wasn't too sure about the words. We've learned a lot since then.

At the same time, the fishermen appreciated McGrath's and Cashin's ability to meet them on their own terms. "They could go any place and talk to anybody," one early union member says, "You could say what you liked to them, and you never felt they were talkin' down to you."

As the organization spread beyond the St. Barbe coast, the two friends became more and more the centre of attention and emerged as colourful personalities, interesting in their own right. Activist clergymen were a recognizable phenomenon of the turbulent tag-end of the 1960s, but there were not many in Newfoundland and for that reason alone McGrath stood out. Cashin was already well known, and almost anything he did would attract attention. Together, they made a team that might have been created by a movie scriptwriter with an eye for dramatic contrast.

Usually in clerical black, McGrath was a solid, imposing figure, towering over most of the fishery workers that came to hear them. Cashin was several inches shorter, a bouncy, slightly pudgy bundle of nervous energy. In personal contacts McGrath was disarmingly soft-spoken and gentle; Cashin brisk and challenging. Both had a lively sense of fun, and they learned to provide each other with openings to exercise it. Cashin, with a computer-bank memory, could tease McGrath for having "no head for figures," given to confusing the price of a restaurant cod-fillet with the price due to fishermen for the raw material. McGrath could act as Cashin's "spiritual advisor," curbing some of his scrappy, impetuous pugnacity. McGrath could speak with earnest moral conviction of rights and obligations; the volatile Cashin could savage merchants and plant-owners with a tongue as sharp and barbed as any fish-hook.

They put on a good show, both on stage and off. As they travelled the province they left the beginnings of a mythology in their wake—

anecdotes that spread through the outport communities about what they did or said in this place or that, and the tales lost nothing in the re-telling. An irascible fish merchant in an isolated outport publicly threatened to throw them off his wharf if they tried to organize his workers. When they flew into the community they made a point of landing at his plant and walking up the wharf into the town, and added another story to the repertoire.

Once, when travelling a lonely stretch of road with Mike Martin, the editor of the union newsletter, near Christmas of 1970, they came upon a scene of apparent tragedy. Tire tracks in new-fallen snow showed that a car had slid off the road, down an embankment, and through the skin of ice on a roadside pond. It was evident that the accident had just occurred: bubbles were still rising and sodden Christmas packages were floating in the icy water. The outline of the car was visible, but there were no footprints to show that anyone had escaped.

They later joked that they were almost an ideal team to come upon such a scene—a priest, a journalist, and a lawyer—but for the moment everything was deadly serious. McGrath waded into the frigid pond, going under completely to wrench open the doors of the submerged car. While he was thus engaged another vehicle appeared and the affair took on a less macabre aspect: the occupants of the car in the pond had, in fact, managed to escape. They had come ashore behind some bushes which hid their footprints, made their way safely to a nearby house, and were now returning to see what could be done about the accident.

When the organizers arrived at their destination, McGrath was fitted out with some dry clothes several sizes too small for him and they proceeded to the parish hall where they were to meet the local fishermen. As usual, the hall was practically unheated, and the audience sat expectantly, bundled in their outdoor clothing. When it came McGrath's turn to speak he was shivering so violently that he could not utter a word.

And so the mythology grew. Behind it were two men of widely different background and temperament whose lives had converged at a point where they were to have a profound and irreversible impact on their society.

Desmond McGrath was born in the paper mill town of Corner Brook, with a twin brother the youngest of a family of six. His father, an accountant for the Bowater paper company, was killed in a freak accident when McGrath was only four years old, struck by an exploding firework during celebration of the visit of King George VI and Queen Elizabeth in 1939. His mother became the first public librarian in Corner Brook, and brought up her family alone. Among young Desmond's chores was collecting the library mail from the post office, and he exploited the job by getting first access to new books and periodicals, thereby gaining, perhaps, a wider perspective than some of his contemporaries. He finished school at sixteen and went to work at the paper mill as an apprentice electrician. After two and a half years in the job, he says, he found himself one day filling out a form relating to the company's pension plan, and faced, at age eighteen, the question of whether he wanted to spend his life in the mill. He decided to go to university instead, and had the priesthood in the back of his mind.

At St. Francis Xavier University in Antigonish, Nova Scotia, he came under the influence of several of the people who had fostered community education and co-operatives among poverty-stricken fishermen and farmers in the 1920s and 30s. The founder of the movement, Father Moses Coady, was retired and ill by that time, but McGrath made a point of visiting the old priest in his nursing home and listening to his stories. McGrath majored in philosophy and English literature, played football and hockey, and involved himself in the full round of student life. In the summers he worked in the paper mill back home.

St. Francis Xavier in the 1950s was something of a hot-bed of student politics, and among those taking part at the time were several who were later to rise to national prominence as both Liberal and Conservative politicians—Lowell Murray, Brian Mulroney, and Warren Allmand, for example—as well as several others who went on to political careers in the Maritime provinces. It was in this company that McGrath first met Richard Cashin, and recruited him briefly into the New Republican Party of which McGrath was a founding member. The party advocated abolition of the monarchy, a distinctive Canadian flag, and a programme of social reform. The two became friends, but this did not prevent Cashin, who now tells the story with mischievous glee, from sitting on a student disciplinary committee when McGrath was caught at some late night revelry in the town during his final year.

After four years at St. Francis Xavier, McGrath had decided on his vocation. He went directly into theology at St. Augustines in Toronto, where he met and was heavily impressed by priests from the Scarborough Foreign Missions—men who were in the thick of revolutionary social change in Latin America. Rather than going back to the paper mill, he spent his summers in officer training with the Royal Canadian Air Force. After his ordination in 1961, he returned to Corner Brook as an assistant in the Cathedral Parish, where his community work was mainly with the Boy Scouts.

When he took charge of Holy Family Parish on the St. Barbe coast in 1968, the amalgam of ideas he had picked up from the founders of the Antigonish Movement, from student politics, from working in the paper mill, and from the priests of the Scarborough Missions suddenly acquired a focus, and he threw himself into union organizing with full commitment. To do the job he had to deal with the fishermen on their own ground, and even before the union attracted much public attention stories spread of the unconventional young priest who could be seen in bars and on fishing boats as often as in church. His superiors and brother priests, he recalls, were not always in sympathy with his actions, but did not actively oppose him. Some of them cautioned him against losing his religious vocation, but on the whole he was left to follow the dictates of his conscience. There were times, however, when the patience of his bishop and his colleagues must have been somewhat strained.

On the west coast of Newfoundland, many fishermen begin their season by hunting seals in March, threading their way through narrow leads of water among the ice floes of the Gulf. In 1970, McGrath went with them, to learn at first hand how his parishioners made their living. The fishermen taught him how to kill and pelt the seals, and subjected him to the traditional mockery when he received the sealer's baptism—slipping through a snow-covered crack in the ice and having to make his way back to the boat in clothing that froze on his body as he walked. The trip was to last for three or four days, but when it came time to head home the boat was stuck fast in the ice, and remained that way for several days. Other boats were stuck nearby, and on Sunday morning McGrath celebrated the Mass for a congregation of fifteen or sixteen fishermen packed into the boat's little cabin.

Apart from other commitments, he was scheduled to attend a celebration in Corner Brook for a retiring bishop. It was a notable event, and the proceedings were broadcast on radio. The master of ceremonies read telegrams from well-wishers who were unable to attend, and made a special point of announcing that Father McGrath of Port Saunders was absent because he was ice-bound at the seal hunt, and the hunt was going well. The men in the longliner heard the broadcast in some dismay. The dates of the seal hunt are strictly regulated, but often the offical dates do not coincide with the best times for hunting. In those days boats frequently put out from the smaller communities well in advance of the official opening. Although the clerical master of ceremonies did not know it, he had informed the radio audience—including any Fisheries Patrol Officers who might be listening—that the incumbent of Holy Family parish was out with his parishioners, taking seals before the opening of the season.

For McGrath, the commitments of a union leader and a priest never presented a moral conflict; sometimes, however, they conflicted in other ways. On one occasion, on union business in Nova Scotia, he realized to his horror that he was scheduled to perform a marriage in a tiny community at the northern end of his parish within the hour. McGrath placed an emergency call to a colleague who set off immediately for a drive of several hours to conduct the rites; he then called the young couple and suggested that they carry on with all the non-essential parts of the festivities, but delay the honeymoon until the arrival of the priest. It is remembered as the only wedding in the parish in which the reception was interrupted by the ceremony.

Like the founders of the co-operative movement in Nova Scotia, McGrath sees his work with the union as an extension of his religious vocation: he describes the essence of a Christian attitude as "a recognition of the value and dignity of each individual":

> When I first went to Port Saunders, parents used to threaten their kids: 'If you don't study hard and go to school you'll only be a fisherman.' Fishermen themselves would say it. They'd say, 'I've only got grade three' or—'grade four'—'and I can't do anything else, but I want my kids to have something better.'
>
> I found that really sad. It wasn't just that the work was hard and dangerous and uncomfortable—they were used to that. It was because fishermen had no control. They were at the mercy of the companies, and they were deprived of dignity. It was much the same for the plant workers.
>
> The union has changed all that. Nowadays there are lots of fishermen who would be proud to see their sons follow in their footsteps.

Ever since his New Republican days, McGrath's political philosophy has been of the liberal left, and he is a supporter of the New Democratic Party, although he does not accept all of its policies—most notably its stand on abortion. In 1977-78, he chaired a Peoples' Commission on Unemployment for the Newfoundland Federation of Labour. Before Pope John Paul II tightened church strictures on the participation of priests in politics, McGrath was asked many times to run for the NDP, and many of the party's members believed that he had been forbidden to do so by the church hierarchy. His own explanation is simply that he does not see himself as a politician:

> It's a noble calling—or *should* be: we've had too many scoundrels in office. I admire a good, honest politician, but it's not my calling. I'm a priest.
>
> I'll encourage a good person to run, and I'll work to help them get elected, but I wouldn't run myself.

From the beginning his work with the union involved him with fishermen of other religious denominations, and as the organization spread, especially across the northeastern areas of the province, he frequently found himself preaching the union message to some of the solidest and most uncompromisingly Protestant of congregations. There can be few Roman Catholic clergy anywhere who have given more speeches in meeting halls of the Loyal Orange Lodge. It was disconcerting, at first, for the one-time founder of the New Republican Party to be holding forth in rooms decorated with Union Jacks, photographs of the Queen, and portraits of King Billy triumphant on his white charger, but the strangeness soon wore off. "I wasn't talking to Protestants or Catholics," he says, "I was talking to fishermen and plant workers. They all had the same problems, whatever their religion."

The union's members seem to share his feelings, and treat him with both respect and affection. When the NFFAWU became successful and financially solvent, they presented him with an automobile, complete with two-way C B radio. They also gave him his radio code-name or "handle"—The Cod-father.

Newfoundland society is still sufficiently small and close-knit that family background plays a large part in the judgements people make of others. At elaborate St. John's dinner parties or in outport kitchens, discussion of an individual's motives and actions frequently includes assessment based upon what his or her parents or grandparents or even great-grandparents may have been and done. The fishermen who rose to positions of leadership in the union were known in their own areas both as good practitioners of their craft and as the sons and grandsons of good fishermen. McGrath, coming from respectable but relatively obscure parentage in Corner Brook, was free to create his own public persona, unencumbered by ancestry. For Richard Cashin, however, the situation was entirely different.

Long before Richard, the Cashins were well and widely known, and not universally admired. The family had a reputation for producing mavericks—headstrong, ambitious, sharp in business and politics, independent-minded, capricious and unpredictable. Their roots are in Cape Broyle, an outport seventy kilometres from St. John's on the heavily Irish-Catholic Southern Shore; for the past two generations they have been in, but not quite of, the St. John's upper-middle class elite.

In Cape Broyle, the Cashins were small-scale entrepreneurs. They bought fish and supplied fishermen, but they were not above catching and "making" fish of their own. Richard's grandfather, Michael Cashin, pulled an oar in his father's boat during the summers from a very early age. At twenty, he took over a debt-ridden family business and within a few years turned it into a thriving operation. To do it, he needed the daring, determination, and pugnacity that came to be regarded as Cashin characteristics.

In the late nineteenth and early twentieth centuries, the Southern Shore was frequently the scene of shipwrecks. The inhabitants gained some part of their livelihood—and occasional windfalls—by recovering cargo from ships driven ashore during storms. And, like poor fishermen on many another stretch of rugged coastline, they were sometimes rumoured to have tampered with navigational beacons in order to bring about the wrecks they salvaged. Although they often saved lives, they were looked upon with mixed feelings by ship-owners: to the captain of a vessel dashed up on some rocky headland the enthusiastic efforts of a group of small-boat fishermen to remove his cargo looked uncommonly like plunder. The fishermen, for their part, regarded what came ashore as the gift of Divine Providence, belonging by right to those who could get it. A middle-man who could gain the confidence of both sides could strike a bargain: the fishermen would be rewarded in money for their efforts, and the ship-owners would be able to retain at least some of their property.

In this chancy business Michael Cashin established a pre-eminence, securing salvage contracts by force of personality and a notable quickness of both wit and hand. He drove a sharp bargain with owners and enforced it among the fishermen, when necessary, with his fists. The reputation he earned is demonstrated in an anecdote recounted by his son, Major Peter Cashin: On one occasion, when Michael arrived to take charge of a wreck that was surrounded by the usual flotilla of dories, the ship's captain implored him to come aboard, complaining that the fishermen were robbing him. As Cashin climbed the ship's side the Commissioner of Wrecks, who was standing by, is reported to have called out to the captain, "The king of the robbers is coming up to you now!" Eighty years later, when Michael's grandson was organizing fishermen into a union, Premier Joseph Smallwood is said to have privately called him "Wrecker Cashin" in reference to the foundation of the family's fortunes.

Michael Cashin married a woman who was easily his equal in drive and ambition—Gertrude Mullowney of Witless Bay, whose father and uncles had earned the sobriquet of the "Mad Dog" Mullowneys for their defiance of the clergy in an age and an area where the power of the church was seldom openly questioned. Her father was a noted sealing captain, and one of her uncles is remembered for having the incredible audacity to stand up in his pew and challenge the priest on some matter of parish business. Together, Gertrude and Michael Cashin built the Cape Broyle store into a thriving business.

Michael entered politics in 1893, and brought to it the same energy and the same tactics that he displayed in business—more than one of his early election meetings ended in a punch-up with Cashin at the centre. At first he ran as an Independent, then as a Liberal. In 1905, when the Liberal government of which he was a member brought in an Act that limited the activities of New England banking schooners in Newfoundland waters, he crossed the floor. His Cape Broyle store did a lively trade with the Yankee vessels.

Cashin was elected for the conservative Peoples' Party in 1908 and again in 1913, when Coaker and the FPU entered the political scene. In that government he was minister of finance and customs, and often crossed swords with Coaker when the "Northern Moses" launched his stinging attacks on government and merchants. When an all-party National government was formed in 1917, Cashin continued as minister of finance, now with Coaker as a cabinet colleague. He was knighted in 1918.

After the war, as plans were being laid for the first election in six years, Cashin precipitated a series of events that stands out as a curiosity in a political history that has more than its share of peculiarities. When the all-party coalition government was first formed, its prime minister was Sir Edward Morris, leader of the conservative Peoples' Party for which Cashin had been elected. Morris retired shortly afterward, leaving the premiership in the hands of the Liberal leader, W.F. Lloyd. In May of 1919, Cashin, as minister of finance, rose from his place on the front bench and proposed a motion of non-confidence in the government of which he was a part.

The action was unexpected, but not as unreasonable as it might at first appear. Although the Peoples' Party had lost its leader, it still held the largest number of seats in the House. By moving a vote of no confidence, Cashin clearly intended to break the coalition and allow his party to become the government again before an election could be held. The response of the Prime Minister, W.F. Lloyd, is less readily explained. Either through inattention or else from political motives so deep as to be unfathomable, he seconded Cashin's motion. With this lead the House passed it unanimously and Sir Michael Cashin, as second-in-command of the majority party, became prime minister.

A few months later his party, re-named the Liberal Progressives, was defeated at the polls by the coalition between the Liberals led by Sir Richard Squires and Coaker's FPU. It was in this election that a small group of St. John's trade unionists ran unsuccessfully as Labour candidates. Cashin sat as leader of the opposition for four years. In 1923, in an attempt to broaden his party's appeal, he resigned as leader to make way for a Protestant. The party remained conservative and merchant-dominated, but to appeal to the St. John's workers it was renamed Liberal-Labour-Progressive. Cashin left his Ferryland seat to run in St. John's West against the prime minister. He beat Squires at the polls, but it was a three-member riding and both were elected. Sir Michael retired in 1924 because of ill health, and died in 1926.

But this was far from the end of the Cashin saga. When Sir Michael ran in St. John's West, the place he had held for so long in Ferryland was taken by his eldest son. Peter Cashin, at thirty-three had already had a varied career. His early life with his father had been stormy; he had left home and travelled west seeking his fortune; he had worked on threshing crews in the Canadian prairies, at a whaling station in British Columbia, and for the Canadian National Railway in Ontario. When the war came, he enlisted as a private and came home a major in the legendary Newfoundland Regiment. For a brief period, father and son sat in the House together as members of the opposition.

Peter Cashin's political career was no less eventful than his father's. Before he had been more than a few months in the House the prime minister, Sir Richard Squires, was charged by several of his own ministers with corruption. In the confusion that followed party lines—never very clearly defined—broke down almost completely. In 1924, Peter Cashin was again elected in Ferryland as a member of a newly-constituted "Liberal-Conservative" government dominated by powerful St. John's business interests. Within a year he crossed the floor and joined the Liberals in opposition. In 1928, he ran as a Liberal under the leadership of Squires, who had bounced back from his disgrace of five years earlier. They won, and Cashin took over his father's old portfolio as minister of finance, a difficult enough post in Newfoundland at the best of times, and one that became almost impossible as the Depression struck. In 1931, Cashin was in Ottawa with a delegation that included the ubiquitous William Coaker, trying to sell Labrador to the Canadians.

In 1932 he resigned his cabinet post and in a dramatic speech to a packed House charged Prime Minister Squires with corruption. The government fell in riot and confusion, with a mob of ten thousand irate townspeople storming the legislature and looting government liquor stores. Squires, with the help of a young aide named J.R. Smallwood, narrowly escaped being caught by the mob. In the ensuing election, which Cashin did not contest, disgusted voters put into office the government that, as he later phrased it, "handed [Newfoundland] over lock, stock, and barrel into the hands of a few second-grade English civil servants and a few subservient Newfoundlanders."

Peter Cashin left Newfoundland again, but returned in 1942 and promptly began to attack the Commission government in speeches and radio broadcasts, advocating a return to independent responsible government. In 1946 he was elected to the National Convention that was to decide the Dominion's political future and, as the campaign for confederation with Canada took shape, became J.R. Smallwood's most vocal opponent. When confederation became a reality in 1949 he sat, again for Ferryland, as the only Independent member of the new provincial House, one of only three who had sat as elected members of a legislature before. The anti-confederates had coalesced around the Progressive Conservative banner, and they quickly recruited Cashin as their leader. He was elected in that capacity in St. John's West in 1951. In 1953 he resigned in an unsuccessful bid for a federal seat. He died in 1977.

Richard Cashin's father, Laurence, was the second son of this remarkable family. He managed the family business in Cape Broyle while Sir Michael was attending to politics and Peter was away at the war. As a young man he displayed an aggressive energy and drive to match his father's, but this phase of his career was brought to an end in 1919 by illness. Later, when opponents taunted Richard Cashin, the union leader, with references to his merchant-family background, he turned the taunts back by wryly observing that his father had been lucky enough to contract tuberculosis and was thereby saved from the dreadful fate of being a fish merchant. The family enterprise was sold, and after a period of convalescence Laurence established Cashin and Company in St. John's, dealing in coal and insurance. For a time the company had branches in other Newfoundland centres.

As an outharbourman and a Catholic he was doubly an outsider among the established and largely Protestant business families of Water Street. Proud and sensitive to slights, he became something of a loner, following his own path and playing by his own rules. He never fully recovered his old energy, but he was a sharp, if somewhat unorthodox, businessman. During the Second World War there was a strike by the

Longshoremen's Protective Union over the unloading of coal. Supplies in the city ran low while a loaded vessel lay in the harbour. As the Coal Importers' Association blustered, Cashin teamed up with another entrepreneur who was also doubly an outsider, being American and Jewish; they made a deal with the union, and got the coal ashore. Thereafter he and his partner prospered, supplying fuel to the American military. Later, Cashin moved into the oil supply business. He made money: not a great fortune compared to some of the ex-fish merchants who diversified their businesses during the war years, but enough to leave his sons a comfortable inheritance.

Among them, the Cashins of Cape Broyle left indelible marks in Newfoundland's history. For succeeding generations of the family they left a reputation to be lived down or lived up to, depending on one's point of view. Certainly, no one bearing the name could make any public move without being closely watched and even more closely judged.

In personal terms, Richard Cashin inherited independence, both financial and philosophical. His father was a private man, gentler and less irascible than Peter or Sir Michael, but he shared their inconoclastic individualism. "Be your own man," Richard remembers him saying. "Go your own way. You want to be able to turn to the congregation when it's all over and tell them to kiss your arse." He disliked pretension, and in later life, as a successful businessman, avoided the formal social events to which he began to be invited. This discomfort with the more formal manifestations of the class structure transmitted itself to his son at an early age. One of Richard's most vivid childhood memories is of a trip he made with his father by car over the new road to Bonavista when he was about ten years old:

> The kids—kids my own age and older—came around the car and stared in at us. They looked at us as though we were some kind of different species. I remember the deference that even adults showed me, because of my father. I hated it. That was when I first really became aware of the paternalism—the inequalities of the class system.

At fifteen, Richard was sent to Loyola College in Montreal for high school. He did not like being away from home, and returned to St. John's before the year was out. While in Montreal, however, he had time to place second in a city-wide public speaking contest for high school students. The contest's judge, making the presentation, predicted a political future for him.

He finished school at St. Bonaventure's College in St. John's and went directly to St. Francis Xavier. During his first year he was a member of the student CCF party, before being recruited by McGrath for the New Republicans. He took a leading role in university affairs as vice-president of the student union and president of the Co-operative Society. When he graduated with a bachelor's degree in political science, he was elected life-president of his graduating class.

From there he entered law school at Dalhousie University in Halifax, where he continued his involvement in campus political life, now as a member of the student Liberal association. During his final year he courted and married Rosann Earl, a beautiful, dark-haired young woman from St. John's who was finishing a degree in education at Mount Saint Vincent. After graduation, Cashin articled and was called to the bar in Nova Scotia. The young couple returned to St. John's with a baby daughter, where Cashin again went through the articling process, was called to the Newfoundland bar, and began to set up a law practice.

His entry into politics was probably inevitable, but it occurred much sooner than might have been expected, and almost by accident.

A federal election was coming up in the spring of 1962. There was no distinction in Newfoundland between federal and provincial wings of the Liberal party. Premier Smallwood ran it all, and he promised the federal leader, Lester Pearson, a clean sweep of the seven federal seats in the province. In five of them the Liberals had good reason for confidence, but their prospects were not so good in the Tory stronghold of St. John's. The premier had picked six of his candidates and was looking for someone for St. John's West when a party lieutenant noticed the announcement of Cashin's call to the bar and suggested his name. Smallwood did not know the young lawyer, although Cashin had interviewed him several years before as a university student preparing a political science essay. In fact, the premier later admitted that he had confused Richard with his younger brother Laurence, who was then still an undergraduate at Memorial University. Smallwood remarked doubtfully that "this Cashin fellow seemed awfully young," but the idea appealed to his sense of political theatre—the nephew of his old arch-enemy in the Confederation battle running for the Liberals in a riding that included large parts of districts once held by both his grandfather and his uncle. Besides, it would have a fine dramatic flavour of sending a Liberal David into the field against a Conservative Goliath, for the incumbent in St. John's West was a formidable opponent.

The Honourable William J. "Billy" Browne was a contemporary of Peter Cashin; he had entered politics a decade before Richard was born. He had been a minister in the last pre-confederation government of Newfoundland. He was a lawyer, a KC, a judge, and an old enemy of J.R. Smallwood. In 1948 he had been one of a group of lawyers who unsuccessfully took action in the Supreme Court to prevent Confederation with Canada from taking place. In 1949 he resigned from his judgeship to run in Newfoundland's first federal election as a Progressive Conservative, accusing Smallwood of pulling strings in Ottawa to have him removed from the bench. Later in the campaign he laid charges against Smallwood for violations of the Elections Act. Browne did not win the case, but with the assistance of Major Peter Cashin he won the election, and then went on to win several more, sitting as a member of the provincial House in 1954 and 1956, and returning to the House of Commons in 1957 and 1958. At the dissolution of parliament in 1962, he was solictor general of Canada.

Smallwood offered the candidacy and Cashin, who had been practicing law for all of two weeks, felt that he had nothing to lose and a lot of experience to gain. His father was more skeptical—he thought that Smallwood would expect him to pay his son's election expenses. In the end, the party paid and Cashin ran. Announcements of his political debut were full of carefully-selected references to the family history and glowing predictions of a brilliant career.

Smallwood led the campaign himself, stumping the province tirelessly and getting more media publicity than all the actual candidates put together. Because of his ancient enmity for "Billy" Browne, he gave special attention to St. John's West, bolstering Cashin's effort with slashing personal attacks on his opponent, which were vigorously returned.

Browne has charged that during the election Smallwood used "bribery and corruption on the retail and wholesale levels," offering voters gifts of groceries, and promising suburban areas large-scale road paving if they returned his candidate.

On election night, Browne came out ahead by a slim margin of fewer than two hundred, but when the military vote was included and official recount held, Cashin was the winner by twenty-four. The other St. John's seat remained Tory. The Conservatives contested the outcome in St. John's West, alleging irregularities in the service vote, and Cashin's election was disallowed, but by that time Prime Minister Diefenbaker's shaky minority government had fallen, and a new election was called for April of 1963. This time Smallwood delivered all seven seats. Browne did not run and Cashin beat his replacement handily, becoming, at twenty-five, the youngest member of the minority Liberal government of Prime Minister Lester Pearson.

The voluble young Newfoundlander, his beautiful wife and their infant daughter soon became favourites among many old Ottawa hands. For the young couple, it was almost like an extension of their university life of student politics, the Model Parliament, and the Debating Society: they both regarded it as a form of postgraduate education. In the House, Cashin was articulate and often impassioned, leaning to the left of his colleagues on many issues—to the point that one of them observed that he seemed bent upon becoming the Nye Bevan of the Liberal Party. In his maiden speech he struck a strong regional note: Newfoundlanders, he said, had not entered the Canadian confederation to become perpetual second-class citizens. Among other things, he argued for a twelve-mile ocean limit for fisheries jurisdiction, something that was not to become a reality for another seven years. In 1964, when his party was in full cry on the issue of biculturalism, he suggested to the House that it was only an aspect of much greater problems of inequality: the most important goals, he said, were the eradication of poverty and the provision of such essential services as a comprehensive medical care plan. At home in his riding he urged fishermen to stand up for themselves and demand reforms in the fishery.

In later years Cashin was to become something of a political enigma, confusing his opponents and baffling those who would want him as an ally, but there was little hint of that in his orthodox, if unusually rapid, development as a Liberal member of parliament. He was cocky, feisty, and independent, but he learned the ropes quickly and was soon acknowledged as future cabinet material. He was re-elected in 1965, and a year later became parliamentary assistant to the minister of fisheries, H.J. Robichaud. Rosann was elected president of the Parliamentary Wives' Association.

In 1967 a cabinet shuffle was in the wind and newspaper speculations suggested that Cashin could become minister of fisheries, but he did not get the post.

Some say that Smallwood feared him as a potential rival in the making and, not wanting him to advance too rapidly, used his influence in Ottawa to see that Cashin did not get the promotion. Apparently the Honourable John Diefenbaker had a different theory. A one-time senior civil servant tells a story of a large public meeting in St. John's where Prime Minister Lester Pearson was to speak. The audience was noisy and challenging, and when Pearson came to the microphone he was drowned out by shouting and heckling. Cashin, who was also on the platform, came forward and berated the crowd for their bad manners, quieted them, and turned the meeting over to the prime minister. The man who tells the story says that when Diefenbaker heard about the event he gave his famous chuckle and said, "Well, that young man will never have a cabinet post. Mike Pearson doesn't like being upstaged!" Cashin says the story is apocryphal.

Whatever the reason, Cashin stayed where he was. Then, in 1968, when the rest of the country swept the Liberals back into power with a new prime minister in a wave of enthusiasm that the journalists labelled "Trudeaumania," the Newfoundland electorate showed Joey Smallwood their feelings by returning six Conservative MPs and Cashin lost his seat.

The defeat was not entirely unexpected, but it was none the less disturbing for that. Cashin had never held any other job than as a member of parliament. He had fallen out with Smallwood and was not on good terms with many of the premier's aides and associates. For all the brashness and confidence of his public image there is a private, protected side to his personality that is vulnerable and sensitive to slights. His friends found him withdrawn and unhappy:

> We were really concerned about him. Everything had come pretty easily for Richard, you know. He did a good job as an M.P., but it never really challenged him. Even as parliamentary secretary he didn't have the challenge he needed. Then, all of a sudden, he's starting out in a law practice, and all the people that graduated with him are five years ahead of him. We really wondered what was going to become of him.

Cashin may have wondered the same thing himself, but he did not wonder for long. In the summer of 1969 the inshore fishermen of Placentia Bay, many of whom had been Cashin's constituents when he was a member of parliament, were at the centre of a swirling controversy over red herrings—not the figurative kind, although those were also present in shoals, but actual fish which had begun turning up in fishermen's nets and on the surface of the water with their bodies blushing crimson from broken blood-vessels under the skin, their gills distended, and their eyes red and bulging. The symptoms were consistent with those of phosphorous poisoning. The fishery was closed, and several hundred fishermen lost the season's income.

On the eastern shore of the bay at Long Harbour, not far from the spot where Churchill and Roosevelt signed the Atlantic Charter in 1941, stood a plant of the Electric Reduction Company (ERCO) which processed ore from Florida into phosphorous to be shipped abroad for industrial use. The company had been induced to establish in Newfoundland by lower-than-cost electric power and lax pollution control standards offered by the Smallwood government. The same company had been the centre of controversy a few years earlier in the Dunville area in Ontario, where crops and cattle—and farm families—began showing symptoms that could be the result of toxic phosphorous.

When the red herrings began to surface in Placentia Bay the Long

Harbour plant was closed for a time and new equipment was installed to reduce the amount of phosphorous being poured into the water. ERCO denied any legal liability for damage to the fish but as self-styled "responsible members of the community" the company offered three hundred thousand dollars to be divided up as compensation among the fishermen. Some of them reluctantly accepted and signed a paper freeing ERCO from any further claim. Others, however, were dissatisfied and began legal action. Some of these, who had known Cashin as an M.P., came to him with their case and he accepted it on a percentage-of-settlement basis. If they lost they would pay him one dollar each; if they won he would receive a portion of the compensation payment.

The case suddenly propelled Cashin into the milieu for which he seemed to be destined by heritage, temperament, and training: a heady, fast-moving whirl of public controversy and confrontation between people, industry, and two levels of government. He did not treat the case as an ordinary piece of litigation—his actions were more those of an organizer than a lawyer. With the help of his clients, he conducted a study of fishermen's incomes more comprehensive than anything that had been done before. Then, as the company dug in its heels, he organized a picket line of fishermen across the entrance to the plant.

The picketing was not the spontaneous and desperate plea for public sympathy that it may have seemed, however. Behind the scenes, Cashin had forged links between his clients and the powerful steelworkers' union which represented ERCO employees, the Newfoundland Federation of Labour, the Canadian Labour Congress, and the Federation of Fishermen. ERCO workers refused to cross the picket line, and Cashin vowed that if the company did not come up with a better offer of compensation, their factory would be the scene of "the biggest demonstration ever seen in Newfoundland," supported by unions all across the province.

The case dragged on for another month or two. Cashin's Ottawa connections came into play in the form of supporting actions by Don Jamieson and Fisheries Minister Jack Davis. O.M. Solandt visited Newfoundland in his capacity as chairman of the Science Council of

Canada, a body with a heavy advisory responsibility to government on matters of environmental protection: Solandt took the opportunity to say a few words in defence of ERCO, since he was also vice-chairman of *that.* Pat Antle spoke up for the Federation of Fishermen, but he always seemed to be up-staged by Cashin.

Finally, just as the case was about to go to court, the company made an offer which has been described as the largest out-of-court settlement in Newfoundland history. Cashin's clients accepted. Another group of fishermen, with a different lawyer, proceeded to court and lost their case. During the height of the public protest part of the campaign, Cashin had told reporters that the affair had forged an "alliance" between fishermen and organized labour in the province that could be a "real breakthrough" for the fishermen. As the excitement wound down, he started getting telephone calls from McGrath in Port Saunders, who was planning a breakthrough of his own.

In light of all this, it is not surprising that journalists would raise questions about the political implications of Cashin's involvement with the fishermen's union. His own public statements did nothing to discourage the speculation. He flirted openly with the NDP, stating that Newfoundlanders should stop thinking of politics solely in terms of Liberals or Conservatives. "I don't think an indigenous Newfoundland party is the answer either," he was quoted as saying. "The only way another party can be formed is to join the NDP with central support." He did not, in fact, join the party, but there were persistent rumours that he had, or was about to. Opinion in the tiny Newfoundland NDP was divided. Its president accused the national leader, Tommy Douglas, of trying behind the scenes to ease Cashin into the position of provincial leader. Douglas denied that he had any such intention, but if some party supporters were outraged by the suggestion others wished fervently that it were true, believing that with Cashin at the helm the party could become a real force in the province.

Cashin clearly enjoyed the freedom conferred by his ambiguous party position. In an address to a group of political science students, shortly after the NFFAWU was formed, he told them that the union would have great political power, and would not hesitate to use it. He appeared on an NDP-sponsored panel discussion of pressure politics and argued the virtue of action outside the usual channels of party and government. When a group of students at Memorial University occupied the university's administration building during a dispute over the use of student fees, he addressed an audience of several hundred of them, urging them to stick to their guns. Like his grandfather and his uncle he is a skillful orator, and he developed and broadened his skills in these new settings. Whether his audience were students, fishery workers, or the Rotary Club, he could deliver an amusing ancedote, a convincing lecture, a rousing call to action, a bitter philippic against some enemy, or a eulogy for a friend, all with practised ease. Newspaper reporters could rely on his speeches to produce quotable lines; television and radio reporters could count on snappy, attention-grabbing interviews.

When the occasion demanded, he could build a speech to a high pitch of passion. With his large head thrown back, its shock of gingery hair slightly dishevelled, shirt collar tugged open and tie askew, small hands moving in choppy, violent gestures, he could electrify an audience with lines that in another context might sound like melodrama. The students who occupied the building at Memorial University were engaged in a dispute over the university administration's plans to use student activity fees in a way that the students disapproved. Their protest was directed primarily at the university's then president, Lord Taylor of Harlow. When Cashin addressed the students he began by reminding them that it was another British peer, Lord Amulree, who in 1933 authored the report that resulted in the suspension of democratic self-government in Newfoundland. Then, as the students waited in hushed expectancy, he thundered, "What that British lord did then, *let not this British lord repeat!*" The auditorium erupted in a roar.

Audiences came to expect this sort of oratorical highwire act, building to daring climaxes where one false move could spell disaster. In the heat of the moment he could also slip into sharply pointed—and highly quotable—attacks on individual opponents, often with a touch of profanity or vulgarity for emphasis.

One result of such high-profile oratory was to convince many commentators that he was not merely the spokesman for fishery workers but rather the dictator of union policy, ruling the members by demagoguery and bluff. Six years after the founding of the NFFAWU, *The Evening Telegram* was still referring to it in headlines as "Mr. Cashin's Union." Far from being abashed by such suggestions, Cashin cheerfully made use of them. "The fact that I am president of the union," he once told a reporter from a mainland newspaper, "just shows how bad things are in Newfoundland." To a hall full of fishery workers he would quote some editorial or news report that suggested he was manipulating the union for his own purposes. "That's what they think on Water Street," he would say. "But, you know, it doesn't show what they think of Richard Cashin." Then, after a moment's pause: "It shows what they think of *you*! It's the same old arrogant St. John's middle-class idea that fishermen [or plant workers] can't do anything for themselves!" Sometimes, with the right audience, he would drive the point home with one of his pieces of homely vulgarity: "You and I know who runs this union. You know that Richard Cashin is like the business-end of a bull—he goes where he's shoved!"

The question of leadership in the union was undoubtedly a little more complicated than that, but the ambiguities of it served the purposes both of Cashin and the NFFAWU. Once, when negotiations with a fish plant were breaking down and a strike was imminent, a member of the management team said, "It's all right for you, Mr. Cashin. You don't need to worry about money. But what about the fishermen? If there's a strike, how will they put food on the table?" Barely looking up from his papers Cashin shot back, "Let them eat hake!" It was a typical Cashin answer, and it was unsettling. Could he say such things because he was an arrogant union boss in the Jimmy Hoffa tradition? Or was he what he pretended to be: the leader of a united body of workers, confident of their support? If they really knew the answer to those questions management could plan a strategy, but the answers stayed ambiguous.

Obviously, some of this enigmatic quality was a pose—and an effective one—but some of it, surely, is rooted in the maze of contradictions that made up Cashin's personal and political life. Born a Cashin and having been an impressionable adolescent during the Confederation battle, he could hardly help but be vividly conscious of his Newfoundland identity. As a union leader he would sometimes play on the nationalist sentiments of his countrymen by reminding them that "We are the only people in the whole world who not once, but *twice*, voluntarily gave up the right to responsible self government"—the first time to the London-appointed Commission, and the second time to Canada. On the other hand, his education and his reading had made him a cosmopolitan liberal, quick to decry anything that seemed to smack of narrow parochialism.

He held strong egalitarian ideals, yet he occupied a position of power and wealth. He was an admirer of Scandinavian-style social democracy, yet he had been a Newfoundland Liberal under the egotistical, ironbound, one-man rule of J.R. Smallwood. He disliked and distrusted the tendency of Newfoundlanders to follow charismatic leaders, yet he was such a leader himself, heading a movement that sometimes looked less like a union than a crusade.

In politics, too, he kept both admirers and detractors guessing. Once the union was firmly established and J.R. Smallwood's government had gone down in defeat, he became in many people's minds "the man who could be premier" if only he could be induced to take on the leadership of either the Liberal or New Democratic parties—a sort of political wild card with the potential to be either the salvation or the ruination of Newfoundland politics, depending on one's point of view.

In two federal elections he publicly supported Tom Mayo, the NDP candidate in his old riding of St. John's West, and in other elections, both federal and provincial, made little secret of his support for NDP candidates. When he took a seat on the Board of Petro Canada and in 1977 became a member of the National Unity Task Force, it was popularly regarded as preliminary to moving back into Liberal ranks.

Nevertheless, in 1979, when he threw his support behind the former minister of external affairs, Don Jamieson, who came home to lead the Newfoundland Liberals in a provincial election, many New Democrats felt a sense of betrayal as keen as though he had actually been a member of their party. Rumours abounded of a shadowy deal in which Cashin's support was supposed to have been traded for some vaguely conceived reward.

Father Des McGrath has grown weary of defending his friend from such rumours:

> At first I used to have to defend him against people who said he was using the union to become premier. Then I had to defend him against people who were upset because he *didn't* go into politics. Some people are always looking for an ulterior motive.
>
> If he wanted to get into politics, he could have done it plenty of times—and he didn't need the union to do it. Now, if he ever does go back actively to politics, people will be able to judge him on what he has done. They'd have more to judge him on than most people who stand for election. I'd say he's contributed more in the role he has chosen than any politician you'd want to name.

In the Spring of 1971, however, most of this was still far in the future. Columnists and pundits referred to him patronizingly as "little Ricky Cashin", the spoiled rich kid who had ridden into the House of Commons on Smallwood's coat-tails and was now playing at being a radical. Some sources say that when a group of fish plant operators expressed anxiety about the union, Premier Smallwood reassured them, saying, "Don't worry about Cashin. He'll never stick with it. In six months he'll be doing something else."

There was little as yet to discount such predictions, but on the southwest coast of the province a confrontation was brewing that would change everything.

Chapter 5

Back in the hectic autumn of 1970, while negotiations were going on for the merger that produced the NFFAWU, things were happening on the southwest coast of Newfoundland that were to have profound results, not merely for the new union, but for the entire province. Burgeo, a town that had gained unwelcome notoriety a few years before, was about to hit the headlines again.

To the visitor, Burgeo seems almost as much water as land. In the haphazard manner of many Newfoundland outports, its houses are spread over a jumbled little archipelago of islands and peninsulas; they sit nestled in miniature valleys, backed against low hills, or perched precariously on rocky outcrops. The roads loop and twine among them, skirting innumerable little inlets, coves, and reaches of the sea, and the network of freshwater ponds that feed into them. Behind the town stretch treeless, wind-swept barrens, dotted with ponds and populated only by moose and caribou. A gravel road now links the town with the Trans-Canada Highway, ninety miles away, but in 1970 only a few miles had been completed; the only way in or out was by coastal steamer or, for those who could afford it, chartered light aircraft.

In 1967, Burgeo briefly gained the unwelcome attention of news media across the continent when a whale became trapped in a narrow-necked inlet near the town. Some of the local men began shooting at the whale from the shore, and author Farley Mowat, who was living in Burgeo at the time, undertook a publicity campaign to save her. The whale died, and the people of the town were left with smoldering resentment at their treatment by the press.

Burgeo has always been totally dependent on the fishery. In 1970, it had a population of about two thousand, a few miles of unpaved road, a fresh fish plant employing about two hundred people, and a new herring reduction plant which employed, at the peak of the season, about fifty. The plants were fed by a fleet of up to five trawlers, each with a crew of about fourteen, and thirty-five or forty inshore fishermen. Another hundred-odd people were employed by government agencies and service industries. As in any small community, there were never quite enough jobs; young people left looking for opportunity in bigger centres, and, in a pattern typical of many Newfoundland communities, scores of men spent several months of the year on the mainland, working on seasonal construction jobs or as seamen on the Great Lakes. There had been a union in the fish plant for a short time in the 1950s, but there was none in September of 1970, when Lawrence Mahoney, the CFAWU's business agent on the south coast, paid an organizing visit to Burgeo.

En route on the coastal steamer, Mahoney met the young minister of Burgeo's small United Church, Joe Burke, and found a sympathetic ear. They talked of the CFAWU's organizing drive, and of the coming merger with the upstart fishermen's union on the Northern Peninsula. Burke, the son of a union railwayman, was already deeply interested in the possibilities of an organization of fishermen and fishery workers, and had been following with great attention the reports of the trawler strike in Nova Scotia and the activities of Father McGrath and Richard Cashin. With Burke's assistance, Mahoney held a meeting in the United Church Hall, attended by plant workers, trawlermen, and inshore fishermen. The response was not enthusiastic, but the union organizer and the clergyman were encouraged by the questions. Although the people attending were wary and somewhat suspicious, they were clearly interested; especially the younger men, many of whom had been union members in jobs on the mainland or on the Great Lakes.

The meetings and discussions continued, and when the union merger was completed in October the NFFAWU already had several members in Burgeo. A month later the union applied to the provincial Labour Relations Board for recognition as the bargaining agent for workers at Burgeo's 2.6 million dollar herring reduction plant, operated by Natlake, a company owned jointly by National Sea Products Ltd., and three members of the Lake family. Spencer Lake, one of the shareholders and the company's chief executive officer, had earlier threatened that if the union were certified he would sell his shares and resign from the company. It was the slack season, and the plant's work force was down to seventeen. Fourteen of them voted for the union and Spencer Lake lost no time in following through on his threat. "I consider that a genuine vote of non-confidence against me," he told reporters, and promptly resigned his position and put his shares up for sale. It was not merely a petulant gesture, for Lake was no simple minority shareholder and no ordinary fish plant manager.

The Lake family's story, like that of the Cashins, spans much of the history of the Newfoundland fishery. They came to Fortune Bay from England in the 1700s. Various branches of the family fished, ran banking schooners, and engaged in business—including a boot and shoe factory, a canning factory, and a furniture factory in the town of Fortune in the days when such small-scale, small-town manufacturing was still possible. Spencer's father, H.B. Clyde Lake, was a general merchant in Fortune, outfitting both inshore and Grand Banks fishermen. In 1928 he was elected to the House of Assembly as a Liberal under Sir Richard Squires; he sat on the government benches with Sir William Coaker and became minister of marine and fisheries in his stead.

When the Squires government collapsed in riot and scandal in 1932, Lake set up a saltfish business in St. John's. Using the knowledge and contacts gained as an outport merchant, he pioneered a new way of dealing: like a William Coaker of the merchants, he bought the outport storekeepers' fish for cash, selling them salt at near cost to keep their allegiance. His company prospered in the declining years of the saltfish trade, importing salt from Spain and the Turks and Caicos Islands, and shipping fish all over the world as one of the largest exporters in the country. It was in this highly successful business that Spencer and his brother Harold learned the trade. When fresh fish freezing began to take over the industry in the 1940s, the Lakes moved into that, diversifying and expanding their operations.

In the early 1950s the Burgeo freezing plant operated by Fishery Products Ltd. was in difficulty. Premier Smallwood encouraged Spencer Lake to take it over, offering considerable financial assistance from the provincial government. At the time, Burgeo was in some senses a new community. Its population had fluctuated for a hundred years with the ups and downs of the fishery: for the first part of this century the people of the area were living in more than a dozen tiny hamlets scattered among the islands; the complex forces of centralization had brought them together around the fish freezing plant, built in 1945, to cluster in a raw sprawl of houses, old, new, and rebuilt. In 1954, with about a thousand people, Burgeo was badly in need of a sanitation system, improved roads, services of all kinds, and especially in need of employment.

Lake, by his own account, could see the potential as well as the problems. With the help of generous loans and grants from both provincial and federal governments, he built up and expanded the fish plant. He became the town's mayor, and successfully lobbied both levels of government for improvements to roads and schools, a water and sewer system, and other services. Where there were gaps in services normally provided by private enterprise, Lake filled them.

In 1956 he married Margaret Penny, heiress of another fish-merchant family centred in the island of Ramea, twelve miles from Burgeo, and the two family groups of companies came together through interlocking ownership and direction to form what was for the time the most completely integrated fishery operation in the province. The interlinked companies owned trawlers to catch the fish, plants to process them, refrigerator ships to transport the product, and a company in Gloucester, Massachusetts, to handle distribution on the U.S. market. Critics suggested that the U.S. company also existed to cream off profits, so that the Newfoundland companies would qualify for government assistance. When he resigned his position with Natlake, Spencer Lake was president, managing director, and a major shareholder in Burgeo Fish Industries Ltd., Burgeo Trawlers Ltd., Caribou Fisheries Ltd., Caribou Reefers Ltd., Gaultois Fisheries Ltd., H.B. Clyde Lake Ltd., Lake Trawlers Ltd., Lake Shipping Company Ltd., Maritime Trading Company Ltd., and Sarah Shipping Company Ltd. He was vice-president of Burgeo Leasing Ltd., on the board of directors of the Newfoundland Shipyard and the Bank of Canada, and held substantial shares in National Sea Products of Nova Scotia. Margaret Lake was a shareholder and director in most of those companies, president of John Penny and Sons of Ramea, and treasurer of Burgeo Fish Industries Ltd.

Besides being mayor of Burgeo, Spencer Lake owned the town's only supermarket, beauty parlour, dairy, barber shop, and oil and gasoline distribution agency.

Although the NFFAWU's first newspaper hailed the certification vote at the herring reduction plant as a "breakthrough," both sides knew it was only a skirmish. Lake's gesture of resigning from the company was a warning, and the threat was clear: he was in a position to close down virtually all employment in Burgeo—most notably the main fish plant, upon which all the rest depended. "In these isolated outports I contend that there is no place for a union," he told reporters. He then went on to make a statement that Richard Cashin was still quoting fifteen years later as characteristic of the old-style Newfoundland fish merchant. "I'm not anti-union," he said, "I just think that in certain circumstances unions are not practical. And this is one of them: isolated outports in Newfoundland. You haven't got the local leadership to run them intelligently, with all due respect to the people—I'm very fond of them."

To coincide with the announcement of the Natlake vote, the union held a mass meeting in the high school auditorium. In spite of gusty winds and heavy rain, nearly six hundred people attended, including the clergymen from both the United and Anglican churches, the managing officers of the fish plant, and Spencer and Margaret Lake. McGrath outlined the growth of the union and gave a spirited version of his usual challenge. When Cashin's turn came, he began in his usual fashion, but suddenly launched a stinging attack on the Lakes, comparing them with the fish barons of past centuries and being caustically sarcastic about their paternalistic role in Burgeo.

It was typical of Cashin's aggressive, confrontational style, but the people of Burgeo were not used to such tactics. Some were delighted to hear the Lakes attacked; others were embarrassed and uneasy. The Lakes did not reply, but after the meeting Spencer delivered to reporters an attack of his own, accusing Cashin and McGrath of "trying to ride to power on the coat-tails of the fishermen," and comparing them to Coaker who, he said, had organized fishermen "and then abandoned them to live somewhere down south."

Both the union speakers stressed that the people need not fear Lake's threat to close the plant. After the meeting, McGrath sent a telegram to Premier Smallwood:

> Today's statement by Spencer Lake regarding the sale of shares in Natlake Ltd. has been interpreted as a threat to the people of Burgeo, Ramea, Gaultois, Englee in particular and Newfoundland in general.(stop) On behalf of the Newfoundland Fishermen, Food and Allied Workers, and other interested Newfoundlanders we would like to know the Newfoundland Government stand on this matter.(stop) Will the government of Newfoundland stand by the people in the exercising of their democratic right to organize?

By its length and style, the reply showed every evidence of having been dictated by the premier himself:

> . . . We believe absolutely and unchangeably in the right of all workers of hand and brain to organize themselves and to bargain collectively. This right is almost as basic and precious as the right to life itself and this government will defend and encourage it to the absolute limit. Mr. Spencer Lake has made a magnificent contribution to the up-building of the fisheries on the southwest coast and it is a great pity that we do not have many Newfoundlanders like him in that regard for leaders in industry are badly needed in our province today. The government do not share Mr. Lake's attitude in the matter of trade union organization of the fishermen or plant employees. We think he is absolutely and hopelessly wrong in his attitude in this particular matter and I would plead with him to change his attitude and re-establish the fine personal relationships he and his family have had on the southwest coast. He is a very able and strong willed man or he would not have been able to build the great fishing industry he has built. This might make it all the harder for him to bend at the present time but as a personal friend I implore him to do so and to throw his welcoming gates wide open to his workers to organize and then sit down and bargain with them. However whether he does or does not do this, the Newfoundland government proudly take their stand beside the fishermen and workers in Burgeo and everywhere else in our province.
>
> Kindest personal regards to you, Richard Cashin and the other organizers of your union.
>
> Joseph R. Smallwood.

With the confrontation fully in the open, the struggle went on. Lake talked to his workers, telling them that the NFFAWU was backed by "gangsters from Chicago" who only wanted their dues. In a letter, he informed workers that he and his wife had talked the matter over and concluded that they could not tolerate a union in the fish plant: "We both feel that Burgeo would not be worth living in under these conditions—therefore we would most likely have to sell the plant and move away . . . I would like you all to think this matter over very seriously before you sign up to have a union in Burgeo, because I am afraid I could not operate under such circumstances."

Some of the workers argued with their mates, telling them of the advantages of organization. One of these was George Coley, a compact, competent young man in his late twenties. Coley had worked on the Great Lakes freighters for several years, and shortly before the organizing drive had returned to Burgeo to settle and work in the fish plant. He had a special reason for wanting the union to succeed.

George's father, Ward Coley, had organized a union in the plant in 1955, during the early days of Lake's tenure. It had no affiliation with any larger union but was one of the small, spontaneous independents, directly chartered by the Canadian Trades and Labour Congress. This meant that it had no source of funds to support a strike, and depended for the usual union services on the single TLC representative for the province, who was stationed in St. John's and had the whole island to cover. In spite of all the difficulties, the union gained certification and actually negotiated a contract. It was an amazing achievement, for Ward Coley, like many men of his generation, could neither read nor write: his wife read all the correspondence and documents to him, and he committed as much as he could to memory.

Although they negotiated a contract, they could not get a union security clause. The management gradually eroded their membership, and the union was decertified; Ward Coley lost his job, a frustrated and embittered man. The experience impressed itself deeply on young George. "I guess I had something to prove," he says. He proved it by working for the new union, with four of his five brothers.

The management resisted. George Coley gives an example:

> I was working in the carpenter shop then. One day Mr. Lake came down and says to the foreman, 'I hears you've got some union boys here.' 'Yes, one,' says the foreman. 'Well, get him out of here,' says Mr. Lake. 'I don't want him around here.' So I was packing up my things to go, but a few minutes later Lake came back. I expect he'd got some advice from somebody because you can't fire a man for joining a union, you know. Anyway, he came back and talked to the foreman, and the foreman told me to stay. But after that, you know—usually the carpenter shop would work, even if the cutting line was shut down. After that, whenever they finished off a load of fish and the boys on the cutting line went home, I got sent home, too.

By January of 1971, the union was ready to apply for certification in the fish plant. They won, but just barely; out of 205 members in the bargaining unit, 105 voted for the union, 65 voted against, and 35 abstained. It was enough to make certification legal, but a precarious margin indeed when dealing with Spencer Lake.

It was clear from the first that the negotiations would be difficult; while the union team was arguing for a contract, Spencer Lake was continuing to resist the whole idea of having a union. A member of the union's executive remembers their first meeting:

> We had it in the United Church hall. We was all sot down along the table, and we was some nervous, I can tell you. Then they come in—Mr. Lake, Mrs. Lake, Mr. Moulton [the fish plant manager] . . . a whole string of them. They didn't even look at us. Mr. Lake, he looks around the hall. 'Nice place,' he says. Then he looks at the drapes. 'Margaret,' he says, 'Aren't these the drapes we donated to the church?' 'Yes,' she says, 'I believe they are.' That's the sort of thing they got on with. They didn't like it that Reverend Burke was letting us use the hall.

> So we had our list of demands. Mr. Lake, he just goes down the list: *no* to this one, *no* to that one, right down the list. And they gets ready to leave.
>
> We says, 'Are we meeting again, or what?' And he says, 'I suppose we might as well. You won't have no trouble with your friend the minister, getting the hall.' That's the way it went.

The negotiations dragged on and months went by. Tentative agreement was reached on fifteen points that would establish general working conditions, but Lake remained intractable on two of the union's demands—for a wage increase and for a clause guaranteeing union security. Finally, a conciliator was appointed. His report, submitted in late May, recommended an agreement that would give the union a measure of security through a compulsory dues check-off, and would give a five per cent wage increase. The union was willing to accept the first, but not the second. Spencer Lake was quoted as rejecting the report "in total": "If I felt the company could afford a wage increase they wouldn't need to put a gun to my back. And I'll never agree to a closed shop union." A strike was inevitable.

Lake now said to the media what he had been telling the workers for months. "If they think I'm going to be dictated to by priests, lawyers, or gangsters from Chicago, they've got another think coming," he told reporters. Dismissing Cashin as a "political cast-off looking for a new base of power" and stating that "priests should mind their own business," he made it clear that the union's victory at Natlake would not be repeated at Burgeo Fish Industries: "My family owns it lock, stock, and barrel, and I just won't give in. If they go on strike I'll close the plant down until they get better sense and come back to work. I'm prepared to shut down that plant as long as I have to . . . until the end of the year, maybe longer."

When a vote was held on June 3, it went overwhelmingly for strike action, and on the following day at noon, when most of the workers were out of the plant, the picket line went up.

"It was raining that day," one of the picketers recalls,

> and we was stood out there. People didn't take us serious, at first. It was a new thing for Burgeo, eh? People wasn't used to it. They sort of made fun of it, at first. They'd say things like, 'Go on in out of it, boy, you're getting wet.' Things like that.
>
> We didn't know much about strikes either, and I expect most of us felt a bit foolish—I knows I did.

Lake encouraged that feeling, urging the strikers to lay down their "silly placards" and get back to work. He said that he would have no trouble negotiating with his own workers, but would not deal with the "outside influences" that had come in to incite them.

That was Friday. By Monday, with the picket line still up, the battle lines were hardening. Lake issued an ultimatum: if the strikers were not back on the job within twenty-four hours, he would direct his dragger fleet to other plants and close the Burgeo operation. This, like his earlier statement, was technically a violation of the Newfoundland Labour Relations Act, which forbids employers engaged in a labour dispute from threatening to move or close their operations; however, the union leaders could see little advantage in pressing the point. Their main concern was to force Lake to recognize the union. The struggle was going to be played out in Burgeo.

Although a few people had joined the union side since the vote, it still represented only a bare majority of the work force—perhaps 110 people. The non-union workers numbered about ninety. Most on both sides were men; of thirty-five women in the plant, only seven were with the union. Of the crews of the five trawlers only a handful were union members; some of the others were sympathetic to the union, some were hostile, and some were indifferent. The workers at the Natlake herring plant were solidly behind the strikers. Most of the rest of the townspeople had clearly formed sympathies, and before long they all would have. Burgeo was being divided into two camps.

Caught in the middle for the moment were the forty-odd inshore fishermen. Most had joined the union and were counting on its efforts to secure bargaining rights for them. Until then, however, they could legally neither bargain collectively nor strike. Besides, they were entering the most productive part of their year and the only buyer within reach was Spencer Lake. He told them that if they ever expected to sell fish to any of his plants, they should turn in their union cards to him. It was a prime example of the problem that critics had been saying would make the NFFAWU impossible. The interests of plant workers, inshore fishermen, and trawlermen are not always alike: how could they be part of the same union?

The answer required some fast foot-work. First, the union advised the fishermen to turn in their cards if that were the only way to sell their fish: the more complex problems of solidarity could be worked out later, when inshore fishermen had gained bargaining rights. When three of the men refused, the union organized a plan to purchase their catch. At first, the fish was distributed free to the hospital and to any private individuals who could use it; later, when equipment and supplies of salt were acquired, the union set up a salting and drying operation, eventually selling the product to the Canadian Saltfish Corporation. In the press, Cashin made use of the incident, accusing Lake of intimidation, "Nazi-like" tactics and "Stalinist purges."

Another pressing problem was money; few of the Burgeo workers could afford to be without income for very long. The union assured its members that they did not have to worry. After two weeks on strike, their massive international's war-chest would provide them with a minimum of thirty dollars a week strike pay and, they were assured, donations from other unions would boost that to at least forty-five. Since average pay rates in the plant during full-time operation were about sixty dollars a week, this would allow them to continue the strike without undue suffering.

Lake countered by offering his non-union workers thirty dollars a week for simply staying home, and up to seventy-two for work on community projects. The first of these was to be a playground that had long been planned for the community. Union strategists believed that Lake hoped the strikers would interfere with the work, and leave themselves open to legal action. Instead, when the non-union workers turned up to start on the playground they were met by a group of irate mothers whose children had participated—along with the children of the non-union workers—in walkathons and other fundraising activities over several years to raise over twenty thousand dollars for playground equipment. The money had been raised in a spirit of unity, one of the more thoughtful women said, and they did not want it used in a way that would divide the community. Lake abandoned that project and set the non-union workers to building a road to a nearby picnic and recreation spot known as "The Sandbanks." Critics said the road looked more like a riding trail for the Lake family's horses, and would facilitate access to pasturage for other Lake livestock. When a sign appeared on the road one morning, reading "Road Built by Scab Labour," it turned out to have been errected, not by a striker, but by someone who had no direct connection with the Lake operations or the dispute.

The little town of Burgeo, used to the complex rifts and divisions of any small community, was dividing into two clear factions. A few people tried to remain neutral, but this was practically impossible; anyone who did not support one side was promptly assigned to the opposition.

Some of the townspeople will say that Burgeo was a happy, united community until the strike divided it. Others will argue that the division was not new; that it was latent in the town all along, and that the strike merely made it more visible and more rancorous. Whichever view is taken, there is no question that the focal point of both factions was the Lake family, for if the Lakes inspired bitter animosity in some, they inspired powerful loyalty in others.

Their role in Burgeo is, perhaps, difficult for the modern city-dweller to comprehend. About seventy-five per cent of the town's five hundred-odd families depended directly on the Lake operations for jobs. The Lake house stood on a rocky rise above the fish plant among a cluster of four or five others occupied by managerial personnel. It was not palatial by the standards set by the merchant princes on Circular Road in St. John's, but it was large and luxuriously appointed; local girls in starched uniforms served there as maids when the Lakes provided lavish entertainment for visitors. Lake sheep were pastured on meadows and little islands around the town. Across the road from the house, a large Lake barn housed a half a dozen riding horses, several cows, a donkey, some exotic goats, and, incredibly, three Peruvian llamas. On fine days the Lake family—Spencer, Margaret, and their three children—fitted out in proper English equestrian garb, rode their horses through the town.

For all their siegneurial style, the Lakes were not remote from the community. Their children attended the local school and got on well with their classmates. Spencer's position as mayor gave him a central role in the town's affairs, and both he and Margaret took a leading part in community activities. Working for the Lakes was a personal relationship in which loyalty was rewarded and disloyalty punished. "There were always two factions," one resident remarks. "You were either in with the Lakes and went along with their way of doing things, or you were out. And if you didn't agree with them, you'd better keep your mouth shut. There was no life for you at all in Burgeo if you tried to buck the Lakes."

The paternalism had its benevolent side; even people who opposed the Lakes during the strike tell of the summer jobs that were found for students each year, of young people helped through university, and of kindnesses done for the old and the needy. One man's testimony in 1981 summed up many of the feelings of the pro-Lake group:

> You couldn't find a finer kind of man than Mr. Lake. Back then before the strike, I had a brain hemorrhage. Mr. Lake, he flied me to St. John's, to hospital, and he flied me right back home to Burgeo. He paid for that.
>
> I was off work three, four months, and I got paid as much for those months just the same as if I'd worked. The way it is now, when a man's finished work, they're finished with him, but it weren't like that with Mr. Lake.
>
> When I got back up on me feet, I went back up to the plant, and they put me to light work. I'd work maybe an hour, an hour and a half at first. I had a pallet right there in the shop, and when I couldn't do no more I'd

> lay back. I was like it for months, and I got paid the same as if I'd worked the whole shift.
>
> At Christmas, all the widows and old-age pensioners, they'd get a forty-dollar order from the store—they'd have their chicken or their turkey, all they'd need for the days of Christmas. No matter did they ever work on the plant or not; if they was widows or getting the pension, Mr. Lake would send them their order.
>
> One time I worked on the United Church, there. Mr. Lake was United. He said to me, 'You keep track of your time.' When the job was done he come and asked me, 'How much time did you put in at the church?', I told him. He said, 'All right. I'm going to donate that to the church,' and he paid me for the time I worked.

On the other hand, the Lakes had the reputation of being tough, irascible and capricious. Tales of arbitrary firings are legion. While the man just quoted concluded, " 'Twas a sad day for Burgeo when the Lakes left," another who once worked on the Lake trawlers takes the opposite view:

> Where's they livin' to now? Boston? Well, by the Jesus, they're handy enough to Burgeo there, so far as I'm concerned. Supposin' they moves to China, it wouldn't be too far for me.
>
> The man's a anti-Christ. Them times, before the union come in, we was just livin' and that's all. And you only did that if Mr. Lake let you. I don't want my children treated the way we was. Them days, you did what you was told and you took what you was give.

Another man, a civil servant who had never worked for the Lake family, sums up his feelings this way:

> Spencer Lake was a nice enough man to talk with. Sometimes he'd ride by on his horse, and he'd always stop and talk to you. But whether he was on his horse or not, he was always up there, and you were down here.

One of those who agrees that the factional division of Burgeo had deep roots was the Reverend Joe Burke, the United Church minister who aided in the first union organizing efforts. At the time of the strike he was quoted in a newspaper article as saying, "There has always been a kind of subliminal feeling of disdain for Spencer Lake in Burgeo. It was there seething under the surface. The union was merely the catalyst that brought it up." In an article in the union newspaper published during the strike, Burke countered the stories of Lake's benevolence to the elderly at Christmas with the observation that in the week before Christmas of 1970, some workers brought home pay-cheques as low as eight dollars. Ten years later he recalled:

> I still think of Spencer Lake as a friend, though I don't suppose he'd feel that way about me. In Burgeo, the Lakes were a kind of gentry, in the old sense. They felt they had a right to run things. But—*noblesse oblige* — they also felt responsible for the well-being of the town. Spencer didn't realize that feudalism was dead.
>
> When I first came to Burgeo, Spencer started sending me two quarts of milk a day. And I could get any fish I ever wanted from the plant. He never stopped it—the two quarts of milk came all through, regardless of the position I took on the union. There was nothing petty about him. I think he was hurt, more than angry, at my position and the Burgeo people in the union, at first. The anger came later.

Throughout the Burgeo strike, as through Newfoundland's history up to the present, religion runs as a counterpoint. The large majority of the townspeople were, and are, Anglicans. Spencer Lake was one of Burke's United Church parishioners, along with a small group mostly made up of managerial staff at the fish plants and small business people. Margaret Lake and their children are Roman Catholics; across the road from their house, the Lakes had built a small A-frame chapel, where visiting priests could say Mass for them and the two or three other Catholic families in the town. The chapel was named for St. Jude: the patron saint, as the local clergy wryly noted, of hopeless cases and lost causes. When McGrath visited the community on union business, he would sometimes say Mass in the chapel, but the Lake family did not attend. "They wouldn't come near me," McGrath says. "Mrs. Lake would call the children in when I passed by on the road."

For Burke, as for McGrath, support of the union was a natural extension of religious commitment. It was not, he insists, an emotional reaction; he was not caught up in the excitement of union organizing. Rather, he saw the union as one possible instrument of social change. As a student, and as a neophyte clergyman in another small south coast town, Burke had thought deeply about his society:

> I always felt Newfoundlanders were deprived—held back from the kind of social and economic developments that went on in other places—by the three institutions that controlled the society: the merchants, the government, and the church. Traditionally, these three reinforced each other.
>
> The people were fragmented, isolated in small communities or as individual fishermen, far away from markets or sources of power. It created a dissonance. People were dependent on the three governing institutions, but resented them, too.
>
> A lot of Newfoundlanders have a love-hate relationship with their culture. They can be proud of their own and their ancestors' survival through hardship and struggle, and, at the same time, they can be bitter about it, and ashamed of it, and turn against their culture.

Burke's reflections led him to a conclusion reached by a number of other Newfoundlanders in the late 1960s and early 1970s: that their province needed a wider range of democratic institutions to act as countervailing forces to the existing power structure. As Burke expresses it, he felt the need of a "fifth column" that would bring about a confrontation with the existing system. In Burgeo, he had fostered a local development association and started a small weekly newspaper, and when the union arrived he saw it as a similar means for confronting the established institutions. Burke was familiar with the history of William Coaker and the FPU, and he accepted the generally-held view that Coaker's movement had foundered largely because of the religious issue. The success of McGrath and Cashin on the predominantly Protestant northeast coast had impressed him, and he felt that his own support, as a Protestant clergyman, might provide an additional impetus. He supported the union both outside and inside his church; his sermons were often devoted to the union issue. As a result his congregation, largely drawn from the management and pro-management side, began to stay home on Sunday mornings. Often, however, the empty pews were filled by Anglican plant-workers and fishermen. Burke was chagrined by what he perceives as a lack of support from the United Church's governing bodies. "At that time, the United Church of Canada was supporting a boycott of California grapes because of the struggles of farm workers, but they couldn't see the similarity with Burgeo. Maybe it was too close and too sensitive, but it seemed ironic."

While the clergymen representing the two faiths of the Lake family battled for the union, the church that represented the large majority of the people of Burgeo tried to remain neutral. It was not perceived that way by everyone; the strikers, particularly, felt some resentment. "It didn't look too good," says one, "with a Roman Catholic priest and a United Church minister out there helping us, and our own church not doin' nothin'. " The south coast, like the northwest, receives radio broadcasts from Nova Scotia, and disappointment with their church was increased for some Burgeo Anglicans by reports of the activity of the Reverend Ron Parsons in the Strait of Canso. The Anglican priest in Burgeo at the time, Charles Abraham, says his personal sympathies were with the union cause, but that he felt it would be wrong to express them publicly: "In the church there were people on both sides of the argument, holding honest opinions. They disagreed with each other, and they remained members of the church.

> I saw it as my business—an the church's business—to help hold the community together. They had their differences of opinion and had to work them out, but in the church they should be together."

Abraham's position was supported by the church hierarchy and a majority of the laymen who made up the local board. The Anglican parish hall was the usual site for large community activities, and when the union planned a social to celebrate the first strike pay after two weeks of picketing, they naturally planned to hold it there. Some of the congregation complained, the opinion of the bishop was sought, and the church wardens decided that neither side would be allowed to use the hall for the duration of the strike. Thereafter, meetings and socials were held in the smaller and less convenient Orange Hall. Since it was primarily the union that would want to hold large public gatherings, many people regarded the church's action as partisan.

The *contretemps* over the hall was one of a long series of moves and counter-moves, with union and management like two wrestlers locked in a hold that neither dares to break, each searching for that extra bit of leverage to weaken the opponent's grip. A few days before, it had been the union's turn. When Lake's refrigerator ship, the *Caribou Reefer,* arrived at Lake's Caribou Fisheries processing and distribution centre in Gloucester, Massachusetts, with a load of frozen fish, it was met by two Burgeo men, Gordon Hare and Ron Swift, who had flown to Massachusetts with Richard Cashin and set up an "informational" picket line. Workers at the Gloucester operation, mostly members of the Amalgamated Meat Cutters and Butcher Workmen, the international parent of the NFFAWU, respected the picket line and refused to touch the cargo. The Newfoundland crew unloaded the ship, but then truckers refused to move the fish from the refrigerated warehouse. After three days of picketing while Cashin fielded calls from the international's lawyers, the Newfoundlanders returned home under threat of deportation. The press reported resolutions by the Longshoremen's Union to boycott the Lake vessel along the entire eastern seaboard, and offers by the United Farm Workers Organizing Committee of the United States to start a boycott of Lake fish similar to the boycott of California grapes they had organized a few years before.

It was a propaganda victory for the union, and a demonstration of the value of an international link, but it was also a bit of a fluke. Although the big American-based unions make much of the advantages of international solidarity, they are less than enthusiastic about such free-wheeling uses of its power. "What we were doing was probably illegal," Cashin now says with a smile, "but I didn't know very much about all that at the time."

The road into the plant was closed by the picket line, but the fish plant, after all, was more involved with the water than the land. Trawlers, inshore boats, and refrigerator ships could still come to the wharf, and if they could, so could non-union workers. By the end of June the plant was operating again with eighty or ninety non-union workers aided by students and a few men and a number of women who had never worked in the plant before. Each morning, dozens of small boats threaded their way through the maze of waterways and converged on the plant. The union countered with a floating picket line. The fish plant was situated on a small inlet known as the Short Reach. With two or three of the larger boats belonging to the union fishermen, and several of the smaller, they stretched a rope across the Reach, effectively blocking entry to the plant. This action led to one of the most dangerous confrontations of the strike.

Both sides were beginning to realize that the struggle was going to be harder than either had thought. The management side, particularly, could see that the strikers were not going to be shamed or ridiculed into giving up, and that some decisive action was called for. The Lake family gathered its forces: Spencer's brother Harold came in from the family business in St. John's, as did Douglas Hunt, the company's legal adviser. Berch Lake, Spencer's son by a previous marriage, took leave of absence from the Toronto investment company where he was working and came to Burgeo to lend his support.

On Wednesday, July 14, a notice was distributed on the letterhead of Burgeo Fish Industries Ltd., signed by Arthur Moulton, plant manager:

> THERE WILL BE A VERY IMPORTANT MEETING OF ALL NON-UNION EMPLOYEES IN THE ORANGE HALL AT 8 TOMORROW MORNING. AT THIS MEETING MR. S.G. LAKE WILL MAKE A VERY IMPORTANT ANNOUNCEMENT. IT IS VERY IMPORTANT THAT ALL NON-UNION EMPLOYEES ATTEND THIS MEETING.

The non-union workers, still on the company payroll, turned out in force and Spencer Lake addressed them, calling on loyalties built up over sixteen years in the community. If they stood firm together, he told them, they could re-open the plant and go back to work. They were going into the plant, and would meet resistance with whatever force was necessary. Two men demurred, saying that they were willing to work in defiance of the union, but would not fight their fellow-workers on the picket line. They were brushed aside. The rest went along with their employer, some reluctantly and some in high excitement. The more enthusiastic of them hurried down to a wharf and boarded the *Limanda*, a sixty-five foot converted fisheries patrol vessel owned by the company.

In press reports of the day the *Limanda* was referred to as the Lakes' yacht, a designation that Spencer Lake contemptuously rejected, calling her a "work boat," but both terms had some validity. While not the luxurious plaything suggested by the first, the *Limanda* was used by the Lakes for picnic outings, and hunting, fishing, and camping trips. She was also, however, used to ferry people and equipment back and forth among family-owned fish plants. As both pleasure craft and working vessel, the *Limanda* was a compelling symbol of the way the Lakes' personal and corporate lives were intertwined.

With the men aboard, the *Limanda* cast off and moved slowly and deliberately up the Short Reach. In front of her went a smaller boat rowed by four men, with Berch Lake standing in the bows. At the floating picket line there was a brief flurry as strikers and strike-breakers thrust and swung with heavy oars. Defended by his oarsmen, the younger Lake heaved the sodden picket rope across the boat's bow and began to chop it with an axe. "It was a big, heavy hawser," he remembers, "a valuable piece of line. It belonged to the company. In the middle of all that racket, I had this sudden, strange feeling: here I am with an axe, cutting our own bloody rope!" Over a hundred pickets were watching from the road at the plant entrance. When the rope parted they surged down to the wharf with a roar of anger.

For a time, all was confusion. Accounts of events on the wharf are varied and contradictory. Spencer and Margaret Lake were there; plant manager Moulton, and lawyer Hunt. While the strikers milled around the wharf shouting curses and challenges at the men aboard the *Liman-*

da, the Lakes raged at the single Mountie to clear them off company property. The mood of the crowd was building. Objects on the wharf—oil barrels, fish boxes, bits of timber—began to fly. "I'll tell you, boy," one participant recalls, "anything that weren't lashed down was hove over the side. I seen men pick up things they couldn't lift, normally, and heave 'em over."

The *Limanda*, with her engines idling, glided to a halt a few hundred feet away from the turmoil while Berch Lake's boat moved in to land him alone on a small float below the plant wharf. It was a tension-filled moment. "With all that heavy stuff flyin' around," one of the union leaders says, "somebody could have been killed. I think if the *Limanda* had come in there would have been real violence."

The younger Lake does not disagree: "I don't know what might have happened," he says, "but things were definitely getting out of hand. I had to go through with it, but I could think of a hell of a lot of places I'd rather be than on that float!" When some of the union men jumped down onto the float with him, most of those who were watching thought they were going to attack him. Among them, however, was one of the cooler heads among the strikers, a man of about the same age as Berch named Calvin Swift. Raising their voices above the din, the two young men tried to find a way to defuse the situation. Members of the union executive shouldered through the crowd and joined them.

Against the cacophony of shouts and curses an agreement was reached. The strikers would withdraw from the plant if the Lakes would abandon the attempt to land the *Limanda* and, instead, meet with the union negotiators. There was an incongruous moment of comedy while Berch tried to communicate the agreement to the men on the boat and his father on the wharf. Everyone was shouting at cross-purposes and no one could hear anything. Gradually, though, the message was passed. Over considerable objection, Berch and the union leaders convinced their respective sides to withdraw, and the strikers moved back to their station on the road as the *Limanda* slipped down the Reach.

The promised meeting was quickly over. By his own account, Spencer Lake stayed only long enough to "tell Cashin what I thought of him," an opinion that, according to some who heard it, blistered the paint on the walls of the United Church hall. There were no negotiations; instead, Lake applied for and received a court injunction forbidding the floating picket line and limiting the number of pickets in front of the plant to eight per shift. Twenty RCMP with full riot equipment were sent to Burgeo to see that the injunction was obeyed. The plant re-opened, the non-union employees went back to work, and the union maintained its now almost token picket line.

In many respects, the Burgeo strike was the classic union struggle, but in Newfoundland few things are exactly as they are elsewhere, and in some respects Burgeo was unique. The strike caused no financial hardship—quite the opposite, in fact. Contributions from other unions soon allowed the NFFAWU to increase the strike pay to fifty-five dollars a week for women and single men and sixty for those supporting a family—rates that equalled and in many cases surpassed earnings when employed. Lake had increased wages in the plant and was paying a number of people, including youngsters, who would not normally be working at all. Merchants in the town reported that business had never been so good. In one of the many convoluted ironies of the situation, among the principal beneficiaries of all this prosperity were the barber shop, beauty parlour, laundromat, and supermarket owned by Spencer Lake.

The division of the community also had its peculiarities. The news media made much of the rifts that set brother against brother and son against father, and predicted that personal relationships in Burgeo were suffering wounds that would never heal. The animosities, certainly, were very real. Old friends stopped talking to one another, and close personal relationships between kinsmen dissolved in heated argument.

Small towns never lack dissension. The romantic ideal of the placid, integrated community is rarely found in real life. But over generations of isolation and social self-sufficiency, Newfoundland outports have developed a resistance to open conflict. Joe Burke sees this as one of the reasons for the slow development of political protest in the province: "Rural Newfoundlanders don't see conflict as constructive—as a means of confronting situations and improving them," he says. "They see it as threatening. That's partly why the power structures were able to push them around for so long." An open division into two factions was particularly threatening, especially when it was exposed to outsiders through the press. Even worse, in a society with strong family traditions, this was a conflict that, in many cases, set younger people against their elders.

But there is another side to the coin. If rural Newfoundlanders would prefer to avoid open conflict, they also have ways of managing and containing it when it occurs. It is worth remembering that people in small fishing communities are constantly surrounded by potentially lethal weapons; fish plants and homes are stocked with the sharpest of knives, and it is a rare household that does not have rifles and shotguns close to hand. Yet, while the occasional fist-fight on a Saturday night is not unknown, homicidal assault has been extremely rare. During the strike, there was one reported instance of a non-union man threatening a striker with a knife. It caused widespread alarm and disapproval on both sides, but was not allowed to escalate; no charges were laid. There were other cases of individual arguments getting out of hand and coming to blows, but when group violence did occur it was directed against property, not people.

The family splits that caught the attention of the reporters were most painful for those near the centre of the struggle; others found them less difficult. One young man walked the picket line faithfully while his fiancée went as faithfully to work with the non-union forces. Their courtship continued during the strike, and after it they married. In another case, a man and his son picketed and drew strike pay while the wife and mother of the household worked for the Lakes. Anomalies like this outraged the international representative of the CFAWU, Fred Locking. He did not approve of supplementing the strike pay beyond the basic thirty dollars in the first place, and such apparent breaches of solidarity infuriated him. "The first thing I'd have said to that man," Locking says, "is 'stop your wife from working or you're cut off.' " The union, however, had very little room to manoeuver. Its majority was still precarious, and it had to deal with its members in the manner of a small town organization—on an individual, rather than a legalistic basis. Locking was overruled. Burgeo, though divided, remained a community. One consequence was that neither side could maintain much secrecy. "We always knew what they was going to do before they did it," a union member says with a laugh, "and they always knew what we was going to do."

For many of the journalists, the divided families and broken friendships were merely a human-interest angle—a sidelight providing an additional sense of drama to the story. In a sense, however, personal relationships were at the very core of the struggle. When Spencer Lake first gathered his non-striking employees together to resist the union he began by reminding them that he knew them all by their first names, knew their wives and husbands, knew their children. He was not exaggerating. For sixteen years he and his family had been part of the community, attending its weddings and its funerals, celebrating its triumphs and mourning its losses.

Even now, Burgeo seems an unlikely place for a man with a taste for good wine, horses, and sophisticated pleasures, and it was far less likely when Lake first went there. In the early 1950s the community had no municipal government or services, no water and sewer systems, no electricity, and no telephones. Life was hard, and the civilized amenities even of a small provincial city like St. John's were far away. But Lake liked the people. They were friendly, open, honest, and hardworking. He admired their toughness and independence. Like many successful middle-class families in Newfoundland, the Lakes identify strongly with their society's rural past. They may rub elbows with soft-handed Bay Street financiers, but their heroes are the rumbustious, two-fisted, half-legendary ship owners and skippermen who knew the oceans from the Caribbean to the Bay of Biscay and kept their crews in line by force of personality and strength of arm. Burgeo and its people provided a powerful echo of that past, and it gave Spencer Lake a place to put into practice talents and ideas that were the heritage of his family and his class. "I suppose I've always been a bayman at heart," he would say a dozen years after the strike, in his office overlooking the Boston fish-wharves. "Burgeo became my home. In some ways, the years there were the best years of my life."

Lake was born in the Burin Peninsula town of Fortune, and came to St. John's with his family as a youngster when his father was elected to the House of Assembly. At school he was bright, handsome, headstrong, popular with the girls, much admired for this athletic prowess at football and as a rower in the annual Regatta. While still in his teens he sneaked away from school, wangled his way aboard a sealing vessel, and "went to the ice", killing and pelting with the hard-bitten fishermen-sealers in a self-inflicted ritual of manhood. He married young and as a matter of course moved into his father's saltfish business in St. John's where he and his brother Harold learned the trade on the deck and the dock as well as in the office.

They learned to manage men in highly personal, face-to-face relationships, able to issue curt orders, fire a slacker, or share a drink and a joke, all with equal ease. As the frozen fish industry developed after the war, both of the brothers put their skills to work building up plants in isolated outports like Englee and Gaultois. At Burgeo, Spencer had the help of family and political connections—to say nothing of $650,000 advanced by the provincial government—but no small part of his success can be attributed to his personal qualities as a manager.

Like the Reverend Joe Burke a decade later, he saw the deficiencies of outport life and believed that the people deserved better, but where Burke approached the problem by trying to help them to improve their own lot, fostering new democratic structures, Lake did things himself. He pushed for a municipal council and became its mayor as the obvious best choice. The position, he maintains, gave him a type of access to higher levels of government that he had not possessed as a businessman, and he used it to get services for the town—and, of course, for the fish plant. His personal, public, and business interests were all of a piece:

> I like fresh milk, and you couldn't get it in Burgeo, so I got a cow. With one cow you don't get a steady supply, so I got another. Cows don't keep producing without being freshened, so I got a bull. Other people like fresh milk, too, so I got more cows and pretty soon we had a dairy business going.
>
> Then, there was no place in Burgeo to get your hair cut. People cut each others' hair, and they weren't very good

> at it. I found out there was a fellow in the machine shop at the plant who had been in the T.B. sanitarium for a few years, and he'd learned barbering, so I set him up in a barber shop.

And so it went. To match the barber shop, Lake sent a young woman to Corner Brook for training as a hairdresser and established her in a shop. There were no banking facilities, so he built a small office building and leased space for a branch bank. Food prices were high and supplies erratic: Lake had refrigerated ships travelling back empty from the Gloucester marketing operation, so he arranged for them to call at a mainland port on the way home for stock to supply a new supermarket. He tried for years without success to find a cobbler to set up a shoe repair business. Even the llamas that so astonished journalists during the strike were part of the pattern. The Lakes already had sheep whose wool was sent to Prince Edward Island for carding and spinning and came back as yarn for sale in the supermarket to Burgeo knitters. Lake knew that lamas produced an extremely valuable wool, and were native to a cold, bleak, and treeless terrain: perhaps they would flourish on the south coast barrens, and provide a new industry. As it happened, the llamas were not enthusiastic immigrants, and instead of becoming the founders of a new race they became family pets.

Lake's first marriage had broken down, and in Margaret Penny of Ramea he married a woman whose family background and ideas had much in common with his own. They worked together to build up the business and the town, and in the process they created a modernized version of the traditional Newfoundland outport. As merchants, they bought fish from the inshore fishermen, hired others to man their trawlers, employed people to process and transport the product; as merchants they sold people the goods they needed to maintain themselves. Like the entrepreneurs that Coaker had set out to displace they were the pivot-point of the community, and it seemed only natural that they should reap handsome returns. Later, when the strike was over, the provincial government released figures showing that during the last twelve months of operation under Lake management the fish plant earned a profit of $200,000 and the supermarket $100,000.

It was all accomplished in the highly personalized, face-to-face style of a small, isolated community. Both Spencer and Margaret were used to making sharp judgements of people. They rewarded industry and loyalty, and had little sympathy for weakness or timidity. Spencer liked and admired many of his employees, including Ward Coley, who started the first fish plant union: "Coley was a good man. But he went sort of sour after that business with the union. I like to be able to have a straightforward, man-to-man disagreement with a fellow, thrash it out, and no hard feelings afterwards." Even now, Lake finds it difficult to comprehend that in an unequal world such dealings are a luxury, much more easily afforded by the rich than the poor.

Even so, many of the people liked and admired Lake in return. Even some of his strongest opponents in the struggle are willing to give him his due. "Spencer Lake did a lot for Burgeo. There's no denying that," says one of the union leaders:

> You know, he said one time something about us not bein' able to do anything for ourselves. Well, I allow he had reason to think it. It was we people who made him mayor. Whenever there was something that needed to be done—like to get in touch with the government or something—we wouldn't do it ourselves. We'd just say, 'Oh, Mr. Lake'll be going to St. John's next week. He'll look after it.' But then, when we stood up and done something for ourselves, he didn't like it.

Berch Lake inherited many of his father's qualities. They were separated for several of his growing years, but when he was in his late teens Berch spent summers in Burgeo, where his father tried to put him through some of the tough apprenticeship that he believed every young man should have. They did not always see eye-to-eye, and Berch seemed destined to make a career far away from the fishing business. When he returned to Burgeo during the strike his loyalties were put to a severe test. Many of the young strikers were his friends. They had worked, fished, and hunted together, got drunk for the first time together, shared each other's secrets. He came with the thought that he might play a mediating role, helping both sides to a reasonable solution, but he found that everything had changed. The battle-lines were drawn, and he was a Lake. In the new Burgeo, Berch and his father developed a new respect for each other, but the taunts and jeers from his boyhood friends on the picket line cut deep.

The severed relationships that caught the attention of the journalists—the sisters who stopped speaking and the sons who defied their fathers—were by-products of the struggle, poignant but accidental. The breach in the Lake family's relations with the strikers had a far deeper significance, for it symbolized the end of a social structure that had lasted for hundreds of years. After the clash on the fish plant wharf and the granting of the injunction, there was no turning back. Whichever side should win, things would never be the same again, neither in Burgeo nor in Newfoundland.

Chapter 6

With the injunction in effect, the battle for Burgeo was at a stalemate, and it became obvious that any resolution was going to have to come from outside. The union concentrated on generating public support, and the Lakes searched for legal means of getting rid of the union. In the town itself, the slow-motion wrestling match continued. One of the union members owned a small fish storage shed just outside the plant. He gave it to the union, and the men re-built it into a strike headquarters, proudly labelled "union made." One wall was filled with telegrams of support from union locals and individuals across the province—including one from the Honourable Don Jamieson—and with copies of receipts for donations to the strike fund. The Friday night gatherings at the Orange Hall, which began with the first strike pay, became an institution with strikers' wives serving a potluck supper, visiting sympathizers giving speeches, and local musicians providing entertainment. The picket line remained at the legal maximum of eight, but other strikers were always near at hand. They could not prevent people from crossing but kept up a constant minor harrassment of management personnel: eggs were thrown and air let out of tires. Union officials shuttled back and forth, providing support—Locking, Cashin, McGrath, and Charlie Borsk, the CFAWU organizer from Toronto, jokingly dubbed "Chicago Charlie" after Lake's repeated references to "gangsters" from that city.

Union people in Burgeo retain a high respect for these visitors, but they have especially fond memories of Ray Greening, the man who had brought the small retail section into the NFFAWU, and was later to become the union's secretary-treasurer. Greening settled in the community and provided continuity in the link with the larger union. "Ray was the man who kept us on the track," they will say now. "He was a real gentleman. Everybody respected him, even the people on the other side." Ward Coley, organizer of the defeated union of the 1950s, was ill with cancer and as his condition deteriorated he sat in his kitchen window overlooking the plant, watching with pride as his sons walked the picket line. Whenever he could, Greening would walk up the hill and give the elder Coley a report on the progress of the strike. Ten years later, still the NFFAWU's secretary-treasurer, Greening himself suc-

succumbed to cancer at the cruelly early age of forty-two.

The management responded to union harrassment with taunts of their own and frequent calls on the RCMP to report infractions. The Lakes threatened legal action against Cashin, McGrath, and Burke for "inciting" the *Limanda* incident, began to collect affadavits from non-union workers in preparation for applying to have the union decertified, and raised wages for their non-union work force above the level recommended in the conciliation report. Union supporters say that members of the Lake family, on horseback or in cars, intimidated strikers on foot and that even Cashin, during a visit to the picket line, was forced to jump into a ditch when brushed by a Lake car. Tension was high and predictions of violence frequent.

News media in Newfoundland and on the mainland were finding the strike made good copy, and both sides made use of the fact. Mike Martin, editor of the NFFAWU's newsletter, kept up a constant campaign of press releases, in which union officials charged the Lakes with intimidation, provocation, and the use of child labour. Joe Burke had left Burgeo at the end of June, preparatory to going to Scotland for graduate study, and along with McGrath and some other clergy, formed a Committee of Concern for Burgeo that got its share of coverage. A green bumper sticker appeared on cars around the island, reading "It started in Burgeo." The phrase, attributed to Mike Martin, was nicely ambiguous. Everyone knew that the NFFAWU had not started in Burgeo, and the sticker caused people to try to put a name to what *had.*

On the whole, the union fared better in the media than did the Lakes, "I suppose most of us should have been fired," a journalist says. "There weren't many of us who were impartial. We bent over backwards to give the union a good press."

Burgeo people didn't always see it that way. After their experience with Farley Mowat and the whale they were delicately sensitive to criticism or anything that could be taken as a slighting reference, and they sometimes took offence at statements a reporter meant as supportive. They complained that journalists "spent more time chasing the Lakes than listening to the people," a charge that was probably not entirely accurate, but had nonetheless some foundation, because the Lakes were good copy. On the whole, the union handled the press skilfully, their public utterances carefully calculated for effect. The Lakes, on the other hand, angry, beleaguered, and harrassed, were much more likely to blurt out something sensational. Ever since Spencer's patronizing reference to the lack of "intelligent leadership" in rural Newfoundland, reporters hoped to be able to quote a similar gem.

Their hopes were frequently rewarded. Lake could usually be depended upon to enliven interviews with denunciations of the NFFAWU as "a conspiracy by the United Church, the Roman Catholic Church, political opportunists like Richard Cashin, and union gangsters from Chicago." Sometimes he added lines like, " . . . and I don't give a damn if you print that," which were duly printed. Lake neither liked nor trusted the press, and reporters often turned his attacks back upon him. *Evening Telegram* reporter Ron Crocker opened one story by quoting Spencer's first words on meeting him: "I don't even know you yet. But as far as I'm concerned you're a p---k like the rest of them."

Most of the vituperation was directed at the "outsiders" whom Lake accused of stirring up the strike in their own interest, but as the battle wore on he also attacked the local strikers, describing them as "morons" and "goons". One of the strikers was a sixty-year-old woman, Mrs. Pearl Warren. In the manner of many small Newfoundland communities where older people are given the courtesy titles of "aunt" and "uncle", she was called "Aunt Pearl" and much admired by many in the town for her strong stand. When Lake, in a radio broadcast, ridiculed her participation in the strike and referred to her patronizingly as "Granny" Warren, he gained few sympathizers. Hugh Winsor, an expatriate Newfoundlander working for the *Globe and Mail*, quoted Margaret Lake to devastating effect as saying, in reference to the townspeople's refusal to allow their playground to be built by the non-union workers, "Can you imagine turning down a gift like that? Now you know how stupid these people are." Some Burgeo people feel that it was slights like these that finally turned the majority opinion in the community against the Lake family.

Their outspoken intransigence did more than supply a few titillating news reports. In George Coley's opinion:

> Lots of people made the strike a success. Richard [Cashin,] Father McGrath—I guess we all did our share. And Ray [Greening]—he was the man that made it all work in Burgeo.
>
> But if there's one man who made this union, I'd have to say it's Spencer Lake. If he hadn't put up such a fight . . . .You know, we weren't all that strong at the start. If he'd just gone along with it, he'd have been better off. Maybe he'd even have done away with the union like he did with the last one.

Many others agree, Father McGrath for one:

> We *had* to win in Burgeo. Once Lake had said the things he said and dug in his heels the way he did—if we had lost after that, we would have been finished. We would have been just another union trying to organize in a tough industry.
>
> Lake was carrying the ball for the others in the fishing industry. If he'd handled it better, we would have had a much tougher job with the rest.

Support from other unions and outside organizations kept up the morale of the strikers, but it could not break the stalemate. Lake claimed to be operating at seventy-five per cent of capacity, and professed to be willing to carry on indefinitely. "We've got our employees," he said, "and the others are on the payroll of the butchers' union." If the "political opportunists" would leave them alone, he suggested, "this little town would gradually go back to what it was."

If the rank and file among the journalists were sympathetic to the strikers, the editorial writers were not. Popular columnists sniped at the union leadership, echoing Lake's suggestion that Cashin had ulterior political motives, and editorials in *The Evening Telegram* supported Lake's desire for a new certification vote. The union kept up the pressure, with other unionized plants holding sympathy strikes and refusing to handle Lake fish, but it was becoming increasingly obvious that, whatever

Cashin's motives might be, the Burgeo struggle would have to be carried into the larger political arena. Early in the strike union spokesmen had suggested that the plant might have to be nationalized to bring about a settlement. Now, they began to call directly on government to intervene.

Toward the end of July, Premier J.R. Smallwood was scheduled to speak at the opening of the annual convention of the Newfoundland and Labrador Federation of Labour. It promised to be a lively event; besides Burgeo, three other major strikes had been dragging on through the summer. Apparently unwilling to face the labour leaders on their own ground, Smallwood cancelled his appearance at the last minute in favour of a press conference in St. John's. John Connors, leader of the small and struggling provincial New Democratic Party, spoke in his place and received a standing ovation, but the news reports focused their attention on a session later in the day, when Richard Cashin put Smallwood squarely in the centre of the Burgeo battle.

He revealed that the premier had promised to bring about a meeting between Lake and the union in front of the provincial cabinet, but had not followed through. "For two weeks we have been consulting with the premier," Cashin said, "and he seemed to be sympathetic to the union, but now he has betrayed our faith. I didn't believe it was possible until today." Cashin also lashed out at the editorial writers of *The Evening Telegram*, ridiculing their attitude to labour and saying that their support of a new certification vote at Burgeo Fish Industries was like suggesting that Smallwood should give John Crosbie another chance at the Liberal leadership.

Delegate after delegate rose to support the NFFAWU. A motion to hold a general strike was narrowly defeated, and in its place the convention passed a resolution calling for a campaign of sit-ins, demonstrations, petitions, rallies, and picketing in support of the Burgeo strikers. "The common theme in almost every speech," one reporter wrote, "was that the Burgeo dispute will decide the fate of the labour movement in Newfoundland for a long time to come." In Burgeo, virtually everyone had been forced to choose between the Lakes and the union. Now, the same choice was being thrust upon the entire province, and especially upon its premier. "The Burgeo dispute," Cashin told the convention and the voters of Newfoundland, "will tell the truth once and for all about whether Joey is for the fishermen or for businessmen, as it appears he is now."

Smallwood made no direct reply. After twenty-two years of almost unlimited power he was in serious political difficulty and the union leader's challenge was only one item in a long list of troubles. During the NFFAWU's short life, the always-lively Newfoundland political scene had been going through a period of upheaval as exciting and turbulent as any in its history.

Only five years before, Smallwood had been at the pinnacle of his career. The industrial failures of the 1950s were behind him, and the province throbbed with massive new projects. Construction was booming. When the Trans-Canada Highway was completed in 1965, finally linking St. John's with the ferry terminus at Port aux Basques, Newfoundland had celebrated by declaring 1966 a "Come Home Year"; expatriate Newfoundlanders in the United States and mainland Canada were invited to come back and marvel at the progress that had taken place in their absence. On September 8 of that year, Smallwood and the Liberals swept thirty-nine of the forty-two seats in the House of Assembly, leaving the "dirty Tories" clinging precariously to only three of the six urban seats in St. John's. The victory was only partly due to Smallwood induced euphoria. It was also a measure of the inability of the Conservatives or NDP to present a credible alternative.

As the decade wore on, however, the vision of prosperity that Smallwood had conjured up began to fade. Construction faltered. Unemployment rose. Fish prices and fish markets together reached their lowest levels for years. Many of the people who left isolated outports for designated "growth centres" expecting jobs found only frustration, bitterness, and the dole. The real progress that had been made—improved services, expanded communications, and better educational facilities—only accentuated the problems. Smallwood's constant promises of prosperity just around the corner had raised people's expectations: now, better educated and better informed, they were increasingly able to see beyond—and through—the visions that he held out to them, and the Conservatives were steadily re-building their party.

Concrete evidence of the changed political climate came with the federal election of June 25, 1968—the election in which Cashin lost his seat. Before it the Liberals held all of the province's seven federal seats; after it, they held only one—Don Jamieson's Burin-Burgeo—and this in the face of a Liberal sweep in the rest of Canada.

In any other province, responsibility for such an upset would at least be shared. In Newfoundland, it was taken as a personal defeat for J.R. Smallwood. His party was not the "machine" of political legend. It was rather, as Richard Gwyn so ably phrased it, "an ill-disciplined, inefficient agglomeration of personal alliances," controlled by Smallwood and a small coterie of advisors. Now that it appeared to be time for him to step down, Smallwood attempted to give the party some structure. He announced that a leadership convention would be held the following year to choose his successor. In preparation for that great event he called, in the autumn of 1968, the first general convention of the Liberal party in Newfoundland to be held since he took office in 1949.

Richard Cashin had quarrelled with Smallwood during the federal election and now, disgruntled by his defeat, he did not plan to attend the meeting. But the political urge is hard to suppress. The day before the convention opened, Cashin was boating with a friend on Trinity Bay and listening to radio reports of the twelve hundred delegates gathering in Grand Falls. On an impulse, they tied up the boat and drove to the convention hall. A rumour quickly spread that Cashin was there to contest the presidency of the party against Smallwood's hand-picked candidate and, according to Cashin, a Smallwood lieutenant confronted him in the lobby with a warning not to run. Cashin maintains that he had no such intention until that moment but, immediately upon receiving Smallwood's threat, made up his mind. He ran for the presidency, was elected, and, he says, almost immediately began to regret the impulse that made him enter the contest.

For several months he stumped the province making speeches and growing more and more disillusioned with the condition of the party, which he felt was on a "self-destructive course." In June of 1969, eight months after his election, he found a way out. Telling newspaper reporters that "the man who fought the good fight in 1949 is not relevant to Newfoundland today," he resigned his position to undertake a campaign to draft Don Jamieson to take over as party leader. But Jamieson's attention was on the national scene, and soon Cashin's was caught up in organizing fishermen.

Smallwood, having announced his intention to step down, began to express fears that the party would "fall into the wrong hands." Among the hands he had in mind were those of John Crosbie, who had already begun the complicated political step-dance that was to carry him and several others back and forth across the House and in and out of the Liberal and Conservative parties. Crosbie spent freely on his campaign, and it began to appear that he would be a certain winner when the convention was held. Smallwood, considering the situation, apparently decided that the only right hands to hold the Liberal party were his own, and that, therefore, his only proper successor was—himself. He entered the race and spent as freely as Crosbie.

The convention, held at the end of October, was the biggest political gathering ever held in Newfoundland. St. John's hotels were filled; delegates and hangers-on slept and partied aboard a ferry moored at the harbour-front and a string of railway cars from the recently-retired passenger train, the Bullet. In a packed stadium, in spite of angry, hostile demonstrations by university students and Crosbie supporters, Smallwood took sixty per cent of the delegates' votes, and again took up control of the party and the government. He still had his massive majority in the House, of course, but the leadership struggle had divided the party and led to the purge of some of the ablest ministers in his cabinet. Outside the House the Conservatives were still growing in strength, and although the Liberal party had supported Smallwood, there was growing doubt about the extent to which the electorate would support the Liberal party.

Smallwood did not call an election after the customary four years in the autumn of 1970; he hung on, hoping for economic improvements. As the summer of 1971 dragged by with its strikes, lockouts, and demonstrations, he still made no move, coolly observing that the five-year constitutional limit should be calculated, not from the September 8 date of the last election, but from the date of the opening of the House in

1966, which would give him until the end of November. When Cashin challenged the premier from the podium at Federation of Labour Convention to do something about Burgeo no election date had been set, but time was running out and the unofficial campaign had been going on for over a year.

Since his telegram to McGrath early in June asserting his belief in the right of workers to organize, Smallwood had been virtually silent on the Burgeo struggle. With the election inevitable and imminent, the union mounted a concerted effort to draw him out, and by now they had captured public attention. Every move was watched. When labour leaders held a meeting to plan a demonstration it received almost as much publicity as if the demonstration had actually taken place. The union challenged Lake's claim of owning the plant "lock, stock and barrel" by pointing out that Burgeo Fish Industries had an outstanding loan from the provincial government of $475,000 and that the government was guarantor for another loan of $402,000. In recognition of this, a senior civil servant had been appointed to the board of directors, making the government, the union said, Lake's accomplice. When the prime minister visited Newfoundland in a honeymoon atmosphere with his beautiful young wife, he was confronted by Richard Cashin and a group of Burgeo workers who reminded him that a lot of federal money, too, had gone into Lake's company.

Smallwood tried to divert the pressure. He appealed publicly to Lake to meet with the union and the cabinet. When Lake said no, Smallwood delivered a sugar-coated rebuke, stating that while Lake could take justifiable pride in his accomplishments, he was making a "very great mistake" in going against the weight of public opinion. "There is such a thing as being too proud and stubborn," Smallwood said, an observation the truth of which he was soon to demonstrate himself.

Wick Collins, associate editor of *The Evening Telegram*, suggested that the whole Burgeo affair was a product of the internal difficulties of the Liberal party: of Smallwood's vulnerability and Cashin's ambition:

> Normally an employer like Spencer Lake, whose ideas on labour are firmly fixed back in the middle ages, would find himself the target of massive and overpowering attack from all angles. But in this peculiar situation, support for Cashin seems to be tinged with caution. For too many people he is a politician-on-the-make and they suspect he is using the plant workers and fishermen as a stepping-stone into the top political job in the province.
>
> People don't trust Ricky Cashin so they feel they cannot condemn Spencer Lake who is being credited with holding a shrewd political schemer at bay. If someone other than Cashin were head of the union public opinion would probably have forced Lake to give in long ago. Even Joe Smallwood doesn't dare do anything that will turn Cashin into the hero of the fishermen. Joey probably feels much safer with Ricky bogged down in Burgeo.

This persistent emphasis on the leading personalities in the struggle was typical of commentary at the time: the NFFAWU was too new and untried to be seen as a force in its own right. In Burgeo and in the NFFAWU, however, the view was reversed: it was a struggle over the rearrangement of power relationships, and politicians were important only as they impinged on that.

While the political arguments went on, the strikers were growing restless. They reiterated charges that Lake was employing children as young as ten, and said that strike-breakers were being imported from other Lake operations. Lake countered with his usual claims that strikers were deserting the union. In mid-August, a group of men broke into the plant after an evening in the bar and damaged a conveyor belt; the man caught redhanded turned out to be neither a Lake employee nor member of the union, but merely a resentful townsman. After this incident, Lake ordered the plant and the staff houses to be enclosed by an eight-foot chain-link fence, topped with barbed wire. The strikers promptly christened the company compound "Stalag Lake."

Although their publicity campaign was highly successful and support for the strikers was strong, the union was in a difficult position. They could not expect to keep the public's sympathy and interest at such a high level for an indefinite period. If Lake could break the strike, it could break the union, or at the very least seriously damage its organizing efforts. He was clearly prepared to go to almost any lengths, but for the present he had only to carry on operating the plant at its reduced level, and wait. The union could not interfere in the operation without violating the court injunction.

Labour and management in Canada carry on their bargaining within what seems to the layman to be a rigid legal framework, but during labour disputes the processes of law often do not operate in the ordinary manner. Illegal actions by unions and companies—like Lake's violation of the Labour Relations Act by threatening to close the plant—are routinely ignored. Injunctions against pickets are often granted on the most doubtful of grounds, and are frequently violated without legal penalty. One analyst sums up the situation this way: " . . . in a strike, if you can enforce your demands on management or on a union, then the law doesn't matter much; and if you can't, the law won't help much." This does not mean, of course, that the game has no rules. It means, rather, that the ideal rules of the law are tempered by considerations of practicality. If one striker, or even a dozen, should violate a court injunction it is a fairly simple matter to charge, convict, and sentence them. But if several hundred do it simultaneously the practical problems of enforcing the law begin to take precedence.

Unions often find themselves in a position where the only way to bring about movement in a dispute that has reached stalemate is by illegal action. If, however, it can be shown that the union's leadership has planned and directed such action, the union can lose certification and its officers can be charged with an offence. On the other hand, if strikers are angry and frustrated enough to take illegal action spontaneously, the consequences can be disastrous.

Such matters were the subject of lengthy discussions in Burgeo. With only eight pickets per shift the strikers had little to occupy them. Their pent-up frustration could spill over in serious violence or—more likely in a Newfoundland setting—it could dissipate and the strike lose momentum. When Smallwood announced that he would visit the community early in September, one group in the union pressed for a mass demonstration. Others wanted to wait. The premier might be ready at last to do something decisive.

The eagerly-awaited visit was an anticlimax. After spending several hours with the Lakes, Smallwood and his minister of labour reported to a large and sullen public meeting that "they . . . categorically rejected everything we suggested to end the strike." Behind the scenes, he dickered with the union leadership. Would they agree to a commission of inquiry? Ray Greening, usually the calm voice of reason, was against it, feeling that decisive action was called for. Cashin, perhaps uncharacteristically, argued for waiting. The election had not yet been called; provided the commission reported within two weeks, the union would still have time to act. Reluctantly, Greening agreed.

On behalf of himself and three other cabinet ministers, Smallwood donated $125 to the strike fund, and flew back to St. John's. The donation did little to mollify the strikers, but the inquiry would buy him a little more time. A few days later, Labour Minister Legge announced that Judge Nathan Greene of Nova Scotia would conduct the inquiry, and would report to him within fourteen days. This would make the deadline September 23 or 24. By September 29 no report was in, and a two-week extension was granted. On October 6, Smallwood could delay his major decision no longer; he dissolved the House and called on the lieutenant governor. The following day he announced an election date—October 28, the minimum three weeks away.

The first week of the campaign passed, and with it the latest deadline for the Greene Commission, but still there was no report. It was now six weeks since Smallwood's visit to Burgeo and the union's agreement to a commission with a fourteen-day mandate. As long as the inquiry was in progress, the premier was relieved of the necessity of doing anything—or even saying anything—about Burgeo. After the election, no matter which side should win, the union's political bargaining position would be very much weaker. Time was running out. Something had to be done to force the premier's hand.

George Coley remembers the decision, taken at a meeting on the evening of Sunday, October 17: "We had to violate the injunction. We had no other choice. It was supposed to be a mass demonstration. We were going to stop the scabs from going into the plant." The plan was for the full union force to gather in front of the plant gates before the strike-breakers arrived for work. "We were worried," Coley says. "We were afraid it could turn violent. At the time, we were thinking about people getting hurt, not about what actually happened."

Coley talked it over with his father, and confided some of his anxieties. "You have to do what you think is right," the elder Coley told him. "Everybody's got to make up their own mind. But, by God, if you shuts down that plant tomorrow, I'll be some proud!" Ward Coley had been given only a short time to live, but he vowed he would hold out until the stike was won. "I'll be here to see it," he said, "and I'll fly the flag."

On the morning of October 19, the crowd gathered early, and by the time the union's local executive arrived the situation was already out of control. Many people in Burgeo must know how it started, but they do not talk to outsiders about it. Mostly, they make vague references to "young fellows" who "shouldn't have been there at all" starting things off by throwing stones. If that is so, the youngsters soon had plenty of assistance. The crowd of strikers and ordinary citizens suddenly erupted in a paroxysm of destruction.

It was a wild scene. A shower of rocks broke out the windows of the plant office and scarred its roof and walls. One witness recalls seeing a group of men with a twelve-foot length of iron pipe: "They had it up over the top of the fence—sort of balanced there, and they was rocking it back and forth. I think they was trying to shoot it at the office like an arrow." Others were rampaging through other Lake-owned enterprises. The RCMP reinforcements had long since gone back to regular duties elsewhere, and Burgeo's own three-man detachment could only stand and watch. Members of the local union executive tried to calm the crowd, but without effect. Some say that even some of the non-union workers took part. The destruction came to an end as spontaneously as it had begun. "I think the people realized it was really getting out of hand and they just stopped," one onlooker said. By that time, an estimated $25,000 worth of damage had been done.

The destruction was curiously selective. The fish plant itself was not damaged, though its office, housed in a separate building, lost all of its windows. Lake's barber shop, beauty parlour, and laundromat were almost completely destroyed, but the Bank of Nova Scotia branch, next in the same row of storefronts, was untouched. Also untouched was Lake's supermarket.

The fish plant never re-opened under Lake's ownership. Spencer and Margaret were not in Burgeo that day, but as the violence subsided union men escorted Spencer's brother Harold and operations manager Arthur Moulton out of the plant and welded the gates shut.

The day after the violence, Conservative leader Frank Moores announced that, if elected, his party would settle the Burgeo dispute immediately by arbitration, outright purchase, or whatever was required; and, at long last, the Greene report came in. It recommended a resolution of bargaining issues still outstanding—a modest pay raise across the board; a requirement for all workers who passed a probationary period to pay union dues, but no requirement for them to become union members.

The best course to follow, the report said, would be for the two parties to accept these recommendations and go back to normal operations. If they did not, there were two other possibilities: the situation could be "left to drift" until circumstances forced an agreement; or the government could step in and impose a settlement by compulsory arbitration or take-over. After a philosophical discussion of collective bargaining, Greene concluded by saying that while the parties are legally bound to bargain, they are not bound to agree. Although letting the stalemate drag on would be destructive, he would recommend it as a second choice, and recommend against government intervention. The Greene Commission had not only gained the premier time; it had provided him with a rationale, if he wished to use it, for keeping the government out of the Burgeo dispute.

The union promptly opted for accepting the Greene report. They shut down their strike headquarters and suspended picketing for forty-eight hours to await Lake's reaction. Meanwhile, Cashin called on the premier to see what he was going to do. It was not a reassuring meeting for the union leader. The two men had been at odds since the federal election of 1968, and neither was comfortable with the other. According to Cashin, Smallwood strode up and down his office, predicting that the Liberals were going to take thirty or more of the forty-two seats and that they needed neither the union nor Spencer Lake to do it. "Then," Cashin says, "he started going on about unions getting too powerful. I decided right there that if he did win he would try to break us." Cashin reported to a union board meeting, and the board decided to do everything possible to unseat the Liberals.

Spencer Lake was in Massachusetts and it took him a week, until the very eve of the election, before he responded to the Greene report. Predictably, he chose the second option. "All we ask of the government of Newfoundland," he said pointedly, "is the rule of law." Claiming that the destruction of his property had occurred because the provincial department of justice had ignored earlier charges the company had made against the union, Lake said that he and his family were "the victims of a degree of lawlessness and political expediency which exceeds the imagination."

The ball was back to Smallwood, but instead of catching it, he tried to juggle it. First, he urged Lake to accept, predicting that if he refused only "dire trouble" could ensue. If Lake should close the plant, Smallwood said, the government would have to expropriate. "If on the other hand he says he is not going to close it," the premier went on, "that he is going to operate it, and violence erupts, then what can a government do except maintain law and order?" In phrases that sound more admiring than critical he described Lake as "stubborn" and "a fighter," and concluded by saying that the government would follow Judge Greene's advice: if Lake and the union could not reach agreement, the government would not attempt to force the issue. The next day an unprecedented eighty-eight per cent of registered voters went to the polls, higher by three percentage points than the previous record set by the Confederation referendum twenty years before.

A political scene that had been slipping occasionally into farce now degenerated into something close to slapstick. The results gave twenty seats to the Liberals, twenty-one to the Conservatives, and one to Tom Burgess, a renegade Liberal who had formed a left-leaning populist New

Labrador Party (NLP) for this election. Neither major party could elect a speaker and form a government. The Conservatives called on Smallwood to resign, but he refused; five of the PC members and one Liberal had been elected by fewer than a hundred votes, and judicial recounts would have to be held. Rumours were rife, naming members of both parties who were ready to cross the floor before even reaching it.

The results were inconclusive but it was, nonetheless, an astonishing upset. Smallwood's vote had held across the northeast, traditionally the area of his strongest support, but almost everywhere else had swung to the PCs; and in at least two of the seats that swung—Burgeo-Lapoile and St. Barbe South—the fishermen's union was a significant factor. Tom Burgess, too, had more than casual links with the union. During the summer, he had made several visits to Burgeo, speaking from the same platform as Father McGrath. He was there when Smallwood visited in September, talking to reporters and scoring points against the premier. One of the other New Labrador Party candidates, defeated in this election, was Mike Martin, the NFFAWU's publicity director and editor of its newsletter. Richard Cashin says that he was never close to Burgess. He had, however, both affection and respect for Martin, and had provided the NLP with legal advice. Newspaper reporters took note of the fact that when Burgess made his first statements to the press after his election, he did so from Cashin's living room in St. John's.

Spencer Lake made one last attempt to hang on in Burgeo. Hiring time on the Marystown radio station, he appealed to the community to circulate a petition asking him to stay. If the people of Burgeo wanted him, he said, he would stick to his guns and carry on the fight. The local union executive promptly circulated their own petition, and quickly got more signatures than the Lake forces. On November 2, Lake announced from Massachusetts that he was closing Burgeo Fish Industries. He resigned as mayor of the town, and workmen began packing the family's personal effects for a move to Ramea. Sounding almost despondent, Lake told reporters that he doubted if any other company would want to take over the fish plant, but, he said, if anybody did want it, they would be "talking several million dollars."

Reaction to the news ranged from elation to outrage to despair. A columnist for *The Daily News* who wrote under the name of Peter Simple memorialized the event for the conservative side: "Once upon a time there was a little town . . . called Burgeo," he wrote.

> It died Monday.
>
> And its undertaker was a rabble-rousing lawyer called Richard Cashin and the funeral services were read by a priest called Desmond McGrath.
>
> . . . the town was truly butchered; butchered by the rampant political ambition of Cashin with his visions of becoming a second William Coaker, and butchered by the misguided visions of McGrath . . .

The battle of Burgeo was not finished, but with Lake retiring from active combat, the fate of the town rested in the hands of a government that could not even open a session of the House of Assembly.

The question on everyone's mind was posed in print by writer Harold Horwood, one of Smallwood's closest allies in the Confederation battle and now one of his bitterest critics: "Who can't be bought, and who can, and for how much?" Burgess was soon flying about in private jets, courtesy of millionaire promoter and Liberal-backer John C. Doyle and construction magnate Arthur Lundrigan. He boasted to reporters that he had been offered cabinet posts by both sides, and could have a "cool million" for the taking. "I'm the guy who is calling the shots," he said. "I'm the guy who is auctioning." On November 5, while St. John's firemen kept an eye on fifteen illegal bonfires lit in commemoration of the failure of another Guy to influence another parliament, Burgess was in Montreal talking to PC leader Frank Moores. A few days later he had made up his mind. He would support the Conservatives.

But Smallwood was not ready to give up yet. Rumour had it that as many as three PC members were ready to come over to the Liberals. Newspaper reports linked Moores with a scandal involving the collapse of Malone Lynch Securities Ltd. in Montreal. Commentators—including Burgess before his conversion—suggested that Moores was in trouble in his own party, and that John Crosbie was acting more and more like a party leader. And the judicial recounts were still to be held.

The tightest of these was in St. Barbe South, where the Northern Fishermen's Union had been born eighteen months before. Ed Maynard, who had been the union's organizer until the formation of the NFFAWU, contested the seat for the PCs and, with the backing of Father McGrath, won it by eight votes. On November 23, the recount in St. Barbe South came to an abrupt halt when the presiding judge discovered that 106 ballots from Poll No. 13 in Sally's Cove were missing; they had been inadvertently burned with the garbage on election night. The Liberals promptly initiated legal proceedings to have the election declared invalid, and the PC's to have Maynard's win confirmed. Suddenly Smallwood had an extra month or so to deal. If, by any of several means, he could pull in an extra seat there could still be another election while, as Horwood caustically observed, "the Liberals would still have control of the paving machines." Whether for a by-election in St. Barbe South or a general election later, fishery workers' votes would be crucial. At long last, Smallwood began to move on Burgeo.

His intention was obvious. He appointed a task force to report on the Burgeo plant that was essentially the union leadership—Richard Cashin, Father Des McGrath, and Ray Greening, with the managing director of Newfoundland Co-operative Services and a member of the provincial Fisheries Development Authority. A few days later, before the task force could have even begun a report, he announced that the government would take over the plant with the ultimate objective of turning it into a co-operative. In the interim, it would be operated for the government by the Research and Productivity Council, a New Brunswick crown corporation. Spencer Lake, still the "stubborn fighter", denounced the action as "probably illegal" and "more like the actions of a dictator in a banana republic than the leader of a democratic province in Canada. It just goes to show how far some people will go to please a bunch of racketeers," but Smallwood was not listening. He was busy on other fronts. Tom Burgess was in Florida, enjoying respite from his political labours, paid for by a Liberal supporter, at a resort not far from Clearwater, where Smallwood owned a condominium apartment. Late in December, Smallwood flew down to his condominium for the Christmas holiday.

Richard Cashin

Mary Martin Rowe

Reverend Des McGrath

Bill White

Union Forum

NFFAWU Convention, 1974
Head table, left to right: Jean Dyer, Cy Dyer, Jane Crosbie, Richard Cashin, John Crosbie, Rosann Cashin, Reverend Des McGrath, Marion Murphy, Matt Murphy.

Demonstration against company joint ventures, Gander, 1978.

Union Forum

Over-the-side sales, Notre Dame Bay, 1978

Fish plant workers, Harbour Breton

Union Forum

Myrna Kielley

NFFAWU Executive Board, 1975
Top row, left to right: Dave McKinnon (Business Agent), George Chafe, Oran Whalen, Matt Murphy, Reg Anstey, Onslow Tulk, Guy Hackett, John Blackmore (Business Agent).
Front row, left to right: Sandy Rideout, Elizabeth Grace, Richard Cashin, Kevin Condon, Ray Greening.

Union Forum

Trawler negotiations, 1977.
Union side, front to rear (right): Richard Cashin, Ches Cribb, Lester Green, Guy Hackett, Calvin Diamond, Dave McKinnon, Mike Myrick, Bern Dooley (centre)
Company side, front to rear (left): Jake Mullins (Booth Fisheries), Harvey Shave (Fishery Products), Bill Wells (FANL), Jim Mahon (Lake Group), Percy McDonald (National Sea Products), Gerry Malone (Burgeo Fish Industries).

Union Forum

Over-the-side sales, late 1970s

Union Forum

Fish plant workers, St. Anthony

Splitting fish

Union Forum

Gooseberry Cove

Union Forum

Union Forum

Port de Grave

Even in the urban areas of Newfoundland the twelve days of Christmas are normally a time when ordinary activities are at a low ebb, but in 1971-72 the politicians and back-room boys were working overtime. By the end of the holiday period, the Conservatives had gone through an internal revolt and were ready to dump their leader, and Smallwood had his game plan well in hand. Burgess was to rejoin the Liberals, with a promise of Smallwood's backing to become leader of the party. This would even up the seats in the House. If the St. Barbe South election were overturned and the Liberals could win the by-election, they would have a two-seat majority. In any case, they could call an election while still the government and while the Conservatives were in internal disarray.

On January 10, Cashin received a tip from a contact in government that Smallwood had on his desk an order-in-council to take over the Burgeo fish plant, but was not acting on it. Cashin called the premier and was invited to lunch at the Confederation Building for the next day, where Smallwood laid out his deal for the union. First, Cashin was to make sure that Burgess kept his commitment. The wandering Irishman was late coming back from Florida, and had insisted that before making his announcement he would have to go to Labrador and square it with his supporters: Smallwood was worried—not without reason—that Burgess would waver again. Second, once the St. Barbe South election was overturned, Smallwood wanted Cashin to contest the by-election for the Liberals. In return, he would have Smallwood's backing to become leader of the party. And the Burgeo fish plant would become a model co-operative, owned by its workers.

Cashin tells what happened next:

> That was the first I knew that Burgess had made a deal with the Liberals—that he was going to cross over again. I told Joey that I had no influence over him. He was no particular friend of mine . . . I had just met him through Mike Martin.
>
> I also told him I didn't think the St. Barbe election would be overturned. On the way home I heard on the car radio that I was right: the Supreme Court decision had

> upheld Maynard's election. After I got home, Mike Martin came in. It was purely by accident; I hadn't seen Mike for several days. I told him what had happened: "Burgess is going to sell you out." Mike was livid. He got on the phone to Labrador. He couldn't get Burgess at first, but he kept phoning and passing out the message: "Don't let Burgess sell us out."
>
> We sat up until two o'clock in the morning, with Mike on the phone all the time. In the course of the evening, I had a call from Smallwood: "Have you heard from Burgess?" I didn't let on. "I told you," I said, "he's no friend of mine. I can't influence him." And all the time Mike was using my phone, calling all over Labrador.

With the St. Barbe election confirmed and no announcement from Burgess, the Conservatives patched up their differences. Smallwood hung on for another day, but on the morning of January 13 Burgess let it be known that he would stick by his agreement with the PCs. In the afternoon, Smallwood gave in.

Later, in fact, Burgess did return to the fold and a PC member crossed the floor, giving the Liberals twenty-two seats, but it was all too late. Frank Moores met the House and went to election as premier of a Conservative government. On March 24 the PCs swept thirty-three seats. The long reign of the "only living father of Confederation" was over.

The Burgeo affair became a bit of business to be tidied up. In the middle of the new election campaign, Moores announced that he had made a deal to purchase the Lake holdings in the community, including two trawlers, and that the plant would be back in operation within a week. He also announced a tentative agreement with the union, subject to ratification by the Burgeo workers. Spencer Lake, the proven master of invective, proved himself capable of fulsome compliment, expressing his "highest respect" for the new premier, who had, he said, behaved like "a complete gentleman all the way through." And well he might say so: a few months later, the new government's first budget revealed that Lake had been paid 2.6 million dollars, and his Caribou Fisheries Company had been retained to market the Burgeo product for a four per cent commission. Lake gladly lent management personnel from other operations to run the plant for the government. John Crosbie, who had joined the PCs, been elected, and become minister of finance, later admitted that the payment to Lake might have been too much—not a *lot* too much, but perhaps a little.

The union agreement, while not quite as spectacular, was a good one, including substantial pay increases, statutory holidays, and a union security clause. In the high spirits of the moment, the day of its announcement, St. Patrick's day, was made one of the statutory holidays—a curious anomaly in an area where Irish-descended Catholics are almost as rare as millionaires. The holiday was later shifted to a more appropriate date. The agreement was signed at the dining-room table in what had been Spencer Lake's house, while on the little hill across the road the Union Jack snapped crisply in the sun as Ward Coley was carried out onto his front porch for a last look at the fish plant he had struggled to organize fifteen years before. He died a few weeks later.

In the aftermath, the divided community had to come back together. Right from the start, men who had been on the picket line for nine months had to go back to work with men who had been crossing it. "It was hard going for a while," George Coley says:

> We had the three groups—the original union people, the non-union people, and the management. The management was good. They negotiated straight out, and didn't try to break the union. Some of our own guys thought because we'd won they could do anything they liked—we had to deal with that. And we had to show the others that the union could do a good job for them.
>
> You know, here we had all these guys we'd been calling scabs for nine months. So we started calling them "fnups"—formerly non-union personnel. It was a joke, but it helped get over the bad feeling. They're all in the union now. Some of them have been shop stewards and officers. Burgeo's a union town now.

In two years, Father McGrath's little group of St. Barbe Coast fishermen had become a comprehensive organization of fishery workers. It had gained bargaining rights for inshore fishermen, done battle with the toughest plant operator in the province and won, and played a crucial—and possibly decisive—role in the defeat of the government that had ruled Newfoundland for twenty-two years.

Chapter 7

The NFFAWU and its well-wishers celebrated the Burgeo settlement with justified pleasure, but for some of them elation was tempered with anxiety. The union had survived a major test of strength, but it had not come through unscathed and it would have no time to recover from its exertions: there were new and more complex battles to be fought.

A new majority government was in office with a mandate for a full term; the political leverage the union had enjoyed during the death-throes of Smallwood's Liberals would be very much reduced. Recruitment had continued, but it was slower. There was a continuing problem with collective bargaining for fishermen: by the spring of 1972 only one group of about three hundred on the northeast coast had actually been certified. Application had been made in a dozen other districts, but the legislation was proving so difficult to apply that the minister declared that it would have to be re-written. There were ominous signs that other fish processors were not going to let Spencer Lake's fate intimidate them. A strike at Marystown dragged on for thirteen weeks before a settlement was reached, but it had little of the dramatic appeal of Burgeo and to the annoyance of the strikers the union could not afford the inflated strike-pay that Lake's workers had received: they got by on thirty dollars a week. Bonavista Cold Storage Ltd. closed its plant in Fermeuse when the plant workers' contract came up for negotiation in the fall of 1971, and as the inshore fishermen were gearing up for the spring of 1972 it showed no sign of reopening.

Not all of the difficulties facing the union came from outside. For some time sympathetic observers had been disturbed and opponents gratified by a chorus of rumour which suggested that the organization was having internal trouble: stories of dissatisfaction with Cashin's leadership and of quarrels within the executive were widely circulated. As the spring of 1972 approached, the rumours began to take on substance. The second annual convention, projected for April, was postponed until October, and onlookers speculated that the leadership feared an open revolt on the convention floor. Shortly before the Burgeo settlement was announced the president of the fish plant local at Fermeuse told reporters that he and his members were "fed up" with the provincial president and executive. In April, it was announced that the international representative of the CFAWU, Fred Locking, was to be transferred to New Brunswick. Locking refused to go, resigned his position to take a job with another union, and gave statements to the press severely critical of Richard Cashin. Members of one of the union's handful of non-fishery bargaining units, at a government-owned abattoir in St. John's, voted unanimously to have Cashin removed as their chief negotiator in contract discussions with the treasury board. Petitions were circulated calling for Cashin's removal as president and the recall of Locking to head the union. Some locals were reported to be refusing to send their monthly dues to the provincial office, remitting them instead directly to the international headquarters in Chicago, though the union headquarters denied that this was happening.

On one level the upheavals seemed to be simply a conflict of personalities; disagreements between Richard Cashin and Fred Locking had been evident within the union for some time. Encompassed in those disagreements, however, and in the clash between their respective supporters, were a set of conflicts over the very nature of the NFFAWU. The union's formation and its initial spurt of growth had been sparked by a general dissatisfaction with conditions of work and wages in the fishery. The overall goal was to improve those conditions, but details of how the goal was to be pursued had been left necessarily vague. The clash between Locking and Cashin was merely the focal point of a process in which the NFFAWU was defining what sort of a union it was going to be.

The two protagonists could hardly have been more unlike in background. Fred Locking was born into a working class family in Yorkshire. His father had to pay to have his son accepted as an apprentice, at the age of sixteen, in a machine shop. Locking's apprenticeship was interrupted by a stint in the army during the Second World War; after the war he returned to his training, became a journeyman, and was elected as shop steward for his union. Growing dissatisfied with prospects in post-war Britain, he and his wife decided to emigrate. They chose Canada because Mrs. Locking had a brother in Saskatchewan, and came over in 1949:

> We landed in Quebec City, myself, my wife, and my daughter, with fifty dollars and a railway ticket to Moose Jaw. We got there on a Wednesday, I went looking for work on the Thursday, commenced work on the following Monday. I never missed a day's work after that until I retired.

For Locking, active participation in union affairs was as natural as working. He held office in his local, in the Moose Jaw Labour Council, and the Saskatchewan Federation of Labour. In 1965 he began to work part-time for the United Packinghouse Workers of America. In 1968, while the international mergers were taking place that produced the CFAWU, he was sent to Newfoundland to organize fish plant workers. At the time Newfoundland was new territory for the meat unions, and they had little information about the place. Locking recalls being told by his superiors that his wages would go further there:"You'll be getting the same pay as you were in Saskatchewan, but wages in Newfoundland are really low, so prices must be low, too. You'll live like a king!" When he moved, he found that although wages were indeed pitifully low for many of the people, the cost of living in his new home was worse than anywhere outside the high arctic. And the political climate was rather different from what he had been used to under the CCF and NDP in Saskatchewan.

Locking's first job was to incorporate the existing fish plant locals into the structure of the CFAWU. He did not find this an altogether easy task. Originally, as has been described, the locals had been independent units, the oldest of them having been directly chartered by a long series of central labour organizations. They had developed their own ways of doing things, had their own constitutions and rules of procedure. Some of them had full-time, paid officers running their affairs. In 1967, before Locking arrived, a beginning had been made at incorporating them into the United Packinghouse Workers of America. This involved only minor changes in structure, since the UPWA favoured a system of separate plant locals serviced by an international representative. However, in 1968, when the UPWA merged with the

Amalgamated Meat Cutters and Butcher Workmen and its Canadian branch, the CFAWU, there was a change. CFAWU policy was to create large locals of the workers from several plants, with officers elected from among people actually working in the plants. When they were large enough they could hire their own staff.

Locking's efforts to institute this new form of organization were resisted. The established locals were reluctant to give up their independence, and their paid officers were reluctant to give up their positions. After nearly two years in Newfoundland, Locking wrote to the CFAWU headquarters in Toronto:

> I have talked to the local union officers explaining the whole thing until I am blue in the face, if I continue to push them the way I have been, I'm afraid they may get out or at the least lose the confidence I have tried to build up . . .

On the other hand, Locking found that the workers in unorganized plants were anxious to be unionized. Looking back on it a dozen years later he said:

> On the mainland, when you'd go to organize a plant it was a question of knocking on doors after hours, meeting them at home, trying to catch them in the pub when they were having a beer . . . But in Newfoundland you could go into a place, find a hall and rent it, and get the word around that there was going to be a union man in town to talk to fish plant workers—and they'd all turn up. They'd all be there.

Locking concentrated on hourly-paid plant workers, but when the strike by the British Columbia fishermen's union took place in Nova Scotia, the CFAWU in Newfoundland also acquired some trawler crewmen: some company officials were afraid that the B.C. union might spread, and gave voluntary recognition to the CFAWU as the lesser of two evils.

When Locking heard of the formation of the Northern Fishermen's

Union in Port au Choix, he promptly telephoned Father McGrath to see if this strange little upstart organization could be incorporated into the CFAWU. McGrath declined the invitation, and Locking wrote to his headquarters urging that more effort be expended on organizing in Newfoundland in order to compete:

> . . . the people want organizing but they won't wait forever. What makes it worse of course is that the church is getting into the act and unless we get cracking right away all expansion will be lost, you know I am sure how hard it is to fight a union that is sponsored directly by clergy . . . . Their membership so far covers two plants . . . if we can confine them to that, very little will be lost, but speed is essential if we intend to expand and if only to protect what we now have.

The international headquarters responded by providing three of the larger CFAWU locals with a subsidy which allowed him to select one person from each area to act as paid business agents and organizers.

Locking also became aware that the Northern Fishermen's Union had appealed for support to the New Democratic Party's national leader, Tommy Douglas. He wrote to Douglas reminding him of the backing that both he and his union had given to the NDP in the past and concluded, "I would object if the party was to give carte-blanche support to the 'Northern Fishermen's Union' . . . "

Clearly, Locking perceived McGrath's efforts as threatening to his own plans. When amalgamation with the NFU was proposed he was against it. When it appeared that CFAWU officials were serious about it, he proposed a two-part structure that would keep fishermen and plant workers separate: if the international wanted to back the NFU they should do it independently of the organizing that was going on in the plants. His superiors in the CFAWU and officials of the Canadian Labour Congress, however, saw in full amalgamation the potential for a much more rapid and comprehensive organization of fishery workers in the province, and concluded the amalgamation agreement. The subsidies the international had been providing, which were intended to amount to no more than fifteen thousand dollars a year, were replaced by the series of fifty thousand dollar grants. Money for organizing was suddenly available on a scale far beyond anything that Locking had ever hoped to receive, but as international representative he found himself administering it on behalf of two men whom he had regarded as rivals, and who had now partly usurped his position at the head of the organizing drive.

Locking had no choice in the matter: he had to go along. He was never convinced that the fishermen and plant workers belonged in the same union, and he never lost his suspicion of Richard Cashin. "It's always been my opinion," he says,

> . . . that before you can be a real trade unionist you've got to have some dirt under your fingernails. You've got to have come through it the hard way. Richard never did. He was wealthy . . . What's a man like that doing with a union?

Like many others, he believed that Cashin had ulterior motives. Even a dozen years later, with Cashin still heading the NFFAWU, Locking said, "he has one goal in mind, and that's politics. He won't stay with the union. He wants to be premier."

At the founding convention Locking put aside some of his reservations, at least publicly, and bowed to the inevitable. He did not support Cashin's candidacy, but in a speech to the membership he recanted from his opposition to bringing plant workers and fishermen together and told the convention that he was now convinced that it was a good idea. However, during the year that followed union members noticed a growing tension between the president and the international representative. They disagreed frequently, and meetings were sometimes prolonged while they argued. They avoided one another in the union offices, and each tended to make decisions without consulting the other. But the problems were created by much more than mere personal rivalry.

No very clear thought had been given, before the convention, to how the NFFAWU was to operate. Under the original CFAWU plan there would have been for some time in Newfoundland several regionally-based locals, with co-ordination among them and communication with the parent union handled by the international representative. Upon the rapid formation of a provincial council, however, the NFFAWU had become a semi-autonomous unit within the national and international union structure, managing its own affairs through an elected executive and hired staff. In a formal sense, Locking's position had become almost redundant. On the other hand, the re-structuring was far from complete, and the Newfoundlanders were mostly neophytes who could certainly benefit from the guidance of an old professional hand, so it seemed reasonable that he should stay on.

Union bureaucracies are not notably more flexible than other kinds, however, and as international representative Locking continued to carry on most of the duties that he had before. He was still responsible to the international for the organizing funds: the letters from Chicago and Toronto demanding explanation were all addressed to him. Kevin Condon had sensibly tried to decline nomination as secretary-treasurer on the grounds that he lacked the necessary skills and experience for the treasurer's job, but had been talked into accepting the position with the promise of help: in practice, it was Locking who handled the finances. He also continued to provide service and advice to the established fish plant locals and to deal with the business agents, leaving Cashin ostensibly to concentrate on organizing fishermen and working out their collective bargaining. This arrangement, as he later noted in a letter to headquarters, left Locking with—in theory, at least—a major part of the work, but he was willing to accept it nonetheless. In spite of his statement at the convention, he was still far from convinced that the experiment with the fishermen would work. If it fizzled out, or if Cashin made the expected leap back into politics, things would go back to the way they had been before.

Inevitably, however, the roles of the president and the international representative overlapped. Cashin was drawn into the full range of the union's activities, making policy decisions, taking the leading role at Burgeo, acting as negotiator for contracts, providing advice to locals. When their opinions differed, each man had his own source of legitimacy: Locking had his staff position with the international and his links with its officialdom, but this was counterbalanced by the fact that those same officials had bet heavily on Cashin and McGrath when they struck a bargain to bring in the fishermen and west coast plant workers. Locking had the advantage of having been the primary contact with the main body of dues-paying members in the established plant locals; Cashin had the backing of the fishermen, his high public profile, and the moral authority of election by the membership. Locking drew upon the experience and knowledge of more than twenty years with organized labour; the union was his career. Cashin, however, had his legal and political credentials, and he was a volunteer: he had other options, but had chosen to work with the union.

They differed widely in approach and priorities. Locking's experience was entirely in industrial settings, and the strategy he favoured was the step-by-step building of plant organizations, moving carefully and deliberately within an accepted framework of established rules and practices. He was not given to taking risks, and in negotiations was cautious, unwilling to push beyond what he believed to be the limits of solid support. In the Newfoundland setting this sometimes put the union at a disadvantage.

For example, in January of 1969, well before McGrath and Cashin came on the scene, the man who became Locking's organizer on the South Coast, Lawrence Mahoney, managed to get certification in a plant owned by the Lake family in the town of Gaultois. Lake treated the situation in the same way as he later began at Burgeo, by simply refusing to negotiate. Writing to his Toronto headquarters, Locking described the dilemma:

> The situation is that Lake has two other large plants on the South Coast which have around 300 to 400 people in each and if we struck him in Gaultois he could just move his operations to the other plants.

Locking felt that the only safe way to proceed would be to organize the other Lake plants before attempting a confrontation. But while that tactic was being pursued the workers at Gaultois grew disillusioned, Lake applied for a decertification vote, and the union lost. The Gaultois plant remained unorganized long after most plants in the province came into the NFFAWU.

In wage negotiations, too, Locking tended to be cautious, unwilling to force issues with strikes, and favouring long-term contracts. In 1970 several locals signed up for minimal wage increases and fringe benefits in contracts that would not come up for re-negotiation until 1973.

Cashin and McGrath, on the other hand, had come into the struggle in the first place on behalf of the inshore fishermen, who did not even have rights of collective bargaining. The only approach that had any hope of being effective was headlong engagement on all fronts, with companies, governments, and general public—and, where necessary, unorthodox bending of established union practice. For the fishermen there was nothing to lose. When he turned his attention to the plants, Cashin quickly concluded that similar tactics were called for. The fishery was a chancy business, fluctuating wildly from season to season and year to year. The Lakes were not the only ones who owned several plants in different regions, and could transfer resources from one to another at need. The plant-by-plant approach, with locals bargaining independently and contracts coming due at different times in different places, Cashin felt, worked more to the advantage of the companies than of the union. To change the pattern would require risk and confrontation.

As the rift deepened, there began to be suggestions that Locking would be nominated to run against Cashin for the presidency. To some members of the old, established plant locals, this possibility seemed to offer a chance to reverse the direction in which the union had been moving. The original CFAWU plan had been to merge the plant locals into a single, large local with sub-locals or bargaining units in the plants. When the NFFAWU was formed, it was intended to be that provincial body, and its constitution provided for all dues to be paid into the central organization. In practice, however, an intermediate structure was operating. Three of the old locals—at Marystown, Burin, and Catalina—were still collecting their own dues and paying their local officers honoraria before contributing to the provincial body. The Grand Bank local had stoutly refused to affiliate with the NFFAWU at all, and continued to remit its *per capita* payments directly to Chicago.

Locking had begun his career in Newfoundland trying to change the old form of organization, persuading the locals to give up their autonomy. Now, however, he seemed more sympathetic to it. If he were in charge, he might be able to persuade the international that the old system should be maintained. Cashin, on the other hand, stood for the provincial council that would take away local autonomy, and for the doubtful alliance with the fishermen. In meetings, Locking argued that the wishes of the plant workers should predominate: the fishermen were, after all, as yet no more than names on a list—only a tiny handful were certified and in a position to pay dues.

When the spring convention was postponed it was said by some that Cashin was afraid of losing his job, but among those who were committed to the idea of a comprehensive fisheries union there was a deeper fear than that. If the cleavages in the membership came to an open fight on the convention floor, the hard-won but uneasy alliance of fishermen and plant workers could be irrevocably broken. If that happened, the presidency would no longer matter very much.

Cashin gives credit to Ray Greening for breaking the log-jam. Greening was liked, trusted, and respected by almost everyone, and people of all shades of opinion confided in him. He came to realize that the division was steadily deepening, and that even those members who took no strong stand on either side were beginning to lose confidence in the organization. Greening had already left one union when he felt that it was not serving the best interests of its members, and he was prepared to do it again. He came to Cashin's house, explained the situation as he saw it, and handed over his resignation. Cashin, thoroughly alarmed at the prospect of losing a man of such demonstrated ability and integrity, urged him to reconsider and promptly telephoned Toronto and Chicago. The international officials, alarmed in turn at the prospect of losing what they had gained in Newfoundland—not to speak of the several hundred thousand dollars invested there—arranged to transfer Locking to the mainland.

Locking protested, but to no avail. He now says that if he had been asked to return to Saskatchewan he would have gone, but the appointment in New Brunswick looked like the beginning of a continuing series of moves, a prospect which, at his age, he was unwilling to accept. This assessment is probably correct. He had not merely lost a dispute with Cashin: within the union hierarchy he had lost credibility, and his chances for advancement were probably over. Some of his detractors, however, suggest that he had another reason for refusing to move: they believe that he took another job in Newfoundland only as a stopgap, and still planned to challenge Cashin for the presidency when the convention came up. If he could win, it would be a vivid demonstration to the parent union that they had backed the wrong horse. Minutes of the April executive meeting where his transfer was announced record that "most members did not want to see him go." A motion was made to hold an immediate convention, but it was defeated by a vote of six to three in favour of a date in October, six months away. The three votes for an immediate convention came from representatives of the plant workers. In an interview after the break, Locking made a point of noting that he was still a member of the union.

Whatever Locking and his supporters may have intended, he did not contest the election when it finally came. He stayed in his new job with the Newfoundland Association of Public Employees, and several years later left that job under the cloud of another dispute to live in retirement in St. John's. His feelings about Cashin remain unchanged, but he allows a note of slightly grudging admiration: "The NFFAWU has been a good, democratic union. Richard has done a good job for them. But I still think he wants to be premier."

Locking's resignation clarified the authority structure, but the disagreements were still there, and Locking was still within easy reach of journalists and disgruntled union members. In statements to the press he and Cashin accused one another of trying to promote "boss unionism" and "one-man rule". Locking said that Cashin had "bought" members with strike pay at Burgeo, given locals bad advice on negotiations, and promised fishery workers more than the union could deliver. Cashin said that Locking had simply been unable to give up direction of the union to the elected officers.

The underlying problems were still there, too, and Cashin began a campaign to clear away some of the difficulties before the fall convention. During the year between the first convention and the announcement of Locking's transfer in 1972, the full executive of the union had met only once. Now, Cashin began to call more regular meetings. He also created a small central committee to handle administrative details and encouraged its members—Woodrow Philpott, Kevin Condon, and plant worker Alec Brown—to take a more prominent role as spokesmen. Cashin, with this committee, took over the functions that Locking had performed in relation to the locals and the business agents. The Grand Bank local was under pressure from the international to join the provincial council, and its president came to an executive meeting to discuss terms. The executive agreed that it could come in and still continue—for the time being, at least—to pay its officers independently.

Ray Greening took charge of the finances and found them to be in an alarming condition. *Per capita* dues payments to the international were seriously in arrears, money had been spent that was not adequately accounted for, bills and expense accounts were overdue and unpaid. Because of the confusion that had existed in lines of authority, responsibility for the mess was hard to assign: Cashin pointed out that Locking had been in control of finances, and Locking said that Cashin and the executive had spent money without his knowledge. Whatever may have been the cause, Greening found that the union had for a year been spending nearly double the amount it could afford—and this was not counting the subsidy from the international. He established a working budget and floated a loan to cover overdue commitments. Barring unforseen problems, he estimated, it would take three years or more of careful management to pull the union out of debt.

While Greening worked to straighten out the books, Cashin was busy trying to do the same with the rest of the administration. There was plenty to occupy his attention. A plan was put forward whereby all dues would come into the central coffers, and fifty cents *per capita* per month would go back to the locals. Even though the union—and some of the locals themselves—were in debt, however, some plant representatives on the executive rejected the plan, wanting to continue paying local officers. The St. John's abattoir workers who had rejected Cashin as their negotiator voted to leave the union altogether, and followed Locking into the public employees' association. Cracks were showing even in the ranks of inshore fishermen. Efforts to get them certified were still ham-strung by complications. At Torbay, near St. John's, they were having trouble finding a buyer for their catch, and the president of the uncertified NFFAWU local there complained that the union was giving them no support. "So far," he was quoted as saying, "the union has been hiding in the background."

Bill Short, amid continuing rumours that Locking was going to try for the presidency, announced that he would run against Cashin when the convention came up, saying that "no president should walk into the convention and pick it up by acclamation." Short now says that he was on Cashin's side all along but was concerned about the depth of the division in the organization. "Richard was the right man for the job," he says, "but if anybody was going to replace him I figured it should be a fisherman." Woodrow Philpott apparently thought so, too: he also announced that he would be seeking the presidency.

Meanwhile, the ordinary business of the union had to go on, and amid the difficulties and rumours were some decidedly bright spots. In June, workers at the new National Sea Products plant in St. John's signed an agreement that was described by a company official as the "best contract ever to be ratified between workers and the company": a two-year contract that provided raises every eight months, improved fringe benefits, and slightly narrowed the gap in pay between male and female workers. It was by far the best contract in the industry in Newfoundland, though it was not yet on a par with some in Nova Scotia.

In July there was another break-through. Each year, by time-honoured custom, the Fisheries Association of Newfoundland and Labrador (FANL) the association of fish-processing companies, announced the prices that would be paid for fish. They usually held discussions first with the Federation of Fishermen, but there was no bargaining. The decision and the announcement were made by FANL. This year, however, there was something new. The union was negotiating with a fish plant owner on the northeast coast on behalf of their only certified unit of inshore fishermen—a group of about three hundred in the Valleyfield–Badger's Quay area. According to some sources, the fish processors had agreed among themselves to withhold announcement of prices until the negotiations were complete: that way, they could announce whatever price was agreed upon at Valleyfield, and the union would not be seen to have made any gain. However, while the negotiations were still open but adjourned temporarily, FANL made its customary unilateral declaration of prices, perhaps with the intention of forcing the union's hand. This put both the union and the Valleyfield plant operator, Boyd Way, in a difficult spot. If the union was to come out of the negotiations with any credibility they had to achieve prices above those announced by the industry, but for this to happen Boyd Way would have to break the customary solidarity of the processors. At first, Way offered the price set by FANL, and the union negotiators asked for more. Neither side was anxious for a show-down: the union had plenty of other problems without trying to carry through a strike with one small group of fishermen, and Way, as a small independent operator, had no wish to carry the ball for the whole of the processing industry.

Way had dealt with the union before: workers in his fish plant had been members for about a year, and were working under a contract. As Richard Cashin remembers the negotiations, "We were in Boyd Way's office. He looked out at the plant, and he said that as far as he was concerned, things were working better with the union than they had without it." Way offered a half a cent a pound above the FANL price on some species, and the union negotiators accepted. The contract that was signed—the first negotiated union contract betweeen a plant operator and a group of inshore fishermen—had other provisions concerning the weighing and grading of fish, but it was the price that caught people's attention. Cashin announced that it would mean as much as $150,000.00 in extra income to the fishermen. Many men who were in the boats that summer remember the news being passed by radio from longliner to longliner amid the crackle of static and the creak of winches: ... *I hear the Union got a half a cent more at Valleyfield* ...

Other developments were less encouraging. Shortly after ratifying their "best ever" plant contract in St. John's the union began negotiations on what they generally agreed was their worst, with Bonavista Cold Storage Ltd. at their plant in the town of Bonavista. The expiring contract, which had been signed before the creation of the NFFAWU, provided practically no fringe benefits and even included a clause that allowed the company to deduct money from all the workers' wages if plant toilets were damaged and no culprit could be found. More than half of the workers were women and were earning $1.40 an hour, which was twenty cents more than they had been getting the year before—not because of their contract but because the government had raised the minimum wage for female workers. Men on the cutting line were earning from $1.44 to $1.56. The plant was a seasonal operation, processing fish caught by inshore boats from about May until September: it might continue on a limited basis until December, but was closed during the mid-winter period. It was owned by the same company that owned the potentially year-round plant at Fermeuse which had been closed when the union contract came due in the previous autumn. The company also owned another year-round plant at Grand Bank, where workers doing the same jobs as those at Bonavista were being paid an average of twenty-five cents an hour more. With the boldness that was coming to be characteristic, the union set out to get the same contract for the Bonavista workers. There was an important principle at stake—that workers in seasonal plants should have parity with those in the year-round operations.

The company offered fifteen cents but the union held out for the full twenty-five, and the confrontation moved inexorably toward a strike. Again, the union faced the problem of how to deal with companies that owned several plants. While negotiations were impending at Bonavista, the company re-opened their plant at Fermeuse and gave the workers there a thirty-cent raise without even consulting the union. To some observers, this move signalled an ominous new development in the war between union and processors. The Bonavista plant was said to be only marginally profitable: could it be that the company was merely using the contract dispute as an excuse to close it? There would be much to favour such a course. Given the paternal position of fish plant operators in rural Newfoundland communities, a company could not easily close even a marginal operation without incurring public disapproval. However, if a plant were seen to be forced into closure by unreasonable union demands, the result would be a double gain to the company: a graceful exit from a money-losing operation and a general weakening of the union's prestige and bargaining power. The union, on the other hand, could not maintain its momentum if it were to fall back to the old pattern of knuckling under to the companies out of fear of losing jobs. At Burgeo the provincial government had been the *deus ex machina*, but they could hardly be expected to continue to buy up fish plants—especially on the sort of terms they had given Spencer Lake.

Paul Russell, Bonavista Cold Storage's owner, was a tough and determined opponent. Some commentators were calling him "this summer's Spencer Lake", but columnist Ron Crocker wryly observed that the comparison "may be unfair to old Spencer." Paul Russell, he said, "is Spencer Lake in overdrive." Russell's style, however, was very different: he simply kept quiet and left the ball in the union's court. The strike began at the end of June, and by mid-August the union had another set-back: Russell gave his Fermeuse workers another raise and they, still disgruntled over their plant's long winter closure, voted to withdraw from the NFFAWU.

Then there was the problem of the inshore fishermen who would normally sell their catch to the Bonavista plant. Like the plant workers themselves, they depended on the summer season to earn the money and the unemployment insurance stamps that would see them through the winter. And, typically, they were the husbands and brothers, uncles, fathers, and nephews of the plant workers. At a large meeting in Bonavista the fishermen were putting pressure on for a settlement: the company had offered fifteen cents, which wasn't bad . . . and with overtime . . . As the meeting wavered, Richard Cashin suddenly leaped up on a table. "What you are doing here," he bellowed, "is exactly what Paul Russell wants you to do!—It's just exactly what Spencer Lake and Dennis Monroe and all the rest of them want to see you do!" For the next twenty minutes he treated the assembly to a high-decibel, arm-waving lecture on the history of the Newfoundland fishery. "If you do what you're planning to do," he told them, "you'll be doing what Newfoundlanders have done for four hundred years. You'll be giving the merchants exactly what they want because you can't stand together and back each other up!" When he finished, the meeting erupted in a roar of cheering and applause.

The strike continued. The Bonavista fishermen, who were not enjoying very good catches that year anyway, were able to dispose of their fish at the Fishery Products plant at Catalina, a few miles along the coast, where unionized plant workers were making pay rates equal to, or slightly above, the rates the union was demanding at Bonavista.

The strike dragged on all summer with no change. In the autumn, when the plant would normally close for the season, a new crisis arose. Before the strike began, workers had not been able to earn the number of unemployment insurance stamps required to qualify for benefits. Some, in fact, were as little as one stamp short. They would not be getting unemployment insurance and, since the plant would be closed in the normal course of events, union policy dictated that they could not continue to draw strike pay, either. The three hundred-odd plant workers faced a bleak winter on the dole if they could get it.

When news of the closure came to the NFFAWU offices in St. John's, Cashin was away. Bill Short, the Pouch Cove fisherman who had announced his intention of running for the presidency was there, and took it upon himself to phone the CFAWU offices in Toronto. CFAWU official Frank Benn tells the story:

> . . . Bill called here and he told us how the people were suffering, and all that. We were sorry, of course, but what could we do? It was hard and fast policy. The union doesn't pay strike pay at a plant that's closed down. We told him there was just no way it could be done. It wasn't even just our policy, it was international policy.
>
> So Bill asks for Pat Gorman's phone number. We told him, 'Nobody just phones Pat Gorman,' and Bill says, 'Well, maybe it's time they did.' We gave him the number, but we never thought he'd get through.

Perhaps Gorman's defensive line of secretaries in Chicago was too startled by the call to know how to react. Whatever the reason, Short was put directly through to the tough old head of the Amalgamated Meat Cutters and Butcher Workmen—boss of a union with more members than there were people in Newfoundland and Labrador, which had already sunk more than a dollar for every member into the effort to organize in the province.

No one, including Short, is quite sure what it was that turned the trick. "If Pat Gorman didn't want to be moved," says Frank Benn, "God Himself couldn't move him." Whether it was just the novelty of the thing, or Short's undoubted sincerity and eloquence, or Gorman's sentimental weakness for the Irish sound of Newfoundland voices, or just a hardheaded calculation of publicity value—or some combination of them all—Gorman moved. The Bonavista workers drew their strike pay through the winter.

The second NFFAWU convention, when it was finally held in mid-November, seven months late, bore little resemblance to the first. In 1971, everything had been staged for maximum publicity: the 1972 gathering was held in Gander, away from the main media centres, and all but one of the sessions were closed to press and outsiders. The minimum of delegates attended—less than half the number that had come to the founding convention—and in public statements Cashin played down the significance of the event, saying it was concerned only with "housekeeping." The more persistent reporters roamed the hotel corridors, looking for the inside story—Father McGrath found one of them stretched at full length on a hall carpet with his ear to the crack at the bottom of a meeting room door, and chased him away.

Even an ordained security guard could not prevent a version of the financial statement from being reported in the press, but the rest of the proceedings were kept very much in the family. Excluded observers were preoccupied with the Locking–Cashin dispute, and attributed the need for secrecy to some inner-circle hatchet-work and the laundering of blood-stained linen. This was not the whole story, but it worked to the union's advantage by diverting some of the attention from other problems. "We didn't want the fish companies to know how badly off we were," Cashin says now. "We were damned near bankrupt, and the whole organization was very shaky for a while."

By most measures, the convention strategy worked, both internally and externally. The eavesdropping reporter that McGrath had chased away concluded that, while the union might have wanted to hush up some details of "managerial sloppiness" the main reason for the quiet convention was

> . . . the fact that the union is no longer attempting to drum up public support to help get itself established. It is firmly established and it has nothing to look forward to during the next couple of years but hard work, with little time for grand-standing.

He predicted that the union was on the way to playing a major role in the development of a third force in Newfoundland politics, either through the NDP or a new Newfoundland party.

Behind the closed doors, Cashin was re-elected without opposition as president, Ray Greening became secretary-treasurer, Woodrow Philpott vice-president for the fishermen's section, and John Blackmore vice-president of the industrial section. A compromise was reached on the matter of paying local officers. A general increase in dues by the international was to take effect the following year. It was agreed that the locals which were paying honoraria could continue doing so until the new rate came into force: after that, if they wished to go on with the practice they would have to do it by raising local dues above the international rate to cover the cost. A phasing-out of paid local officers was thus virtually guaranteed.

In the aftermath of the convention, the last of Locking's organization faded away. Hubert Sutton, one of the business agents he had recruited, followed him into the public employee's union: the others left their jobs either voluntarily or under pressure from the executive to be replaced by a new staff more oriented to the new policies. Although the reporter quoted above may have been a little premature in saying it, the union's structure was indeed on the way to being "firmly established", and over the next few years moved steadily in the direction of incorporating all the fish plant workers and the small retail section into one local—number 1252—and the fishermen, both inshore and offshore, into another—number 465.

It had been a difficult period for the NFFAWU, and for a time the future of organization in the Newfoundland fishery hung in a rather delicate balance. Although the division went much deeper than personal differences, that balance may have been tipped by individual judgements by union members of the two key actors—judgements that involved particular features of the Newfoundland culture and system of social class. Locking's attitude to Cashin was firmly rooted in his British industrial working-class background. It was an attitude he expected workers anywhere to share, and he was frustrated by the apparent reluctance of many union members to accept the conclusion to which it led. The Newfoundlanders were not unaware of the class differences that so preoccupied Locking, but they perceived them differently, with that peculiar blend of egalitarianism and elitism that is evident in so much of the province's history.

The structure of the traditional rural Newfoundland community was relatively simple. It consisted of a group of fishing families who, although they might differ from one another in success and material prosperity, were of the same class by virtue of their trade; one or more merchant families who bought the fish and sold the necessities of life; and—in larger places, at least—a few resident professionals such as clergy, teachers, and so on. In social terms, the merchants and professionals constituted an upper class, having in common the fact that each was the point of contact with institutions of the larger society, and that they shared, to some extent, a style of life. The mass of the people were a lower class within which strong egalitarian ideals were held. There was practically no intermediate middle group of independent tradesmen and entrepreneurs. The resident professionals, moreover, were usually "outsiders", doing a tour of duty in the community, but not "belonging" to it—for in rural Newfoundland one does not say that someone "comes from" a place, but rather that he or she *belongs* to it, even if the person concerned is living elsewhere.

In a society like this, status divisions are clear and sharp but they are also highly personalized. By contrast with a large-scale industrial setting, the merchants are seen less as representative of a class with interests different from those of the fishing families, than as individual *patrons* like the *hacienda* owners of old Mexico or the feudal landlords of Highland Scotland: people who control the local resources and with whom it is necessary to establish and maintain personal relationships. With the shift from saltfish production to fresh fish freezing plants, the merchants became more explicitly employers, but on the same model. Government subsidies for the development of the fishing industry reinforced the relationship, for the subsidies went to the companies for modernizing equipment and building large offshore catching vessels: the patron was now channelling government expenditure to the people in the form of jobs. And frequently, as with Spencer Lake in Burgeo, he or she was also the channel by which the community acquired other benefits: roads, schools, hospitals or even a laundromat or a bank.

One analyst of Newfoundland society has suggested that this pattern was particularly characteristic of the south coast of the island, in the area where there was some of the strongest initial support for Locking, but the analysis has validity for all areas. It goes a long way, for example, toward explaining some aspects of the career of William Coaker. While he was lambasting the merchants as a class and trying to institute a "new way of dealing", forces within the society and, probably, within himself as a member of it were pressing him into the paternal role. In the end, he became very much like what he had set out to destroy.

This structure and its accompanying set of attitudes are also evident in the early local unions that formed in the fish plants; they were groups of clients dealing with individual patrons. The point is underscored by a report on labour relations in Newfoundland which notes that until 1970 the fish plant unions tended to use strike action not as a bargaining tool but as a way of expressing dissatisfaction with their treatment by plant owners or managers. Until Burgeo, strikes in the unionized plants were typically "wildcat" walk-outs touched off by an over-eager foreman or some dispute over the use of toilets. They were occasioned, that is, not by disputes over the fact of the patron–client relationship, but disagreements over its details.

For many workers, at least at the beginning, the formation of a more comprehensive union structure did not represent a change to a new level of class consciousness, but rather a shift of allegiance to a different patron. In some places the plant-owning companies had become large and remote: in others—as in Burgeo—there was an undercurrent of resentment against the landlord. If the union was to become the channel for resolving dissatisfactions and achieving benefits, its leader would become—symbolically, at least—the new patron. For some workers, indeed, a union could not become a credible alternative until it could throw up a leader who fit the role. Among other things, Locking could never reconcile Cashin's position in the union with his lifestyle. For a union leader to live in a large, elegant, historic house on the fashionable Rennies' Mill Road in St. John's, among the mansions of the old "fishocracy", seemed to him a violation of the natural order. To be sure, some of the union members shared this view or something like it, but for many others, Cashin's house, like his law degree, was one of his qualifications.

It is an anomaly that has dogged Cashin through more than a dozen years with the union. He has railed against the merchants, he has denounced and derided the paternalism of fish companies and governments, he has exhorted union members to see themselves as the locus of power in the industry and the society. There has been growth within the union of a new set of attitudes, a new analysis of the social structure, yet much of the success that the union has achieved is rooted in the personal allegiance that many of its members felt and still feel for Richard Cashin and Father McGrath—an allegiance that is not altogether unlike the loyalty that some people in Burgeo felt for the man who got them a road and a sewer system.

If Locking and Cashin were, for a time, in competition for the symbolic position of patron in the developing union, Cashin had another advantage: he, after all, was a Newfoundlander and Locking was not. Some observers have concluded that Newfoundland's people are insular and xenophobic, instinctively disliking outsiders. This is an oversimplification: the reality is more complicated than that.

To begin with, Newfoundland has a long history of colonial domination, both in its political and economic forms. For well over a hundred years, her population has been by North American standards homogeneous and relatively stable, apart from out-migration: Newfoundlanders have left home in large numbers, but since the early nineteenth century movement of people to the island has been no more than a trickle. And whereas in most of Canada immigrants have entered in greatest numbers at the lower end of the socio-economic scale, those who came to Newfoundland after the main waves of immigration were over tended to come as managers and professionals. There was, not unnaturally, some resentment. In 1946, a newspaper editorial remarked:

> Newfoundlanders in semi-important jobs find themselves working for twenty years as assistant manager in one job or another only to find that when the manager finally dies another is imported from England or Canada . . .

After Confederation in 1949 the flow increased somewhat as Canadian government and business moved in. Both the federal and provincial governments tended to make liberal (and Liberal) use of "experts" and consultants from outside, giving rise to a wry little joke in which one Newfoundlander asks another what degree is required for a particular government position and is told that to get the job one must have a "CFA" degree. On inquiry, it is revealed that CFA stands for "Come From Away."

Since Newfoundland was chronically in economic difficulty, constantly struggling to catch up to more affluent places, many of the CFAs, whether they worked for business, government, or international unions, came there to bring "improvement"—a role that, though it may be pursued with the noblest of motives, has inevitably bred resentment wherever it has been undertaken. A St. John's columnist in the mid 1970s remarked that the Canadian government officials who came to the province went about their work with "the priggish attitude of a Ladies' Auxiliary which sends knitted socks and toothbrushes to the starving blacks in the Congo."

Coming from other English-speaking societies, the CFAs tended to regard Newfoundland's society and culture as merely a variant of their own—and an inferior variant, at that. It was hard for them to realize that over hundreds of years there had built up in this little, isolated, wind-swept place a distinctive culture with subtleties and complexities that require time and, more important, effort to grasp. Many did not put forth the effort and, often without realizing it, imposed their own ways of thinking and behaving, in an almost unconscious assumption of superiority.

Newfoundlanders, therefore, are not inherently antagonistic to outsiders—they may, in fact, be at times overly willing to defer to them—but from long experience they have learned to be wary. In-comers who work at it can gain acceptance—H. Landon Ladd, the mainland Canadian IWA organizer who led the loggers' strike in 1959, is still a folk hero in many central Newfoundland homes. But such acceptance has to be earned, and it is gained on an individual basis. When J.R. Smallwood wanted to crush the IWA, he could easily invoke in the minds of the larger public a threatening image of the "outside agitators" who did not understand or care for Newfoundland. And even committed unionists who supported Ladd and the IWA will say that Ladd made tactical errors because of his lack of understanding of the local culture.

Fred Locking had also gained acceptance among many of the south coast plant workers, but when the dispute came into the open, the fact that he was "not from here" told against him. What in another context would have been his greatest asset, his background of union experience, could become a liability. "Fred's an Englishman, eh?" one union member says. "He was always tellin' us how much better things was done someplace else. Seems like he thought Newfoundlanders couldn't do nothin' right by theirselves." Ultimately, in spite of class differences, Cashin and the workers shared a sense of belonging expressed in nuances of speech and attitude, in knowledge of local history and personalities, from which Locking could be excluded. Another member of the first executive recalls:

> They said Fred was going to run for president. What the hell would we want with a guy out of some flour mill in Saskatchewan? He didn't know nothing about the fishery. — Of course, Richard didn't, neither, as far as I'm concerned. But that's another story. He knew Newfoundland, and he could learn. We could teach him, and he could understand.

In part, the convention of 1972 was a confirmation of the NFFAWU's identity as a Newfoundland union, an identity that is acknowledged by officials of the CFAWU with a slightly puzzled admiration. "It's more than just a union," one of them says:

> There was a time there when it was a bottomless barrel — money was just pouring in and disappearing. The reason the international stuck with it was because they could see it was a peoples' movement.
>
> It's not like our other divisions. We don't always understand it, but we're proud of it.

Much of the subsequent history of the NFFAWU is understandable in terms of a continuing tension between its two identities: as a social movement and as an international labour organization.

Chapter 8

The NFFAWU had been born into a complex and chronically troubled industry. Even in its best years, in the nineteenth century, while some companies and merchants did very well, there was also a record of failure and bankruptcy. In this century it had stumbled from crisis to crisis, constantly plagued by competition on foreign markets, poor quality of product, lack of regulation, inept marketing strategies, and cut-throat rivalry among rapacious companies. By the time the NFFAWU came on the scene, to this list had been added massive competition by foreign fishing fleets and the consequent depletion of the resource.

As has been mentioned, the major part of the catch in the traditional Newfoundland fishery was taken in traps or on hand lines from small boats, within a few miles of the shore. This inshore fishery was complemented by an offshore effort, conducted from schooners which carried small boats to the underwater plateaus of the continental shelf, a hundred miles and more at sea, where the fishermen took cod on baited hooks. In both fisheries, the catch was salted and dried. As early as the 1890s experiments were taking place with a different fishing method: *trawling* or *dragging*, in which a bag-shaped net is towed across the ocean floor by a powered vessel, scooping up the fish in its path. This did not become an established method in Newfoundland until the 1940s, and then only a few such vessels were in use.

After the Second World War, as fresh fish freezing expanded and the saltfish industry declined, the banking schooners disappeared: the last of them to sail from Newfoundland ports made their final trips in the early 1950s. Their place on the Grand Banks was taken by a small fleet of trawlers that could scoop up large quantities of fish quickly, pack them in ice, and bring them back to the freezing plants for processing. On the banks, the Newfoundland trawlers competed with their traditional rivals from France, Spain, and Portugal, some of whom were still hand-lining and salting their catch. Others had been trawling for a long time, and by the 1950s some of the foreign trawlers were equipped with freezers.

In the mid-1950s, the first factory trawlers, built in Britain, began to appear: large, powerful vessels three times the length of the Newfoundland ships, carrying crews of up to eighty, and dragging nets the size of a football field. The big ships were highly successful: in those early days they often caught more fish than their nets and winches could safely handle—twenty tons or more on a single tow. When the fish were brought aboard they were processed by a factory crew operating a variety of compact, semi-automatic machinery for gutting, splitting, filleting, skinning, and freezing to produce a marketable product. The offal and unusable species were converted to fishmeal in grinders and dryers.

The British were quickly followed by others. By the mid-1960s, the Grand Banks were being swept by hundreds of vessels from the Soviet Union, Poland, both Germanies, Rumania, Spain, Portugal, France, and a half a dozen other European nations. The tonnage of cod being caught shot upward, reaching a peak in 1968 and then falling sharply as the stocks were depleted. The factory ships and fish plants ashore diversified their intake, processing species that would have been scorned and discarded only a few years before.

The true dimensions of the resource crisis were masked for a time as the fleets of trawlers shifted their effort from area to area and species to species, depleting each in its turn. In one area, as an almost-random example, the catch of redfish fell from 486 million pounds in 1959 to 42 million in 1972. Quotas set by international agreement continued to be above the levels established by biologists as the maximum sustainable yield, even in areas where actual catches had fallen well below either figure. In Newfoundland, the decline in volume of fish landed was offset by improvement in prices on the American market. A government report for 1972, for example, noted that "The fishery . . . may be regarded as a failure . . . " because of decreased landings, " . . . but from a marketing and prices point of view, the year was a remarkable success."

In such findings there was a clear threat for the future, but in spite of foreshadowings of disaster, fish processing companies in the province were in an expansionist mood as they entered 1973. The year started badly for the inshore fishermen: heavy coastal ice delayed the beginning of the season for most of them, but when they did get their boats into the water they received prices up to forty per cent above those of the previous year. Landings of cod continued to fall: for the first time in four hundred years it was not the dominant species, but other species filled the gap and with the increased fishing effort the total landings for the year were four per cent above those for 1972. The improved prices in the USA meant that the total value of the catch showed a thirty per cent increase.

Several companies undertook major expansion of their facilities. On the Burin Peninsula the companies reported that two hundred jobs were "going begging" because of a lack of housing for workers needed on the cutting and packing lines: the union suggested that low wages and poor working conditions were also a factor. In Bonavista, after nearly eleven months of strike, plant employees went back to work without much fanfare but with a contract that gave them pay rates well above their original demand.

For the union, 1973 was a period of plain sailing between the storms it had just weathered and another that was building just over the horizon. It was a time to consolidate gains. The strikes at Burgeo, Marystown, and Bonavista had effectively dispelled any idea that the NFFAWU would be easily broken from the outside, and the Gander convention had crushed any hopes the companies may have entertained of its disintegration from within. With plants expanding and prices for the product bouncing up by fifty per cent and more on the U.S. market, it was obvious to almost everyone that pay and working conditions in the fish plants were out of line both in comparison with other industries and in respect to the companies' ability to pay.

Most fish plant jobs were—and are—hard, uncomfortable, and tedious. The majority of the workers stand for hours in one place, repeating the same simple operation over and over, hundreds of times an hour, as an endless stream of fish moves by on belts. The noise is deafening; hands and feet are numbed by the cold water that flows everywhere. Hours of operation are controlled by the supply of fish, and under some of the seasonal plant contracts in force in 1973 workers could put in ten-hour shifts for six days of the week without getting over-time pay. Men did the cutting and filleting, and the heavy work of moving fish about in bulk, but a growing number of women worked at trimming, grading, weighing and packaging. Women had always been part of the traditional saltfish production process, and now that the old self-sufficiency of the outport household was disappearing their earnings were needed to meet the array of monthly bills so familiar to city-dwellers. For men and women alike a major objective each year was to gain a sufficient number of weeks' work to qualify for unemployment insurance to tide them over the inevitable periods when no work would be available, but conditions in the plants meant that many people had little motivation to work longer than was necessary to qualify. Turnover was high. A plant employing three hundred people could have as many as nine hundred names on its payroll over the run of a year.

From the union's point of view, the improved market conditions and the plant expansions were a fortunate coincidence, for the leadership had targetted 1973 as the year to make substantial gains in the fish plants. The battles they had fought so far had been primarily for recognition: they had made important contract gains with National Sea Products and Bonavista Cold Storage, but the biggest negotiations for wages and working conditions were still to come. Back in 1970, before the formation of the NFFAWU, several CFAWU locals had signed three-year agreements which incorporated only minimal gains. Some of these, with Fishery Products Ltd., were so inadequate that in 1971 the company had voluntarily, and without prejudice to future negotiations, added twenty cents to the base rate to keep the lowest-paid workers ahead of the minimum wage. Since then the union had signed some one- and two-year contracts, with the result that in the second half of 1973 about seven collective agreements were up for re-negotiation.

In mid-summer, the union called together the local committees from all the plants concerned and agreed upon a joint proposal that they would carry to the negotiations, a proposal that would ask for changes in almost every aspect of the contracts. Negotiations began in August with two companies—Atlantic Fish Processors Ltd. of Marystown and British Columbia Packers at Harbour Breton. By the end of September, with the help of a conciliation officer, an agreement was reached with BC Packers, and the fish plant committees were called together again to see if it was acceptable to everyone. It was, and not surprisingly: virtually all of the union proposals had been accepted by the company. Under the new contract the Harbour Breton workers would have a seniority clause, improved grievance procedures, overtime pay for the sixth consecutive day of work, eight paid statutory holidays, and a health scheme. Most remarkable of all, they would receive a pay increase of $1.25 per hour over the two-year life of the agreement, with seventy cents of it immediately and retroactive to the first of August. Over all, it meant a seventy-two per cent increase in the basic pay rate over the two years. The contract was signed in mid-October.

It was a landmark agreement, but its full implications did not become apparent to the news media and the general public for another two weeks. In September, while negotiations were still going on with BC Packers, the troublesome three-year contracts with Fishery Products Ltd. had come due, one covering three year-round plants in the south and the other covering three seasonal operations in the north—six important plants employing about fourteen hundred people. By custom, workers in the seasonal plants received hourly rates that were about twenty cents below those in the year-round operations and had inferior arrangements for overtime and holidays. The union asked for a master agreement covering all six plants, with fringe benefits and rates to be equal to those in the Harbour Breton settlement, allowing for some differences in fringe benefits for the seasonal plants.

In late October Fishery Products signed, and the newspapers took account of the historic nature of the agreement. For the first time there would be entrenched parity between seasonal and year-round workers. For the first time, there would be parity between male and female workers in the same jobs. And for the first time Newfoundland fish plant workers had moved ahead of their counterparts in Nova Scotia. Because the Fishery Products workers had been receiving somewhat lower rates than those at BC Packers, the effects of the pay increases were even more spectacular: some of the lowest-paid workers in the seasonal plants would receive increases of ninety to a hundred per cent over two years, and overtime and bonuses besides.

The new contract set the standard for the rest of the industry. Booth Fisheries at Fortune and the Lake-owned John Penny and Sons at Ramea had both given their still-unorganized workers raises in August which had put them ahead of many of the unionized plants, hoping to forestall entry of the union. After the Fishery Products settlement they had little choice but to raise their rates again to match the union-negotiated agreement. "We've set the pattern now," said Richard Cashin, giving the knife a deliberate twist and serving notice that the NFFAWU intended to stay in the forefront for plants in the Atlantic region. Fish company spokesmen put the best face they could on the situation, announcing that the new rates would attract a more permanent supply of skilled and professional labour. "Attract" might not have been the most appropriate word in the circumstances, since in the outport communities the companies had a virtually captive labour force, but the sentiment was basically correct. A job in a fish plant was becoming something worth keeping.

The NFFAWU was now firmly established in the processing sector. As Cashin had said, the pattern was set. Most of the major plants were organized and the others were falling into line on wages: it would be only a matter of time before they would be organized too. For the fishermen, however, things were not so clear-cut. The NFFAWU was certified as bargaining agent for only three groups of inshore men and for crews on about three-quarters of the offshore trawlers, but much of the organization was not very firm and thousands of fishermen remained outside the union. The fishermen had benefited from some important price increases, but the process of establishing prices was not yet clearly defined. In 1973, the union had negotiated prices with Fishery Products Ltd., and the rates agreed upon were applied throughout the industry for organized and unorganized fishermen alike, but this was merely at the choice of the companies: they were in no way bound to continue the pattern and it was questionable whether the union was in a strong enough position with the fishermen to force the issue. In light of all this, the leadership determined that 1974 was to be the year for fishermen as 1973 had been for plant workers.

The circumstances, however, were very different. The plant employees, like other industrial workers, share a basic organization by the nature of their work. Jobs can be clearly defined in categories by the technical operations carried out; workers must interact with one another on the job, and must live within a reasonable distance of the plant—and hence of each other. Even at that, organization is not always easy to achieve but the basis for it, at least, is inherent in their situation. Inshore fishermen, by contrast, carry on their work in small, independent units. Although they may frequently co-operate with one another they are also fundamentally competitors for fish and fishing locations. The number of fishermen required to constitute a bargaining unit may live in several different communities in the vicinity of a fish plant, widely separated from their fellows, and during the fishing season they work extremely long hours, leaving little time for meetings. Also, the same bargaining unit could include men operating widely different types of boats and gear, from the sixty-foot, hundred-thousand-dollar longliner operated by an owner-skipper and a crew of three or four sharemen, to the home-built twenty-eight foot trap-skiff powered by an outboard motor and crewed by her builder and a son or a brother. Their common ground was that they sold their fish to the same companies, and the price structure affected them all.

The year did not have a propitious beginning. Ice conditions were even more extreme than in 1973. The start of the season was seriously delayed for most of the fishermen, and when they finally got their gear into the water in the north and northeast, an unseasonal movement of the pack ice destroyed thousands of nets and traps. Fishermen who, as usual, stopped receiving unemployment insurance benefits in May in anticipation of the start of the fishing season, spent six weeks and more with no income, unable to fish. Cashin and others described it as a "disaster in the making." To add to their troubles, the ever-uncertain U.S. fish market went into one of its cyclic down-turns. Newfoundland fish company spokesmen said that the market conditions were the worst in twenty-five years, and that they were still holding stocks of processed fish unsold from the previous year. Reasons advanced for the drop in the market ranged from the arrival in the U S A of cheap fish from Japan and Korea, to a drought in American cattle areas which led ranchers to sell off their stock at depressed prices, resulting in lower consumer prices for beef.

The union campaigned for a programme to compensate fishermen for their lost gear and for an emergency unemployment insurance programme to help them over the period of lost fishing time. "One thing is certain," Cashin was quoted as saying, "between the federal and provincial governments, one hundred per cent compensation must be paid . . . for gear losses, or no more fishing." But the fundamental problem was the price of fish. Early indications were that the fish companies would be looking for decreases rather than increases in the rates to be paid to fishermen.

At the time, the union was still negotiating separately with the different companies for their bargaining units, but they hoped to be able to do this year what they had done in 1973—negotiate a price structure with Fishery Products Ltd. that would hold for the rest of the industry. Fishery Products was the major single purchaser of inshore fish, and among those selling to their plant at Port au Choix the union had its oldest and firmest organization of fishermen, the men who had formed the Northern Fishermen's Union in the first place. Negotiations went on from May into June with the union and the company both remaining firm—and a considerable distance apart—in their proposals. The government appointed a conciliator, but while the conciliation was still in process the association of fish companies pre-empted the initiative. Reverting to the old practice, they unilaterally announced fish prices for the year. On most prices there was to be no change from the 1973 level, there were to be slight increases for some specialized species such as shrimp, but for cod under twenty-four inches—the mainstay of the inshore fishermen—there was to be a decrease of a cent and a quarter a pound.

In vain the fishermen protested that their costs for fuel, rope, and gear had escalated far above 1973 levels—that the proposed price structure would mean decreases in their earnings by as much as a third compared to the previous year. In the press, Cashin blasted fish companies and government impartially. "Fishermen, it appears, are the only workers in Canada," he said, "who will earn less in 1974 than they did in 1973 for the same effort." The provincial government's inaction on compensation for lost gear he put down to the fact that most of the fishermen affected were on the still-Liberal northeast coast, where the Conservatives "get no votes." Government members, he charged, were "in the pockets of the fish buyers, who assist with their election expenses." As for the companies, he said that if they could not absorb the effects of a temporary down-turn in markets they should not be in business at all, but should be replaced by a government agency like the Saltfish Corporation: "Why should the primary producer, the fisherman, suffer because of poor industry organization?"

The negotiations with Fishery Products now took on a new—and for the union—sinister significance. If it was to retain any credibility at all as a union of fishermen, the NFFAWU simply had to gain something better than the prices announced by the industry. "We practically pleaded with them," Cashin says now. "We would have settled for almost anything—a half a cent, a quarter of a cent over the industry price . . . " Such a settlement would have done little to alleviate the problems of the Port au Choix fishermen in the face of vastly inflated costs of operation, and nothing at all for the others, but the issue at stake had become the very survival of the union. "We had to get some little thing," says Cashin, "just to recognize our existence." He now cites it as one of several examples in which, as at Burgeo, company intransigence forced an issue that helped to establish the union:

> If they had given us anything, we'd have settled, and that would have been it for 1974. We wouldn't have been happy, but we'd have taken it.
>
> I told them. I said, 'Look, don't back us into a corner,' but they did. We had no choices left.

When the conciliator failed to bring about an agreement, the minister of labour declined to appoint a conciliation board and the union was in a position for the first legal strike by inshore fishermen in Newfoundland's history. At the end of June, men from seventy of the seventy-three boats in the bargaining unit took part in the vote and decided for a strike by 173 to 9. "It is almost unbelievable for them to go out on strike, given these [market] conditions," said Gus Etchegarry, general manager of Fishery Products. Cashin replied that "If the fishery is to have a long-term future, the primary producer cannot be the one to bear the brunt of temporary and cyclical difficulties in the marketplace."

Although the strike was essentially for union recognition, the striking fishermen had their own grievances. Unlike most other plants in the province, the Port au Choix operation required them to unload their own vessels onto the weighing-scales, and at the height of the season fishermen claimed that they might have to wait six hours or more for a place at the wharf, losing sleep and fishing time. One of them, Joe Plowman, estimated that once costs were deducted they made less than two dollars an hour for their work. "If we worked an eight-hour day, we'd starve," he said. The union leadership predicted that the strike would spread, and compared it to the plant workers' strike at Burgeo. The vast improvements in the earnings of plant employees were still fresh in the public mind, and union officers made use of the fact: those gains were a direct result of the Burgeo strike, they said, and this strike would have the same effect for fishermen. Cashin reinforced the parallel with the charge that "conditions on the wharf in [Port au Choix] would make Spencer Lake seem like a benevolent socialist." Bill Short elaborated on the theme, saying that the strike was an indication of "a whole new era in the fishing industry." Fishermen, he said, were younger and better educated than in the past:

> [They] have been treated like dirt for years, but now they realize they've depended too long on industry and politicians. They realize they've got to solve their problems themselves.
>
> . . . We are going to break the system [of setting prices]. If it takes ten years we are going to break that system!

Like the Burgeo strike, this one had its peculiarities. Although the fishermen were striking they were able to continue working at a reduced level. Fish plants belonging to other companies refused to take their fish, giving Cashin the opportunity to charge that the fish industry was a "cartel", but the union found an out-of-province buyer for their halibut who gave them twenty cents a pound more than Fishery Products had been paying; they were also able to split and salt their cod, and sell it to the Saltfish Corporation. On the other hand, the Fishery Products plant workers, who were *not* on strike, could not work because there was no fish for them to process. Newspapers picked up rumours that they were unsympathetic and rebellious, but reporters sent to the scene could find little evidence to substantiate the stories. As elsewhere, many of the plant employees were from fishermen's families.

In the midst of it all a strange little drama unfolded in St. John's, totally.unrelated to the Port au Choix strike and yet in a curious way placing it in a larger perspective. It involved the crews of the last vestiges of the once-great Portugese "White Fleet" that in days past had annually marked the beginning of spring by sailing in magnificent array into St. John's harbour, now reduced to four decrepit vessels that still fished the Grand Banks using two-man dories and hand-lines. One of the ancient ships had burned and sunk on the fishing grounds, and the other three had brought the rescued crew in. Since they had left Portugal the ruling dictatorship had been overthrown, and the dorymen learned that the new revolutionary government had doubled the wages of crews on the modern trawlers. They demanded assurance that they would get the same treatment, and went on strike. Clearly, the winds of change were blowing in other fisheries besides Newfoundland's, but officials of the Newfoundland government and fish companies might have taken some comfort from the differences when they read the crudely-lettered signs in the windows of the Portugese Seamen's Centre on Water Street: "With hands clasped in democracy we will kill the fascists."

The Newfoundland union's invective was less violent, but cutting nonetheless. Harold Collins, the provincial minister of fisheries, was "more to be pitied than blamed," Cashin said. "You can't really say that the fishermen of the province are disappointed in Mr. Collins, because that would imply that they expected something from him in the first place." Meanwhile, the federal and provincial governments were putting together a programme to deal with the fishery crisis. Much to the union's anger and chagrin, indications were growing clearer that it would not be the programme they wanted. There would be compensation for gear lost to ice, and some income support for fishermen who had lost weeks of fishing, but the basic problem of the market was to be handled as it had been in 1968—"bailing out the companies," as the union put it, with no guarantee of a different deal for the fishermen. When the strike had begun, Cashin predicted that it could force the governments to act because they had put so much money into the fishery. Now, after nearly four weeks with the boats tied up and with government about to take what he felt was inadequate action, he underlined that the strike was not merely against Fishery Products, but "a demonstration going to the root of the whole fisheries charade . . . We are not just negotiating for today—we are demonstrating that they have to take the fishermen seriously." The Port au Choix tie-up, he said, "could be the action that triggers fishermen right across the island."

No one—and perhaps Cashin least of all—would have taken that possibility very seriously at the time. Organization among fishermen was too uncertain and too uneven for any comprehensive action to be likely. They were used to ups and downs, to good years being followed by bad, and when prices were low they could always stretch out their already long hours of fishing a little more, try to bring in a little more fish, and somehow make ends meet. The newspapers seemed to make a special effort to seek out fishermen like this in unorganized areas who could be expected to say that things were "not so bad" and that the strike was not a good idea. On the other hand, there was no question that all the fishermen were feeling the pinch, and that a great many of them were solidly behind the Port au Choix strike.

To give a little extra force to Cashin's words, Bill Short led a group of the strikers to the town of Burin, on the peninsula of the same name, to picket and talk to crewmen on the Fishery Products Ltd. trawlers.

Their conversation had an immediate effect: on July 24 and 25 the crews of four ships, in various stages of unloading and preparing for sea, refused to sail for the fishing grounds. A collective agreement was in force between the trawler crews and the company, so the tie-up was not a legal strike. The men did not call it a strike at all, but said that they wanted a mass meeting of all Fishery Products crews to discuss "the general situation with regard to the fishery." They wanted assurances, they said, that the fishery had a future, given the "gloom and doom picture being painted."

Fishery Products had sixteen deep-sea trawlers serving their three year-round fish plants in a constant shuttle to and from the offshore fishing banks. At any time except Christmas some vessels would be at sea while others were discharging their fish at the plants or taking on supplies to sail again. A mass meeting of their crews, of course, would tie them all up.

One by one, the ships came in to Burin, Trepassey, and Catalina, discharged their fish, and stayed tied to the wharf. With the shuttle broken, the company announced that within a few days the three plants would have to close, and not only the 224 trawlermen but also over a thousand plant workers would be idle. "We just wanted to put a bit of extra pressure on Fishery Products," Cashin says, "to get them to settle the inshore strike at Port au Choix.

> . . . And it was working. I was negotiating with Gus Etchegarry [manager of Fishery Products] and he was ready to give us something on the price of fish to get his boats back in operation.
>
> Then Atlantic Fish Processors' boats began to tie up at Marystown. I was on the phone: 'Get the Atlantic Fish boats back to sea!' I'm saying. Then I get a call from Bill Morrow [manager of the National Sea Products plant in St. John's] and he was mad as hell. He was furious—one of *his* boats had tied up.
>
> So I'm still on the phone: 'Get the Atlantic Fish boats back! Get the National Sea boats back!' but there was

> no way. If there was going to be a mass meeting those guys were going to be in on it. If we'd been able to send any of them back, they'd have all gone—but, anyway, we couldn't get them to sail.
>
> So that was it. Etchegarry withdrew his offer. We went ahead with the mass meeting, and by this time all of Fishery Products, all of Atlantic Fish, all of National Sea—they're all tied up. So we thought, 'Oh, my God, we're into it now!' There was nothing we could do but go ahead with it.

Temporarily, at least, the situation was out of control. Events were moving rapidly ahead of the union leadership, and they found themselves in the midst of an illegal strike by workers for whom no clear demands had been formulated and no bargaining strategy planned.

The reasons for the situation were complex, and at the time not clearly understood. For one thing, the union had a new business agent working with the trawlermen: a huge, boisterous Prince Edward Islander named Dave McKinnon, an ex-trawlerman who had moved to the NFFAWU from the CFAWU in Nova Scotia shortly before, when the Port au Choix negotiations were going on. He was an enthusiastic organizer with a hearty, back-slapping style and a belligerent, confrontational attitude toward employers. Later, he and Cashin would have a falling-out over the union leadership. Perhaps McKinnon's enthusiastic entry into his new job had some influence—"Dave might have got a bit carried away," Cashin says—but that is far from all there was to it. Many of the tie-ups were spontaneous actions by the tough and independent trawlermen themselves, a group of men whose circumstances and problems had not been brought to public attention in the way that had been done for other fishery workers.

Unlike the inshore fishermen and the plant workers, many of the trawler crews had not been organized into the union in the conventional manner. Back in 1970, the CFAWU had played a somewhat nefarious role in the trawler strike in Nova Scotia, accepting voluntary recognition from the companies to squeeze out the radical UFAWU from British Columbia, and at the time Fishery Products in Newfoundland also gave the CFAWU voluntary recognition for their crews to keep the British Columbians out. It was popularly regarded as a "sweetheart" arrangement, and somewhat tarnished the CFAWU's reputation with other unions.

The NFFAWU had inherited these bargaining units when it was formed, and incorporated other trawler crews as organization of fish plants proceeded, but not always easily: the Lake crews at Burgeo, for example, were not part of the union during the big strike there. When the illegal tie-up began, the union represented about fifty of the seventy-four trawlers sailing from Newfoundland ports. They had recently been certified for about eight vessels with Booth Fisheries at Fortune and were engaged in negotiations for a contract, and a certification vote was being held on their application to represent another group of about eight boats fishing for Bonavista Cold Storage at Grand Bank. Trawler contracts were mainly variants on those in force in Nova Scotia, though with lower rates of pay in Newfoundland. Thus far, the NFFAWU had had little time to devote to the trawlermen, although the contracts they had negotiated had brought about substantial improvements in conditions of work. One of the tasks Dave McKinnon was expected to perform when he came to Newfoundland was to create a greater degree of order in the trawler sector in preparation for more systematic negotiations.

As was mentioned at the beginning of this chapter, the trawlers were a relatively recent phenomenon in the Newfoundland fishery. From their small beginnings in the 1940s they had steadily increased in numbers, and shot up dramatically in the 1960s. Between 1956 and 1974, the capital invested in them had increased sixteenfold.

Trawlers vary in size and sophistication of equipment, but the basic principles of their operation are the same. They are large steel vessels driven by powerful diesel engines, which fish by dragging behind them a long open-ended bag net adjusted by vanes to travel along the ocean bottom, scooping up the fish that are feeding there—hence the common colloquial term "dragger." The development of complex electronic fish-finding equipment in recent years has led also to mid-water trawling, in which the net may be adjusted to catch schools of fish at any depth. On the fishing grounds the draggers fish almost continuously, steaming back and forth over the undersea banks. The net is "shot" or placed in the water and allowed to run out on its tow-cables to the desired depth; "dragged" or "towed" for a period of about an hour or longer, depending on fishing conditions; then "hauled" or winched up to the ship and its contents dumped on the deck. On the large, modern factory trawlers the fish are fully processed—cut, skinned, packed and frozen in a marketable condition, and the offal and unusable fish converted to meal—but the Canadian companies had no vessels of this level of sophistication, and still have not. On the Newfoundland trawlers, the fish were sorted, and the usable catch packed in ice in the hold. The rest was dumped overboard.

The Newfoundland trawlers typically carried then, as they do now, a crew of about fourteen—a captain, a mate, and a bosun, responsible among them for the operation and navigation of the ship; a cook; an engineer and his mate to operate the mechanical equipment; and a crew of eight or nine hands to attend to deck duties, shoot and haul the net, handle, sort, and pack the fish, and maintain and repair the gear when it is damaged in use.

Even now, a deep-sea trawlerman has one of the toughest and most demanding jobs in the world, but the conditions of their work in the early days of the industry in Newfoundland, during the 1950s and 60s, seem like something from another century. The work was almost continuous. From the time the net was first hauled and its slippery contents dumped on the deck, it was a relentlessly repeated round of shooting the net again; sorting, packing and icing the fish; then clearing and hosing down the deck for the next haul. "The captains was pushed to the limit by the companies," one ex-trawlerman says,

> . . . and the captains pushed the men beyond their limit. Keepin' men on deck sixty or seventy hours at a stretch was routine. If you couldn't take that, well, you weren't a fisherman. There was nobody to complain to—if you didn't like it you could stay ashore.
>
> There was times you'd hardly get out of your rubber clothes for a week. If you got a few hours to sleep, you'd just kick off your boots and crawl in. One time, I remembers, when the fish was comin' good, we left on a Monday morning and we was back the Friday night. We fished steady from early Tuesday mornin' until Thursday night—sixty hours without a break, only for meals and mug-ups.

When the men could get below decks for a respite, their living conditions were as harsh as the work. Quarters were cramped, crowded, damp, and often dirty. Some companies provided only bare bunks with skimpy, smelly mattresses: the men brought their own blankets. The food, prepared under the most difficult of conditions, varied with circumstances and the skill of the cook, but sometimes it was barely edible. "You wouldn't feed it to your cat," one man says, "only when you're workin' like that you'd eat anything."

Union contracts negotiated by the NFFAWU and in force at the time of the illegal strike in 1974 addressed some of the more extreme of these conditions. Among other things, the signing companies agreed to provide "clean mattresses . . . and clean covers as necessary." Even under these agreements, however, the men had little time to enjoy their bunks. Work schedules allowed watches of six hours on and six off, for a work day of twelve hours out of twenty-four; or eight on and four off, for a work day of sixteen hours, depending on fish and weather. During heavy fishing, these hours might be extended, but the contracts stated that "no crew member will be required to work longer than sixteen [consecutive] hours, after which he shall have his watch below." Even that allowance, according to some trawlermen, was often exceeded.

Such hours would be hard to endure at any job, but the trawlerman's back-breaking work is carried out on a slippery, heaving deck that is rarely still, often in seas that make it a punishing task just to keep upright. On the older vessels, a few of which are still in use, the net is shot and hauled over the side of the ship and the fish are handled on an open deck, unprotected from the elements: on the newer stern-trawlers, the net is put into the water and recovered from a sloping ramp at the rear of the vessel and the catch is handled in a partially covered area in the waist of the ship. In either, however, the men do much of their work exposed to wind, rain, snow, and driving spray. "I'll tell you, boy," one fisherman says, "there's been many times I wished to Christ I was the captain's old dog instead of a human bein'. At least he was up in the wheel-house in some kind of shelter."

Besides being hard and uncomfortable, the work of a trawlerman is also dangerous: the rate of injury and loss of life is higher than for almost any other industrial occupation. The fishing banks off Newfoundland provide some of the most hazardous marine conditions in the world. At various times of the year they experience heavy fogs, high seas, pack-ice, icebergs, unpredictable winds, freezing temperatures, and extra-tropical hurricanes. In winter, the entire crew of a trawler may be required to clamber over the rigging and superstructure wielding axes to chip off the ice that builds up from the driving spray. More than one trawler has rolled over and sunk, rendered top-heavy by an uncontrollable build-up of ice. In 1982, when the oil-rig *Ocean Ranger* carried eighty-four men to their deaths during a February storm on the Grand Banks, landsmen across the country were appalled at news reports of the ferocity of the sea—sixty-foot waves driven by hundred-mile-an-hour winds making any hope of rescue impossible. Most were not aware that there were scores of trawlers on the Banks that tragic night, from Newfoundland and other jurisdictions, riding out the storm and waiting to begin fishing again when the weather moderated.

In their cramped, tossing work-place the men are surrounded by other hazards—razor-sharp knives, straining cables, grinding winches, and always the slippery ramp that leads down over the stern to deadly cold water. Most old trawler crewmen have stories like this one:

> I seen a young fellow one time get his arm caught in a winch. Tore it right off. And we brought him in like that—no anaesthetic or nothing.

> All he got for compensation was a couple of months work as a watchman, after he got better, then they laid him off. Some of us tried to get up a collection to get a lawyer to fight his case. When we got a lawyer, we found out he was workin' for the company. That man got his arm tore off, and he got nothin' for it.

Although the trawler fishery is a highly mechanized industrial operation, comparable to other resource extraction industries like logging or mining, the trawler crews in 1974 were not regarded in the same light as other industrial workers. By tradition, they were "co-venturers" with the companies that owned the ships and were paid on the basis of a share of the value of the fish caught. Under the contracts in force at that time, the crew's share or "lay" was set at thirty-seven per cent of the gross catch: money was deducted from this to pay for provisions consumed during the trip, and the remainder was divided into equal shares. "Learners" received five-eighths of a share; officers and cook received additional amounts from the company share ranging from two and one-eighth to five-eighths per cent. Captains were not covered by the agreements, and made their own arrangements with the company. If crewmen were required to work on the vessel while in port they were paid an hourly rate, under the 1974 contracts, of $2.25. Before the union agreements came into effect, the trawler crewmen also used to pay a portion of the cost of fuel and ice used on the trip, and were required to unload the vessel or pay for the cost of unloading: in 1974, Nova Scotia trawlermen still paid for unloading.

Besides the physical risks of the occupation, therefore, the trawlermen also shared in the financial risks. They outfitted themselves with rubber boots, gloves, and oil-skin clothing, all subject to rapid deterioration in use. If, as occasionally happened, a trip to the fishing grounds produced only a small amount of usable fish, they might earn barely enough to cover their costs for clothing and provisions. If, because of mechanical breakdown or other causes, the trip was completely unproductive —colloquially called a "broker"— they could earn nothing at all, or even owe the company money for their food. A union publication at the time of the strike described one such trip in 1974 on which a Fishery Products trawler landed a volume of fish that would, in normal circumstances, have given each crewman a share of about $300.00. In the plant it was discovered that the fish were worthless because something they had been eating made the flesh unusable. According to the union's account, the workers who unloaded the fish, the cutters who discovered its condition, and the labourers who eventually dumped it were all paid at their regular hourly rates: the fishermen, after ten days of hard work at sea, received nothing at all.

Irregular and fluctuating income was, of course, nothing new in rural Newfoundland, but other features of the trawler industry meant that it presented special problems. In the past, the banking schooners recruited their crews of dorymen from the scores of tiny settlements dotted along the coast, where the men lived in a network of kin and friends in houses they or their fathers had built on family land: living expenses were low, and income could be supplemented by a variety of subsistence activities—fishing and hunting for the table, cutting firewood, gardening, and so on. But the trawler industry is highly centralized. A typical trip takes about ten days, allowing for about twenty-four hours steaming time to reach the fishing grounds and a similar period for the return voyage. Under the union contracts, the vessels were required to spend forty-eight hours in port between trips, discharging fish and outfitting for the next trip. The operation is year-round: the ships tie up only for mechanical breakdowns or extreme weather conditions, an annual two- to three- week refit, and a week of holiday at Christmastime. Trawlermen, therefore, had to live in, or very close to, the trawler ports, where they were subject to all the costs of town life—rents, mortgages, heating fuel, supermarket prices, and all the rest, most of which are geared to the pattern of a regular industrial wage, and must be paid on a monthly basis.

With the men at sea for ten days at a time and home for only two between trips, the trawlermen's wives bore almost the entire burden of child-rearing and household operation. When house or car required attention—the sort of thing an ordinary worker could do in his time off—the wives had to cope with it themselves or hire an expensive professional. In most of the little emergencies of family life—illness, school problems, financial crises—the women struggled through alone. Because times of sailing depended on fish and weather, they could not count on their men being home on any given day, apart from the Christmas tie-up. Sometimes, to meet the demands of the plants, trawlers would be diverted from their home ports to land their fish at another plant, and the men might not get home at all between trips, or would spend part of their precious time ashore travelling overland to their own communities.

The union contracts had improved some of the conditions of work, but in other respects the situation of the trawlermen was deteriorating. Particularly, they were feeling the effects of depletion of fish stocks due to over-fishing. According to one report, the offshore vessels were putting in triple the effort they had expended six years earlier to bring in the same volume of fish. The men were working longer for less return. They had other grievances: for one thing, they complained that they had no control over the grading of fish when it was landed. They charged that at times fish delivered in good condition was given a lower grade because of delays and mishandling by the plants, and the loss was passed on to the fishermen. They said that sometimes a portion of a catch would be converted to fish meal simply because the company could not handle the volume being brought in, and again the fishermen would lose. But the central problem was declining earning power. According to an independent study, the earnings of trawler crewmen, averaged over the year, had risen by only fifteen per cent between 1970 and 1974, well below the rate of inflation. In the same period workers from two other industries in the south coast area of Newfoundland, miners at St. Lawrence and shipyard workers at Marystown, had gained increases of fifty and sixty-six per cent respectively. Fish plant workers, of course, had done even better.

Even at that, the averaging may have made the trawlermen's earnings look somewhat better than they actually were, and it did not take account of the incidental costs of pursuing the occupation. One trawler crewman summed up the feelings of many of his mates when he said,

"It's better to stay home for nothing or get the welfare than to spend sixteen hours a day for so little money. I've been at the fishery all my life and I can see the industry going down. There's less fish and if we can't get more money we'll have to quit the fishery." Many did just that when the opportunity presented itself, and the turn-over of manpower was high. Men drifted off to jobs in mainland Canada or on the Great Lakes, but among Newfoundlanders the pull of home and family and familiar surroundings is always strong, and many drifted back to marry and ship out again on the trawlers.

The industry was plagued with many problems, but from the trawlermen's point of view the central issue was the manner in which their earnings were calculated: the system of setting the price of fish and calculating the value of the catch. The companies were vertically integrated—like the Lake operation at Burgeo, they owned the trawlers that caught the fish and the plants that processed it. Thus, when they transferred fish from trawler to plant, they did so at a price set by themselves. Since the crewmen's pay was based on a share of this price—and, more than incidentally, since the price stood in a fixed relationship to the prices paid inshore fishermen—it was very much in the companies' interest to keep those prices artificially low. As a result, the trawler operations typically operated at a "loss", paying no income taxes, and frequently qualifying for government assistance. The "loss" could be made up in profits on the processing, where workers were paid by the hour. A major economic study of the time gave this blunt assessment: "Obviously, very large book losses on trawler operations have been an accounting device." Equally obviously, it was an accounting device that the companies would not willingly give up.

This, then, was the background to the illegal strike that snowballed through the trawler ports at the end of July. Altogether, the nine Newfoundland trawler operations employed about a thousand tough, independent, disgruntled, hard-pressed men, sailing in units of fourteen or fifteen from a dozen ports. It was a work force difficult to handle at the best of times, and as the tie-up spread the NFFAWU was riding on the crest of an unpredictable wave, struggling to gain control.

The mass meeting demanded by the Fishery Products crews was held. It was closed to press and public, but when it was over the union reported that 250 trawlermen had voted unanimously to go on with the strike. In the days that followed the news media hummed with constantly changing and often contradictory reports. It was said that the Booth Fisheries crews, who were the only group in active union negotiations and had begun a conciliation process, had decided to join the strike—then that they had not, and would sail after all. BC Packers' crews at Harbour Breton tied up. Bonavista Cold Storage crews, still voting on union certification, continued to sail. The Booth conciliation was ineffective, and Booth crews tied up—the only ones to be legally on strike. A Booth trawler still at sea came in with a large catch that netted the crewmen $570 each: the men were prepared to sail again, but after what was described as a "hurried meeting with union officials" decided not to. Fishery Products reported that one of their boats had sailed with a full crew of union members, and the union said that it was a pick-up crew of unqualified non-union men. Plants were picketed and injunctions taken out by companies. Sixty trawlermen staged a demonstration at the Confederation Building in St. John's, the seat of provincial government.

Through the confusion, one fact became increasingly clear: the major part of the Newfoundland trawler fleet was tied up to the fish plant wharves, and it seemed likely to stay that way for some time. Both sides called for government action. The companies wanted the government to force the men back to work, but what the union wanted was not so clear. They wanted changes, and they wanted to be involved in the setting of fish prices, but as a newspaper editorial pointed out, they had made no specific demands. Premier Frank Moores declined to intervene, saying that it was a labour dispute and should be settled by the parties involved, and both companies and union responded angrily. Dave McKinnon, the south coast organizer, was quoted as saying that the premier's statement was "bloody ridiculous . . . The time is right to correct a lot of wrongs."

As frequently happens in Newfoundland labour disputes, the issue was being fought out in the public press. The fish companies purchased large newspaper advertisements in which they emphasized that five collective agreements between trawlermen and companies had been "indiscriminately and illegally broken." As they had done since the union's birth, they focussed their attack on the "union leadership," which essentially meant Richard Cashin, who had chosen, they said, "to break . . . valid collective agreements and act in complete defiance of the law. This type of leadership cannot be tolerated if the fishing industry is to survive." The advertisement challenged the government to act: "Is the government of Newfoundland prepared to accept . . . open defiance of the laws of the province?" Spokesmen for the companies said that they were contemplating legal action against the union and Cashin.

The attacks gave Cashin the opportunity once again to score his usual points. Clearly, he said, the companies regarded the fishermen as "dumb brutes" who could be manipulated by their leaders. As for legal action, he said that the union was considering its own action against the companies under Restrictive Trade Practices legislation. It was they, he said, and not the NFFAWU, who had broken the collective agreements and precipitated the stike.

After two weeks, the companies began to take out writs for damages against the union. Cashin says that he was advised by a lawyer friend to see that his house and assets were transferred to his wife's name. "They are really out to get you this time," he was told. By the third week of August the provincial minister of labour, Joe Rousseau, stepped in and began holding talks with both sides. One condition of his involvement was that the media battle was to stop: a blackout was placed on pronouncements by either companies or union. The press continued, of course, to report on which trawlers were sailing and which were not, and on the picketing of plants and issuing of injunctions.

The talks and the blackout dragged on for a further two weeks, and by September 5 an unidentified industry spokesman—whose style was readily recognizable to the participants—lost patience and broke the silence: "I've had enough of this," he was quoted as saying. "If we don't resolve this thing tomorrow, all hell is going to break loose . . . We've got absolutely nothing done since this news blackout started. This is no way to achieve an end to this thing. We have to make people aware of what is going on!"

"All hell" did not, in fact, break loose just then, but the stage was being set for something to happen two months later that the industry might with only slight exaggeration have described that way.

Leaks from the negotiations indicated that an agreement was very near: the only remaining point of contention was the union's demand that any adjustment of fish prices be retroactive to June 1, the start of the inshore strike at Port au Choix. There were also reports of cracks in the union's support. Children were going back to school, winter expenses were looming, and the fishermen had not been making any money. One of them was quoted as saying that if a vote were held to go back to work, it would be "close."

A few days later, a government plan was announced, which had been accepted by company and union negotiators. It had three main parts. First, a Fisheries Advisory Board was to be established. This was a provision that had been included in the original collective bargaining legislation for fishermen in 1971, but had never been fully implemented: now the Board was to be set up on a firm basis and provided with funds for collecting information. An industrial inquiry board was also to be named, to investigate the situation of the fishery and report back within six months. The third provision was to become the centre of the next stage of the controversy: a conciliation board was to be established to consider the particular matters of the current strike. Although the only legal part of the strike was against one company, Booth Fisheries at Fortune, the board was empowered to consider the matter as a dispute between the NFFAWU and four other companies besides Booth—B.C. Packers, Atlantic Fish Processors, National Sea Products, and Fishery Products. Bonavista Cold Storage and the Lake companies, whose crews had not participated in the strike, were not included.

The terms of reference of the conciliation board were unusually broad, and its task was, as its eventual report noted, " . . . more appropriate to a full scale industrial enquiry than a Board of Conciliation." Besides considering "all items of a monetary nature affecting the relationship between trawler fishermen and operators, including fish prices, lay arrangements, shore time, and work in port," it was also empowered to "investigate and report on any other matters which may affect the relationship between the parties with respect to collective bargaining." Starting without specific demands, the union had succeeded in getting an independent investigation into the entire muddled situation. Whatever might happen next would start from the conciliation board's report. Having gained this, the union conceded on the matter of retroactivity: adjustments in fish prices, when they came, would be retroactive only to the time when fishing recommenced.

When the vote was held, two hundred fishermen did not turn up, and it was speculated that they had drifted away to other jobs, something they were in the habit of doing anyway when times were bad. Those who did attend voted by a seventy-four per cent majority to go back to work, indicating that the level of disatisfaction was still high, and one by one the trawlers again put to sea. In some ports there was confusion over details, and it was not until September 24 that the last crews sailed. Fish companies and union, in a rare unanimity, praised the provincial government for its efforts and took the opportunity to criticize Ottawa for lack of action.

For the time, at least, operations returned to normal, but everyone concerned was aware that it was no more than a temporary truce. The dispute had not been resolved, but only postponed, and Cashin sounded a battle cry for the conflict yet to come. Fishermen had been fighting for years, he said, for the right to representation in the process of setting fish prices, and "finally we have been given that opportunity." The fishing industry of Newfoundland, he said, "will never be the same again." Only a few people were aware of it at the time, but he was speaking with the confidence of a poker player with an ace in his sleeve.

Chapter 9

Unusual as the circumstances may have been, the board of conciliation was appointed in the usual manner, with three members: a representative of each of the two contending parties and a chairperson acceptable to both sides. The fish companies named Paul Russell, the hard-bargaining head of Bonavista Cold Storage Ltd.; the union was represented by Ed Johnson of the Canadian Labour Congress, who had been instrumental in bringing fishermen and plant workers together in the NFFAWU four years before. The chairman was Dr. Leslie Harris, a professor of history and the academic vice-president of Memorial University of Newfoundland, later to become its president.

It was not a new experience for Harris. He had conducted conciliations in several other labour disputes, including the NFFAWU strike against Atlantic Fish Processors in Marystown in 1972. But he also brought to the task another sort of experience: he had grown up with the deep-sea fishery. He was born and raised in the village of St. Joseph's on the Burin Peninsula, and his father and uncles were Grand Banks skippers. "Our fathers were away from home for most of the year," he recalls:

> My father usually spent about six weeks at home, from the 23rd or 24th of December until about the 10th of February. During the rest of the year we would see him perhaps three or four times for a few hours or overnight, if he was passing by and could get in. In winter he would be fishing out of Burgeo or Rose Blanche on the Southwest Coast; in summer he'd be on the Grand Banks and coming in to Calvert or other places on the Southern Shore.

As Harris grew up and the banking schooners were replaced by trawlers, his brother, his cousins, and many of his schoolmates became draggermen. Harris himself had summer jobs in the engine rooms of trawlers in for re-fit.

Although the terms of reference for the board of conciliation were unusually broad and took in matters that would not normally be considered, the board had no staff to assist with documentation and research. They met almost daily with union and company representatives, and meetings often lasted late into the evening. The board members themselves kept track of documents, and Harris's university secretary handled filing and typing. When he took on the task, Harris says, he was aware of the peculiarities of the situation and the unusual breadth of the mandate he had been given, but it was not until the union and the companies began to present their arguments that he realized the full implications. Some aspects of what was presented were matters for straightforward conciliation: whether or not mates and captains should be members of bargaining units, or questions of sailing schedules and tie-up time. Underlying the dispute, however, were fundamental questions about the structure—and the very existence—of the Newfoundland fishery.

When the hearings were over, Harris wrote a report of eighty-two typewritten pages, with appendices of charts and graphs amounting to another twenty. After some minor revisions, the three Board members signed it, but at the last moment the companies' representative, Paul Russell, added a hand-written postscript to his signature stating that of the thirteen conclusions listed at the end of the report he would give his agreement to only twelve. Conclusion number eight, referring to the manner of calculating trawlermen's pay, he excluded. On November 14, the completed report was passed on to the government and to the two parties to the dispute who now had, under the Labour Relations Act, two weeks to consider it and give their response.

Two days before, the final result had been announced of the certification vote taken by crews on Russell's Bonavista Cold Storage trawlers at Grand Bank and Fermeuse. They had voted to join the union by an eighty-eight per cent majority. Now only the Lake family's ten trawlers at Gaultois and Ramea were still unorganized.

In the meantime, the union was preparing for another convention.

In 1972, it had been decided that they would meet biennially, and the two years was up. A few days before the November 30 date, the news media began, as was becoming usual, to report signs of disunity in the ranks. Woodrow Philpott, sitting as vice-president of the fishermen's section, announced that he would be running for the presidency, saying that he was "completely dissatisfied with the leadership of Richard Cashin." Like Cashin himself, Philpott is a volatile and colourful speaker, and in his statements to the press he seemed to corroborate many of the charges that had recently been made by the fish companies: "Cashin has become more a dictator than a leader . . . He has been ignoring the executive . . . he has taken things into his own hands." It was not merely himself who felt that way, Philpott said, "but all of us."

When the convention was held a few days later, however, there was little sign of dissension. In his presidential report, Cashin reviewed the union's achievements in bringing about "dramatic changes in the status of the people who work in the fishing industry." The year 1974, he said, had been historic. The strike at Port au Choix had been "the most significant thing fishermen have done since Confederation. For the first time fishermen—or some of the fishermen—refused to accept the idea that the fish companies and/or the governments are the ones who make the final decisions." The convention passed a series of resolutions calling for various reforms, and gave almost unanimous support to ones calling for nationalization of the whole industry, the establishment of a single government marketing agency, and the creation of a crown corporation to distribute fishing gear. Philpott did contest the presidency and lost, with eight votes to Cashin's seventy-eight, but he accepted the defeat graciously. "If there is one enemy of Richard Cashin," he was quoted as saying, "it is not Woodrow Philpott. And if he has one supporter it *is* Woodrow Philpott." Both men now describe his challenge to the leadership as the result of a temporary misunderstanding.

During the convention, Cashin said that he would not comment publicly on the Harris report until the union negotiating committee had made its recommendation. The newly-appointed provincial minister of fisheries, the Honourable John Crosbie, also spoke at the convention and went only a little farther: he said that the government agreed with "the report's main findings as to what the problem is and what needs to be done," but that its recommendations were open to "argument and debate." A day or two later the report was made public.

Harris says that he expected an "immediate and vociferous reaction" to the document, but in fact there was little stir after its release. He received no official word from either the companies or the union, and there was a surprising period during which no one seemed to be giving it much attention. On December 10, Cashin announced that the union negotiating committee had recommended acceptance of the conciliation board's report. Anticipating the companies' reaction, he added that unless there was a signed collective agreement embodying its contents, "there will be no fishery in 1975." And gradually, as Harris's friends and acquaintances read it, they began to let him know that they thought he had made a dreadful mistake.

> Almost everybody I knew—in St. John's at least—accused me of heresy and apostasy. People told me that if the report was implemented it would be the end of Newfoundland. Some hinted that I had turned pink, if not bright red. The more generous felt I had been taken in by wicked unionists.

By the intensity of their criticism, Harris's friends were acknowledging what was shortly to become publicly apparent: that he had authored an historic document.

It was written in a flowing, erudite, often elegant style, quite unlike the stilted quasi-legalese of most conciliations. After a brief review of the circumstances of the establishment of the board, Harris plunged headlong into a strongly-worded statement on the problem of the supply of fish. He pulled no punches: "The profligate, if not actually criminal, manner in which we have permitted depletion of what ought to be an infinitely renewable resource will probably rank as one of the great asininities of the twentieth century." He demonstrated the validity of the charge with examples of the decimation or near-extinction of stocks of various species, and of international quotas that were far above what the stocks could stand. The data were not new: the problem had been bandied about in government reports and news media for several years, but Harris's brief ten pages were one of the most pointed and powerful statements that had been made on the subject until that time. Two major points that were often obscured in other discussions came through with abundant clarity: the annual catch quotas that were being set by ICNAF—the International Commission on the North Atlantic Fishery—were based much more upon international politics than on realistic information about fish, and, in any case, the biological information that was available was totally inadequate for the task of rational management. If that problem could not be solved, Harris said, there would soon be no fishery for companies and union to dispute over.

> . . . We are consequently disposed to urge, in the strongest possible terms, that the united pressures of the union, of the companies, and of the provincial government be exerted in an effort to convince Ottawa that absolute control of the resources of fish on the Continental Shelf must be assumed; that that control must come about through unilateral action should international negotiation fail to achieve the desired end; and that catch quotas must be drastically reduced until sufficient scientific data are available to provide firm projections of the maximum sustainable yields.

The report then moved to a consideration of the condition of the companies and concluded that, although in the bouyant U.S. markets of 1973 all had made substantial profits, in 1974 they were sustaining losses of from twelve to thirty cents per pound on marketed fish.

But neither of these were the sections that drew the criticism and controversy: that was generated by the report's discussion of the "social needs" of the trawlermen and its recommendations regarding the pay they should earn and the manner in which it should be calculated. On the first point the report stated:

> . . . taking into consideration earnings possible today throughout industry within the province and considering further the legitimate expectations of skilled tradesmen in all fields, we believe that a skilled trawler fisherman, who, through productivity, demonstrates his

> skills should, at the present time, be able to claim earnings in the range between $13,000 and $20,000 per annum, for a work year averaging 240 days.

This was a startling statement, considering that the dragger crewmen had been earning an average of about $8,000 to $9,000 on the stern-trawlers, and considerably less than that on the side-trawlers.

On the second point, the report recommended an end to the co-venture system: " . . . we believe that whenever a fisherman returns from sea, having spent up to ten days or more at work, he should not be put in the position of having absolutely nothing to show for his labours." It went on to suggest a rather complicated system of calculation based upon an average catch of 150,000 pounds of fish per trip. The fishermen's pay was to be based not upon a share of the price, as in the existing system, but upon a fixed charge per pound, regardless of species. No matter how small the catch, fishermen were to be guaranteed wages amounting to what they would receive in poundage on two-thirds of an average catch, which Harris calculated to be $360, or $36 per day for the usual ten-day trip. Thus, a fisherman who sailed on all twenty-four trips could not earn less than $8,640, and would certainly earn more, because if trips fell consistently below that catch figure the industry would not be viable anyway. If the trips produced average catches over all, he would earn $540 per trip, or $12,960 for the year. If the catches were above average he could earn proportionately more, but earnings above the $540 per trip level were to be paid in the form of a twice-yearly "adjustment" to *bona fide* fishermen—that is, to men who had sailed on at least half of the available trips. The essence of this system of calculation was summarized in the report's recommendation number eight—the one that Paul Russell refused to accept: "That trawlermen should negotiate with companies not the price of fish but rather the income level that will be attainable for full-time work." If this recommendation were to be accepted, the trawlermen would no longer be "co-adventurers" but would be paid, like other industrial workers, for work done—plus additional amounts for high productivity.

During December the union and company negotiating teams met and sorted out their reactions to the conciliation report. As Christmas approached it became clear that they were not going to reach an agreement. The companies were now offering considerably more than they had been prepared to offer in August: the "lay" arrangement was to remain the same, but they offered to add an average three and a half cents per pound to the price of fish and to provide a per-trip guarantee, but only for men who sailed on twelve consecutive trips. Average attainable earnings under the scheme would be about $11,000 or $11,500, but the fish prices on which these estimates were based were valid for only six months, and could have gone down after that time. Cashin brushed the offer aside saying, "We are much further apart than just monetary items. The companies are not willing to negotiate a new contractual relationship, and that's at the heart of the matter."

While the discussions were going on, the federal government announced an emergency twenty million dollar assistance programme for the east coast fishery, intended to tide the industry over the four-month period until April of 1975. Bill Wells, spokesman for the fish companies, said that about half of this amount would go to the trawler industry in the four provinces, but declined to estimate how much would come to Newfoundland: whatever the amount, he said that the companies proposed to keep 11/20 of it and pass on 9/20 to the fishermen. It was this subsidy, plus $325,000 from the provincial government, that allowed them to make their offer. Cashin replied that by his calculations the companies planned to keep something closer to 2/3 of the subsidy for themselves. In the past, he said, the government had no way of knowing whether their assistance to the industry benefited the fishermen, but now they had—the collective bargaining process. A signed collective agreement would demonstrate that the fishermen were getting the benefit.

Normally, the first trawlers to stop fishing for the Christmas break would be coming into port around the middle of December, and the last would tie up a few days before Christmas. Immediately after Boxing Day, the ships would sail again in the same order, giving each vessel about a two-week break. This, in fact, was one of the non-monetary items the union wanted to change—they wanted no sailings until January 2. And this year they did not sail after Christmas. Instead, the crewmen attended a series of union meetings in the trawler towns and voted by 450 to 5 to give the negotiating committee authority to sign an agreement based on the recommendations of the Harris report. They also agreed that no trawlers would sail until that agreement had been reached. The strike was on again. And this time, according to the union at least, it was legal. They had accepted the conciliation report and the companies had not.

The publicity battle began almost immediately, and from the outset the provincial government was in the centre of it. A few days into the new year, in the first of several government actions that brought widespread criticism, Minister of Social Services "Ank" Murphy announced that no social assistance would be paid to strikers' families. There was an immediate chorus of protest. Trawlermen picketed welfare offices and charges were laid against some of them for obstruction. Art Kelly, president of the Federation of Labour said that by their action "the government has declared itself on the side of the companies": Cashin echoed the sentiment and said that doubt had been cast on the government's ability to act as a mediator in the dispute. Liberal MHA Steve Neary, once minister of welfare in the Smallwood government, said that the strikers should challenge the action in the Supreme Court, and announced that he would be taking up a collection among the Liberal caucus to support the strikers. Jim Morgan, a Conservative MHA, later to become minister of fisheries, gave a personal contribution to the union fund.

The government back-tracked and explained, saying that the decision had been made months before as general policy and had nothing to do with this particular strike. Premier Moores admitted that the timing of the announcement was unfortunate and said that exceptions would be made in cases of extreme hardship, but each pronouncement called forth further criticism. The situation of the trawlermen had been well publicized during the summer strike, and support for their cause was quickly offered by such organizations as the New Democratic Party, the Council of the Student Union at Memorial University, the Association of Public Employees, and even the Police Brotherhood of the Newfoundland Constabulary.

Because the summer strike had not been a legal work stoppage the strikers had not received strike pay. This time they were eligible to receive it from the international's strike fund, but not until after two weeks had gone by. Even then, it amounted to only thirty dollars a week for married men, plus five dollars for each child, and twenty a week for single men. Families that had already lost income during the summer and were now trying to meet the high expenses of mid-winter faced real hardship. The plant workers' situation was as bad, or worse—they, too, had lost work in the summer and now sixteen hundred of them were idle when the plants did not re-open after Christmas, but were not eligible for strike pay. Children demonstrated in Marystown and some parents said they might have to keep them out of school because they were unable to buy proper winter clothing. Contributions from other organizations and private individuals went into a fund to help people in special need.

On January 9, company and union negotiating teams got together again for an eight-hour meeting at which the companies made another offer, this time with a more secure guarantee of $150 after each ten-day trip and fish price adjustments that would bring average earnings up to about $11,500, as in their previous offer. After the meeting, Fisheries Association spokesman Bill Wells was reported as saying angrily that "the bloody union won't budge," but later said that his remarks had been quoted improperly. Demonstrations and picketing continued in front of welfare offices and fish plants, injunctions were issued and charges laid. Several trawlermen were convicted of obstruction for preventing people from entering welfare offices, and burly Dave McKinnon, the union's south coast business agent, was convicted and fined $300 for intimidation of supervisory personnel trying to enter the fish plant at Grand Bank. As one fisherman remarked later, "If McKinnon just stands next to you, he's intimidatin'. "

The fines were paid, but not without difficulty. The union was still in dire financial straits: it had not recovered from the deficits run up in its first two years, and the summer strike had curtailed revenues from dues and added heavily to the expense side of the ledger. In this one, about twenty-five hundred members were not working and not paying dues. It was a closely-guarded secret, but for a time the union staff up to and including the president did not draw their salaries, and Cashin raised money on his own securities to make a personal loan to the union of over fifty thousand dollars. With such extreme measures as these, Ray Greening managed to keep the NFFAWU afloat, but just barely. One staff member comments wryly, "We were really just about as bad off as the companies were pretending they were, only we didn't want to talk about it."

On January 13 the union received some powerful support from a not entirely expected quarter. The St. John's *Daily News* — the newspaper that during the Burgeo strike had published Peter Simple's virulent attacks on "wrecker Cashin, the butcher of Burgeo"—carried a front-page editorial that began, "Newfoundland trawler fishermen have one important thing on their side in their dispute with the fish companies: they are right." The editorial went on:

> The companies rest their case on the cruel myth of "co-adventure"—except when complaining they're broke. "Co-adventure" is a foolish anachronism that might once have described very well the situation in a two-man dory, but loses all relevance when applied to the modern trawler fishery . . .
>
> Who but the merchants, steeped in historic arrogance, would dare cling to the idea of equal risk, more or less, between a trawlerman and his "co-adventurer" fish baron?

The editorial was signed by James R. Thoms, editor, and William Callahan, publisher—the same William Callahan who, a few years before, as J.R. Smallwood's minister of resources, had given Father McGrath a ride home in a government helicopter on his return from the negotiations in Chicago that founded the NFFAWU. On three succeeding days, the newspaper published front-page articles by Callahan in which he presented an analysis of the dispute that was severely critical of both provincial government and fish companies.

In the same issue of the *News* as one of Callahan's articles was a full-page advertisement signed by W.D. Morrow, president of National Sea Products Ltd., which suggested that the fishermen were being deceived by their negotiators about the company offer. Using the actual figures for two December trips by National Sea trawlers as a base, the letter purported to show that the companies' last offer would, if applied to the same catches, result in an increase in earnings of nearly eighty per cent. "Has Mr. Cashin told you this?" the letter asked. "I doubt it."

The advertisement also made clear the company position on the Harris proposal "Has [Cashin] told you that the $13,000 figure, while quite attainable under an incentive system, is not the least bit practical on a straight guarantee and will NEVER be agreed to by the fishing industry?"

In this and other company publicity, the "guarantee" being sought by the trawlermen was spoken of as though it were a guaranteed annual income rather than a guarantee of payment for work. This confused same observers, and letters-to-the-editor columns were filled with arguments about work and incentive. The companies insisted that the incentive represented by the co-venture system was neccessary to maintain production, and the union replied that other industries had abandoned this line of argument long ago: what, they asked, was so different about fishermen? Cashin offered some figures of his own. A full-time trawlerman, he said, would work about four thousand hours in a year: at that rate, the proposed income of $13,000 worked out to about $3.20 an hour. If overtime were allowed for, it would be closer to $2.40. "What the fishermen are on strike for," Cashin concluded, "is $2.40 an hour"—they were on strike, he said, for the minimum wage.

In St. John's, a Trawlermen's Support Group was formed to raise contributions for the strike fund and arrange billets for strikers who were to come to the city for a demonstration at the Confederation Building, the seat of the provincial legislature. Many of those who volunteered to provide beds and meals were white-collar intellectuals, supporters of the NDP and progressive causes. As a result, many of the two to three hundred draggermen who came to the city found themselves staying in the middle-class homes of university professors and civil servants, surrounded by stripped pine furniture and Christopher Pratt prints. For both them and their hosts it was a novel experience of crossing class barriers.

The demonstration provided further drama for the news media and another opportunity to accuse the government of underhanded opposition to the strikers. The trawlermen, joined by students from the nearby university and other sympathisers, massed on the broad concrete stairs outside the legislative building and heard speakers from government, opposition, and labour organizations. They booed Premier Frank Moores and his minister of mines and energy, Leo Barry, whose district included some of the trawler ports, and applauded Opposition Leader Ed Roberts; but their loudest cheers were reserved for their president, who treated them to a rousing example of his oratory. The fish barons, he told them, "will do anything to destroy the union, and to destroy the fishermen, in order to keep the same old system." It was up to all Newfoundlanders, he said, to "get on the bandwagon and tell the fish companies we are no longer the coolies of the north!"

In his speech, Cashin skilfully interpreted the government members' cautious remarks as support for the union. It was all the more dramatic, therefore, when a group of strikers attempted to carry a petition into the legislature and other demonstrators moved to follow them into the building's capacious lobby, out of the biting sub-zero wind, only to find the doors locked against them.

Dr. Tom Farrell, minister of public works, dismissed the incident as "a mistake," saying that other doors to the building were to have been locked to control the flow of people, but that it was intended that the front doors should have been left open. Someone, he declared, had misunderstood the intention. Mike Martin, still sitting as an MHA for the New Labrador Party, had a different story. He reported that when he found the doors were locked he went in turn to the minister of manpower, the minister of justice, and the premier himself to try to have them opened. If they were locked by mistake, he indicated, they were kept locked on purpose.

Meanwhile, behind the scenes, a more serious and complicated story of government involvement was brewing. From the beginning, both union and companies had been urging government intervention: the companies wanted the strikers sent back to work, and the union insisted that the only possible action the government could take would be to accept the report of the conciliation board set up under its auspices.

In response, both the premier and the minister of fisheries, John Crosbie, had consistently maintained that government had no intention of becoming involved unless the situation reached a point "where the public interest is in jeopardy." All the while, however, there were signs, disquieting for the union, that the government's sympathies were with the companies.

When the companies made their second offer, Crosbie said that it represented an agreement to change the co-venture system. Cashin replied that Crosbie was "either badly misinformed or . . . arguing the companies' case." In late January, National Sea Products asked permission of the Department of Justice to sue Cashin and the NFFAWU under the Collective Bargaining Act, saying that the strike against them was illegal, since they had a collective agreement with the union that would not expire until January 31. Cashin replied that by agreeing to be named in the terms of reference of the Harris conciliation board they were now part of a legitimate labour dispute, but the government gave permission for the suit to proceed. Early in February, Cashin and Crosbie were scheduled to meet, but the day before the meeting Alex Hickman, the minister of justice, whose constituency included the trawler port of Grand Bank, said that a number of trawlermen in his district had told him that they wanted a vote on the companies' offer and that he felt the union executive should comply. Cashin promptly cancelled his meeting with Crosbie, saying that Hickman's statement undermined the union's bargaining position, which forced Crosbie to reply that Hickman was merely expressing his own opinion, not government policy.

All this was highly disconcerting for Cashin, because since the very beginning, before the conciliation board was even set up, he had been carrying in his pocket what he believed was the winning card. Away back in August and September, when negotiations were going on to end the illegal summer strike, both union and government had been concerned that conciliation could result in a standoff: that the board might recommend a settlement that the companies would be unable to pay. After lengthy discussion, the premier agreed—or appeared to agree—that, in this event, the government would make up the difference. The minister of labour, Joe Rousseau, in consultation with Cashin, drew up a letter incorporating this agreement, which the premier signed on September 6:

September 6, 1974

Dear Mr. Cashin,

Further to the discussions between government, the NFFAW and the Fishing Industry over the past week or so, this is to confirm certain undertakings by the provincial government in respect to the existing dispute between certain members of the Fisheries Association and the NFFAW.

As government understands the situation, it is that there appears to be, or is alleged to be, certain incongruities between the operators' ability to pay for their fish and the ability of fishermen to live on the basis of current fish prices. I can assure you that Government understands the situation and, in an effort to rectify it, will undertake the following:

> To have included in the terms of reference of the proposed Conciliation Board a study into the economic aspects (the ability of the companies to pay) and social aspects (the ability of fishermen to live on the basis of these prices). Where there exists an agreed difference between the companies' ability to pay and the fishermen's ability to earn a fair wage, the Provincial Government will undertake to lead a delegation to Ottawa, such delegation to be a united effort headed by the Provincial Government and including representatives of the industry and the NFFAW, which would attempt to convince Ottawa to provide the necessary funding to cover this difference or, failing that, any part thereof. Where the Federal Government does not agree to complete funding of the agreed difference, then the Provincial Government will undertake to fund the remainder of the total difference as agreed to following the report of the Conciliation Board. It is further agreed that the new fish prices which are arrived at as a result of the process will be effective on the date of sailing.

It is the Provincial Government's understanding that, on this basis the trawlers will return to normal operations and government's offer, as outlined above, is contingent on this point.

Sincerely yours,
Frank D. Moores
Premier

This was the union's ace, but it was not an easy card to play. According to Cashin, the premier had wanted it kept as secret as possible, with only the necessary minimum of people knowing of it. Moores was, a union publication later said, "particularly concerned that Ottawa would learn about the existence of the letter and it might prejudice their position with the federal government as far as future assistance for the industry was concerned." The union negotiating committee knew about it. Leslie Harris knew about it—though only unofficially. Cashin made judicious use of it to convince wavering supporters that a strong union stand was indicated. But when the winter strike occurred and then dragged on, the government seemed to be acting as though the letter did not exist. Cashin says that he tried several times to contact the premier to discuss it, but could not get through. Several times he considered making the letter public, but, he says, "Once I'd made it public, what would I do for an encore?" and he continued to use it behind the scenes to convince influential observers that the strike would be won.

After the demonstration at the Confederation Building and several fiery public speeches by Cashin, the companies stepped up their own publicity campaign, buying advertisements on radio and television to put their case to the public—and particularly to the strikers and the plant workers and business people of the trawler towns, all of whom were beginning to be in considerable distress. The Fisheries Association also opened a telephone "information centre" to answer questions about the strike and to receive calls from trawlermen who wanted to go back to work. Cashin derided the use of the companies' lawyer, Bill Wells, as a "public relations man" and said that "the pig squeals loudest before death," but there was evidence that the company campaign, along with statements by government officials, was having some effect. Early in February, he was travelling in the Burin Peninsula and met with a small group of clergymen who expressed concern about the effects of the strike on their towns and urged him to make a settlement. Cashin mentioned the premier's letter and, to his surprise, the clergymen replied that they already knew about it and had been told that the government did not regard it as a commitment. This, of course, was a disconcerting revelation. Until then, Cashin had suspected that even some of the cabinet ministers did not know about the letter: now it appeared that they did, and were working to counteract it. The government was trumping the union's ace.

The denouement came a few days later at a meeting in Marystown, called by the Joint Town and Community Councils on the Burin Peninsula. The municipal politicians had not taken a clear side in the strike, much to the annoyance of the trawlermen, but their anxiety to see it ended was growing stronger and they now seemed to be shifting in favour of a compromise solution. Besides Cashin, the meeting was to be addressed by Fisheries Minister Crosbie; Leo Barry, MHA for Marystown and minister of mines and energy; and Val Earle, MHA for Fortune and minister of finance. Cashin made his presentation to the meeting and was about to leave. "Crosbie hadn't been there for my speech," he says, "and I wasn't going to stay for his." One of the councillors urged him not to go, however, and he stayed. To his surprise and chagrin, he heard the fisheries minister begin to talk about the ostensibly secret letter, explaining to the mayors and councillors of the suffering towns that it did not constitute a commitment to make up the difference between the conciliation recommendation and the amount the companies could afford. The guarantee in the letter concerned an "agreed difference between the companies' ability to pay and *the fishermen's ability to earn fair wage*," and there was no agreement about the latter figure. By the time Crosbie was finished, the letter was no longer secret, and it had been interpreted to mean something very different from what the union president had been selectively telling people it meant.

Cashin's discomfiture grew when the minister of finance, Val Earle, defended his cabinet colleague Alex Hickman, saying that he had taken the right course for a representative of a district with a large number of trawlermen, and that course was not to "jump on the union bandwagon." The strike, said Earle, was "ridiculous." Cashin could no longer contain himself, and from the audience he made one of the most dramatic speeches of his career. He said that because of Moores's letter he had never expected a strike to occur in the first place—he had expected the government to honour its commitment. The union negotiating team had negotiated on the basis of the letter, he said, and Harris had known of it when he wrote his report, but the government had "welshed on the agreement and I can only imagine there is a split in cabinet . . . First Premier Moores makes this commitment, then we have Alex Hickman coming out against the union, and then Val Earle." The union, he said, would not stand for such treatment. In a voice full of emotion, he said that the trawlermen were engaged in the biggest battle since Confederation:

> If the government turns against us, if the South Coast turns against us—indeed, if the whole province turns against us, the only way they will stop us from fighting is to clap us in irons and deport us from the province . . . And, by God, we won't go without blood on our hands!

Outside, a heavy snowfall had begun, driven by the usual Burin Peninsula winds. After the meeting broke up, John Crosbie's was one of the last cars to leave Marystown: when Cashin tried to leave a few hours later the road was blocked. He spent the next few days stormbound on the peninsula, fuming and pacing in his hotel room. Back in St. John's, Crosbie repeated for the news media his explanation that since the companies and the union were not agreed on a settlement, there was no "agreed difference" for the government to make up. Premier Moores said that, in his opinion, there was a "substantial difference between 'a fair and reasonable wage' and thirteen thousand dollars a year, fish or no fish"—although the latter was not, in fact, quite what the Harris report had recommended. Harris, who had made no comment since submitting the document, broke his silence to say that apparently the government did not accept his conciliation report. He said he had known of the agreement: that the government had told his board to make separate and independent assessments of the situation of the companies and the needs of the trawlermen, and "not to worry where the money came from. The implication was that government would make up the difference." The second member of the conciliation board, Ed Johnson, confirmed Harris's statement, but Paul Russell denied it, saying that any understanding beyond the written terms of reference, if it existed, was "between, presumably, the government and Dr. Harris." Crosbie, having made his statement, left the province for a holiday.

When Cashin finally got back to his office in St. John's, he called a press conference, where he delivered a lengthy statement explaining the background of the letter from Moores and the union's understanding of its meaning. As he answered questions following his prepared statement, the anger and frustration built up during his days of being snowbound in Marystown boiled over. He says that in his agitation he forgot that the television cameras were still rolling and reporters' pencils still recording. Skeptical observers are inclined to think that Cashin is rarely unconscious of the effect his remarks create, but, in any case, he delivered to the journalists a salty, free-flowing personal attack on government members. The premier, he said,

> is incompetent, or he is a weak man being bullied by Crosbie, or he is not an honourable man . . . When Hickman questions the leadership of this union he should first look inward to his own government . . . One figures when you get a commitment from the premier you don't need it in writing. I didn't ask for it in writing . . . he offered the letter.
>
> What credibility does this government have in dealing with any organization? The whole moral authority of the government is in question when you have a situation like this.

Fisheries Minister John Crosbie he described as "the most creditable spokesman for the right wing in this country," who had

> prolonged the trawlermen's strike by [toeing] the company line. John Crosbie's words parallel those of Bill Wells . . . It's almost as if they have the same script writer. Crosbie and his buddies sit around drinking scotch and they don't know shag all about what's going on in this province!

Warming to the subject, Cashin turned his guns on the minister of justice:

> Jesus Christ, do I get boiled about Alex Hickman! Alex Hickman makes me sick. He turns my guts! What he and Crosbie wanted me to do was to add my name to the long list of Newfoundlanders who sold out their own people. What does credibility mean to Alex Hickman? . . . What kind of God-damned province are we, that's what I ask.
>
> If they want to drive us out of the province, let them. If they want to fight, they'll get a fight!

The government, he said was "trying to bust the union as Joey did with the IWA," but "enough of us are prepared to be put in chains first and deported from the province before going back to the old co-adventure system . . . and I'm certainly not going to go peacefully."

In a final, sweeping statement Cashin described the trawlermen's dispute in the sort of language that has from time to time led right-wing observers to identify him—erroneously— as a closet Marxist:

> The politicians of this country, by and large, listen to the fish companies—not to the fishermen.
>
> . . . When it comes to the crunch, Moores, Hickman and the rest of them go right back in there with their own class, and in that event I guess we're just going to have to rely on ours.

Riding home in his car, Cashin says that he heard his pithier statements being broadcast, uncensored, on the radio news. "I thought, 'Oh, my God, I'll be getting some phone calls now'. " When he got home, the telephone rang. It was a priest of his acquaintance—not Father McGrath. "I said, 'Hello, Father. I suppose you're calling about what I said on the radio.' He said, 'Yes. It's about bloody time somebody told those fellows what he thought of them. Give them hell!"

Father McGrath backed up Cashin's outburst with a statement of his own, and although he avoided profanity he was no less direct in his condemnation of the government. He sent a telegram to Premier Moores which said, in part,

> I am thoroughly appalled at the reprehensible action of your government in denying your personal commitment to the trawlermen. This action has cast serious reflection on the honour and integrity of the office of premier.

In statements to the press, McGrath said that he felt he had to "alert the people of Newfoundland to a lying premier—to an untruthful premier." He described Crosbie's leaving town for a holiday as a "disgraceful" action:

> It shows a complete lack of concern and feeling for the people of Newfoundland. It's typical Conservative arrogance.
>
> The merchants must be laughing up their sleeves at the inaction of the provincial government . . . You have a fish merchant premier and a fish merchant Minister of Fisheries . . .

Premier Moores, clearly stung by all the invective, defended Crosbie's "few days off to relax, which he badly needed," and accused McGrath of delivering "a blatant, vicious, personal attack, deliberately misrepresenting the facts," but things had gone too far, and too much had been said, for the government to continue its policy of waiting out the strike. Cashin's blast had been delivered on Friday, February 15, and McGrath's on the following day. At the beginning of the next week, Premier Moores was in Ottawa consulting with Joe Morris, president of the Canadian Labour Congress, and by the next Friday meetings were under way which included, besides the union and company negotiating teams, representatives of the provincial government and Joe Morris himself, along with Ed Johnson. The involvement of the top brass of the CLC was most unusual in such a clearly provincial dispute, as was the holding of the meetings on "neutral ground" in Ottawa.

The talks went on for five days, and then were adjourned for the two sides to reconsider their positions. While they were in adjournment the news media had yet another opportunity to criticize the activities of Premier Moores and his cabinet. On March 3, *Daily News* publisher William Callahan announced that the government had cut off all advertising in his newspaper as punishment for the stand it had taken on the strike. Callahan quoted the minister of supply and services, Dr. Tom Farrell, as having offered a blunt explanation of the ban: "Boy, it's those damn editorials you've been printing on your front page." Callahan said that he had been told of the action ten days earlier, but had found it difficult to believe that the cabinet would support such a blatant attempt to muzzle the press. He said that he had contacted some cabinet ministers who did not support the action and left them time to have it withdrawn: they had been unsuccessful, and he now felt that the matter must be made public. Premier Moores denied that any such ban existed, but Callahan cast doubt on the premier's veracity with another quotation from the minister of supply and services who had, he said, told him that he had "no choice" but to cut off advertising in the *News*: "I've got a directive," Farrell was quoted as saying, "and I can say that it comes right from the top." For several weeks thereafter the newspaper kept the story alive, printing denials, explanations, charges and countercharges, all of which left little doubt in anyone's mind that the premier had, indeed, attempted to take revenge for the pro-union editorials.

Meanwhile, talks were resumed in St. John's, adjourned again, and re-convened in Ottawa. On March 20, the *Daily News* carried a banner headline on its front page: "THEY'RE OVER $13,000." Agreement had been reached, subject only to final ratification, and the strike that had started among the inshore fishermen of Port au Choix nine months before was effectively over. Ratification was quick and complete on the part of the trawlermen, who voted by ninety-two per cent to accept the agreement: Bonavista Cold Storage Ltd. delayed signing for a time, arguing over the inclusion of mates and engineers in the bargaining unit, but finally joined in. By the end of March, Newfoundland trawlers were again butting their way through tumbling grey seas, dodging ice-pans, heading back to the Banks, their crews no longer "co-adventurers", but wage-earning employees.

The settlement was not, finally, what the Harris report had recommended, and to someone who did not read the reports carefully it might have seemed to be closer to the offer made by the companies back in January. At that time they had offered a trip guarantee of fifteen dollars a day and an increase in the price of fish: the settlement reached in March was for twenty dollars a day plus poundage. But there was a crucial difference. The company offer was still based on the old system of the fishermen dividing a portion of the "price" of the catch: the companies were saying simply that if a fisherman's "lay" for a given trip did not amount to fifteen dollars a day for time at sea, they would make it up to that amount. The collective agreement that the union fought for and achieved was a twenty-dollar-a-day basic wage, plus a fixed rate for every pound of fish brought in to the plant. The daily guarantee was lower than that recommended by Harris, but the difference was made up in the rates for fish delivered. Harris expressed satisfaction with the agreement, suggesting that it would result in earnings about the same as would have been achieved under his proposal, and "possibly a very little more." The union calculated that catches similar to those of the previous year would earn fishermen from $11,800 to $14,000. Other calculations suggested that on low-catch trips it would mean an increase in pay of eighty to ninety per cent over the previous year, and on bumper trips an increase of fifty per cent. In addition, the agreement provided trawlermen for the first time with some fringe benefits enjoyed by other employees—four per cent vacation pay, and a company-funded life insurance scheme.

Entering its fifth year of life, the NFFAWU was still in shaky financial condition, but its stock was as high and its support as solid as any union's in the country. In four years of struggle, it had brought about fundamental changes in the relationship between fishery workers and their employers, and it had now brought two major groups of those workers into the modern world of industrial collective bargaining.

Chapter 10

From its very beginnings, the Newfoundland fishery was the subject of government policy-making and of argument among interested parties over what that policy should be. In fact, the very question of whether people should live in Newfoundland at all was a matter of fisheries policy: during the sixteenth and seventeenth centuries, British governments, with varying levels of enthusiasm at various times, discouraged permanent settlement in favour of a seasonal fishery controlled by the merchant companies of Dorset and Devon. Even at the end of the eighteenth century, when the resident population was beginning a period of rapid increase, some West Country merchants were still urging their government to halt immigration and repatriate the settlers. Throughout the rest of Newfoundland's history up to the present, questions of population, settlement pattern, and economic development have been inextricably linked with fisheries policy.

In 1933, when Lord Amulree undertook to investigate the causes of the Dominion's economic collapse and to set out a plan for its reconstruction, the fishery was naturally of central concern. Like many others that would follow, Amulree's report concluded that a major impediment to the development of the industry was the distribution of Newfoundland's people. His suggestions embodied two principles that came to be reflected in government policy-making for the next forty or more years: first, that the efficiency of the industry had to be increased by some form of centralization of effort; and, second, since private enterprise could not be relied upon to bring about the needed re-organization, that financial involvement by government would be required. As put into practice, first by the Commission and then by provincial and federal governments, the first of these principles came to mean the encouragement of greater industrialization and concentration of capital, the development of fresh fish freezing operations, greater emphasis on the capital-intensive offshore trawler fishery, greater reliance on the U.S. market for the product, and the decline of the saltfish trade and the small-boat inshore fishery. Under the second principle, governments put up money through grants, loans, subsidies for trawler construction, and the building of wharfs, roads, and water systems to encourage the industrialization process—the sort of assistance that Spencer Lake received at Burgeo—and spent money in other ways in an attempt to ease the social dislocation that would be caused by the expected disappearance of the inshore fishery.

These objectives were pursued neither consistently nor coherently. They constituted a set of attitudes rather than a master strategy. In 1953, a provincial plan for fisheries development was vetoed by the refusal of the federal government to put up the necessary funds. Another provincial plan met the same fate in 1963. The federal government did spend money through the Department of Regional Economic Expansion and a variety of joint agreements to encourage the centralization of rural population, the promotion of "growth centres," and the building of infrastructure for industrial development, all of which implied acceptance of the inevitable decline of the inshore fishery, but there were also countervailing forces. The extension of unemployment insurance and other benefits to fishermen helped to keep some of them in their boats. Expanded road networks and services reduced the isolation of many fishing communities. Loan and grant programmes encouraged the building of larger and better-equipped inshore boats: between 1956 and 1970, while the demise of the inshore fishery was part of the conventional wisdom, the number of longliners increased more than ten-fold, from 41 to 464. In spite of market uncertainties, small seasonal processing plants continued to be viable. Responding to a crisis in the market in 1968, the federal government created the Canadian Saltfish Corporation—too late to play a major role in development, but nonetheless providing another alternative that inshore fishermen could turn to. In short, in spite of predictions of its demise, the inshore fishery remained what one report termed "an astonishingly durable operation", providing work and income for an average number of fishermen that some observers said to be as high as fifteen thousand, and contributing to a persistent, though depressed, rural economy.

Popular acceptance of the central growth strategy reached something of a peak in 1966, when Smallwood's Liberals gained their massive electoral victory on the promise of industrial mega-projects. In the following year a report to the provincial government recommended that no public investment be made in communities throughout the entire northern part of the island and in Labrador—above a line drawn from Cape Bonavista in the east to the Bay of Islands in the west—unless they had some other economic activity than inshore fishing. Government assistance to the fishery was to be concentrated on the offshore sector and the South Coast. This approach was repeated in another planning document in 1970, but by then, public attitudes to development were beginning to change. The mega-projects were failing. The "growth centres" were not producing expected levels of economic activity. Unemployment was creeping up again, and new jobs were not being created. There was growing rural resentment of centralization policies and a movement to demand improvement, rather than abandonment, of rural areas—as expressed, for example, in the Northern Regional Development Association and the Fogo Island Co-op. The initial rapid spread of the Northern Fishermen's Union among inshore fishermen was a part of this backlash against the trend of development policy—as was the defeat of Smallwood's Liberals in 1971-72.

The NFFAWU, by its very existence, became an influence in the formation of fisheries policy. At first, there were those who predicted that by winning collective bargaining rights for fishermen and working to increase fish prices it was hastening the demise of the inshore fishery: others saw it as an instrument of rural revitalization. From the beginning, the union raised its voice in criticism both of government policy and the structure of the industry, calling for nationalization and the establishment of a fresh fish marketing system on the model of the Saltfish Corporation. In May of 1972, only a year after the founding convention, a delegation of fishermen members of the union went to Ottawa to appear before the Standing Committee of the House of Commons on Fisheries and Forestry—the first time that such a thing had happened. Their brief ranged widely over issues from collective bargaining to resource management on the continental shelf, urged that the federal government "drastically change its approach to fisheries development" in Newfoundland, and indicated the union's intention to play a role in policy formation. In the years following, the union did not hesitate to speak out on policy issues, but its main attention was focused on its own survival and, in any case, the major debates on fisheries policy had not yet taken shape. Besides, during the early 1970s, the attention of all parties came more and more to be focused upon the growing crisis caused by depletion of the resource. After the trawler strike of 1974-75, questions of the structure of the industry were forced into second place by pressing concerns about Canadian control over, and management of, the rapidly declining fish stocks off the eastern coast. It was not until the latter half of the 1970s, therefore, that the NFFAWU emerged fully into the spotlight beside the federal and provincial governments and the fish companies as a major player on the stage of policy formation.

On the whole, 1975 and 1976 were good years for the fishermen. In the spring of 1975 the union for the first time negotiated fish prices in a comprehensive way, with all companies who bought fish in certified areas participating. After the disastrous markets of 1974, the negotiations produced no great change in the prices, but the fishermen received the equivalent of a price increase by a different route, for the strike that had begun in 1974 among the inshore fishermen at Port au Choix had an additional outcome besides a new deal for trawlermen. As the union had tirelessly pointed out, the practice of the federal government in subsidizing the fishing industry was to provide its assistance to the fish companies without concern over how much of it—if any—was passed on to the fishermen. When the government allocated funds to help out the industry after the crisis of 1974, however, it heeded the union's urging and the subsidy was split, with two cents per pound of groundfish going to the fisherman—or, more accurately, to the boat owner—and three to six cents per pound of fillet going to the processor, depending on quality. The provincial government added a half a cent a pound as a gear subsidy. Of course, since the big companies owned both trawlers and plants, they got both catching and processing subsidies, but for the inshore fishermen it meant an effective rise of two and a half cents per pound of groundfish.

Measures taken by international agreement in 1974 to limit foreign catches began to pay off, and in 1976 the total catch for Newfoundland was the highest it had been in three years. Markets rose again, the total landed value went up by twenty-five per cent over 1975, and the union negotiated further increases in the price to fishermen. But the big news was that at long last something was going to be done about the resource problem. The government of Canada announced its intention to claim jurisdiction over a management zone extending two hundred miles from the coast, to become effective in January of 1977. There began to be talk of a new era for the fishery. The Department of Regional Economic Expansion (DREE) put money into boat service centres, haul-outs, and water systems for processing plants. The provincial government, during the calendar year of 1976, put out over seven million dollars in loans for boats and gear. The industry that had been near collapse in 1974 was moving into yet another upward swing.

In late 1976, the new provincial minister of fisheries, Walter Carter, began holding a series of fifteen conferences in the fishing districts which culminated in March of 1977 with a large gathering in St. John's attended by fishermen from across the province and representatives of government departments, union, and fish companies. The tone was set by a twenty-foot banner stretched across the front of the hall proclaiming in bold letters, OUR FISHERIES—OUR FUTURE. Carter promised a "revolution in the fishery in the next 1,000 days," and announced plans for major expansion. Efforts were to be made to convert seasonal processing plants to year-round operation. A hundred new longliners were to be built at a rate of twenty per year, and $4.5 million was allocated for the first twenty in 1977. The entire trawler fleet was to be replaced over a ten or twelve year period and the number of trawlers was to be increased, which would involve the building of about ten new vessels a year. Spending estimates for the Department of Fisheries were increased by fifty per cent over 1976.

The premier was equally exuberant. Newfoundland, he said, could have "the world's biggest fishery." The province's representative in the federal cabinet, Don Jamieson, also joined the chorus, stating that the big industrial projects of the past were. "all will-of-the-wisps; here today and gone tomorrow," but that the real future was in the fishery—a pronouncement that may have been prevented from sticking in his throat by the fact that he was no longer minister of DREE, but now of external affairs. Almost overnight, the image of the fishery underwent a Cinderella-like transformation, from a backward, declining industry to a new Eldorado that would bring prosperity to all.

The basis of all the excitement, of course, was the bonanza that was expected as a result of Canada's declaration of the two hundred-mile management zone. Hundreds of foreign trawlers had been taking millions of pounds of fish in areas within that limit: now Canada was to control the allocation of the catch. Premier Moores foresaw the opening of "huge new markets" for Newfoundland fish in Europe, and a scheme by which the foreign trawlers that were to be excluded from the Canadian zone would be available for charter by Newfoundland firms. He estimated that there was seven hundred million dollars worth of vessels involved, of which Newfoundland might eventually charter "some or all." With Smallwood-like enthusiasm, he said, "We'd get fantastic employment on shore. You're talking about thousands of jobs. The only difference is we won't have to pay for the boats but we can use them."

At the conference in March, the union's reaction was guarded. It was reported that Cashin and Carter had joined forces to send a telegram to the federal minister of fisheries, Romeo LeBlanc, protesting arrangements approved by the federal department under which firms in the other Atlantic provinces contracted with European vessel owners to catch some of the new Canadian allocations for landing in Canadian ports. These "joint ventures," as they came to be called, were to be a focus of controversy for some time to come. The Newfoundlanders were complaining that the mainland firms were getting access to fish that ought to go to Newfoundland, and they were dissatisfied with the response. LeBlanc, Cashin said, "is telling us to go to hell."

The provincial government carried its plan for fisheries development to Ottawa in May. The union expressed disapproval, but did not launch a comprehensive attack. The scheme, they said, had been formulated without adequate consultation with fishermen, and at least one part of it would not gain their applause; the government was proposing an auction system for setting prices, an arrangement that worked well enough, the union said, in British and European ports where there were several potential buyers for a fisherman's catch, but was totally unsuitable in Newfoundland, where most fishermen were limited by distance to dealing with a single buyer.

As the summer progressed, however, the debate took on a clearer definition, and the union's opposition to the government plan became more inclusive. At the centre of the controversy was the question of how the newly-available fish were to be caught. The arguments were more complex, but it boiled down to the old question of offshore versus inshore. A particular bone of contention—and an instructive example—was one of the last great stocks of cod to be exploited by offshore fishing methods: the fish on the northern banks off Labrador and the northeast coast of the island. In recent years these banks had been exploited on a year-round basis exclusively by large, refrigerated European factory vessels with reinforced hulls—ships that could fish while ploughing through ice. The banks were now within the Canadian management zone, and seemed to offer the potential for fulfilling part of the government's plan, but Canadian firms had no ships of the size and design necessary to exploit them.

The provincial government's solution to the problem had two parts. The first was by means of joint ventures. A Newfoundland arrangement of this kind had already been made at the beginning of 1977 with a West German company under which the Germans would land six thousand metric tons of northern cod at Harbour Grace and Marystown. It had been accepted by the federal government and agreed to by the union, but only on a one-year, experimental basis. The second part of the solution was to construct Canadian vessels to do the job: the provincial government's fisheries plan was followed later in the summer by a proposal to Ottawa, offered jointly with the government of Nova Scotia, for a $900 million capital outlay on vessel construction, which included $135 million for nine ice-reinforced freezer trawlers.

The union did not like either part. Joint ventures they were willing to allow, but only in certain clearly defined circumstances. They had to be temporary, and they had to be arranged in such a way that they did not interfere with the catching or selling of fish by Newfoundlanders. In arguing the point, the union used the example of an experiment in shrimp fishing being carried on by Norwegian boats on the northern coast, where there was no indigenous shrimp fishery. The foreign involvement was acceptable, the union said, only until the feasibility of the venture had been proven and the Newfoundland fishermen had learned the techniques.

To the plan for building the freezer trawlers the union was completely opposed. In their view, this would mean opening the northern cod stocks to exploitation on a year-round basis by all five of the eastern provinces, and sound the death-knell of the inshore fishery on Newfoundland's Labrador and northeast coasts. There was some disagreement at the time among biologists about the relationship between the cod on the northern banks and those that were caught by inshore fishermen, but the fishermen felt they had practical evidence: the period of heavy fishing offshore by the European vessels had coincided with the virtual disappearance of cod in what had once been the richest inshore cod-fishery in the world. The union proposed that no expansion of offshore effort should take place until the inshore fishermen were assured of an adequate supply of fish. It was particularly galling, the union felt, that at a time when "the fishery is starting to bring a hint of prosperity to our inshore fishing outports," the government should be following the old line of "putting emphasis on the offshore fishery."

As the arguments went back and forth there were growing indications that—in spite of the earlier disagreement—the union's developing position and that of the federal government had a lot in common. The union was lobbying extensively with the federal department, giving rise to suggestions that Cashin was making good use of his Liberal links in Ottawa, an impression that was reinforced when he accepted an appointment to the federal Task Force on Canadian Unity. In any case, the union appeared to find a sympathetic ear in the federal minister responsible for fisheries, Romeo LeBlanc, an Acadian from an inshore fishing district in New Brunswick. Shortly after the provincial plan was submitted, LeBlanc spoke to the Rotary Club in St. John's. Although his audience at the luncheon contained no working fishermen, it appeared to be fishermen to whom his remarks were addressed: "I want to say to Newfoundland and its fishermen that this government is committed to building a solid foundation for the fishery as a way of life." Referring to the fish stocks now within Canadian jurisdiction, he said:

> Who gets first crack at these fish? Here I must say, as I have said publicly before, that I have a clear bias for the fisherman. Not because of some romantic regard, not because of his picture on the calendars, but because he cannot travel far after fish, because he depends on fishing for his income, and because his community in turn depends on his fishery being protected.

Given these sentiments, it is perhaps not surprising that by late August the federal government had rejected the provincial fisheries plan. The Newfoundland minister of fisheries, Walter Carter, expressed the outrage of his government and more fuel was added to the fire of animosity that was building between Ottawa and St. John's; a fire that was to grow higher and hotter over the next half-dozen years. There was little, however, that the Newfoundland government could do, for reasons both of finances and of jurisdiction. Any major development plan would require an outlay of money far beyond anything that the province could afford: most of it would have to come from Ottawa. Even if the province could find outside investment—and Walter Carter had already stated that "considerable foreign capital" was available for the fleet expansion plans—Ottawa would still have the last word. With respect to the fishery, the division of responsibility under the BNA Act has been neatly described as giving the federal government jurisdiction over live fish and the provinces over dead ones. That is to say, the government of Canada controls the territorial waters and hence has responsibility for management and allocation of fish stocks: it is Ottawa, therefore, that decides what fish shall be caught, and by whom. The provincial governments have jurisdiction over onshore facilities for processing and handling the fish once it is landed. The division is not quite as clear-cut as this makes it seem, of course: such matters as the ownership of processing firms, or the marketing of fish products across international—or even provincial—borders, also come under federal scrutiny. The division of powers, while making conflict over policy almost inevitable, gave the union an opening to exert its own leverage on the policy-making process.

The controversy carried on through the summer, with the NFFAWU keeping a sharp eye on the provincial government, and insisting that the fishermen be represented in decision-making. Early in October, the union got wind of a meeting to be held in Gander between officials of the government and the fish companies to discuss joint ventures and fleet expansion. Union members demonstrated in the rain outside the hotel where the meeting was being held, carrying signs reading "Stop Selling Us Out," and "Carter and Moores Not Listening to the Fishermen." In December, Don Jamieson, minister of state for external affairs and member of parliament for Burin-Burgeo, took time out from attempts to mediate between Israelis and Arabs to try to perform a similar office between St. John's and Ottawa, by organizing a meeting in Marystown that brought together senior officials from both provincial and federal departments of fisheries, the fish companies, and the union, for an exchange of views.

The meeting allowed some face-saving and at least the appearance of greater agreement. Federal officials outlined management plans which indicated that there was to be no immediate fisheries gold-rush. Catch levels were to be set in such a way as to allow for regeneration of the fish stocks. The relationship between offshore catching of northern cod and the decline of inshore catches was acknowledged, and an inshore allowance was to be established. Some of the potential Canadian catch was to be traded off to foreign catchers for other international considerations including, most importantly, management agreements governing catches outside the two hundred mile limit, for parts of the banks and therefore portions of the fish stocks lay outside that area and uncontrolled foreign fishing there could have profound effects on the resource within the Canadian zone.

All together, the federal government put forward a policy of cautious management. LeBlanc had harsh words for "under the table" joint ventures, and condemned the provincial arrangement with the West Germans as "a quick deal to make a quick buck." In a vivid but rather curious turn of phrase he expressed fears that the provincial plan put forward in May would result in the "re-rape" of the fishery. He said that he had not seen the nine hundred million dollar provincial proposal for fleet expansion, but only read of it in the newspapers. Walter Carter said that it was not so much a proposal as a paper outlining the needs of the fishery that his government had put together in co-operation with the three Maritime provinces: LeBlanc would find it on his desk when he got back to Ottawa. LeBlanc said that there was no justification for building big new trawlers—the first priority should be to increase the catch levels of the existing fleet—and Carter said that this was what he had intended all along: any impression to the contrary was the product of distortion by the news media.

Cashin, speaking for the union, put forward a position consistent with the federal government's, and repeated that the fishermen must be part of the policy-making process, saying that if they were not included they could become the "most militant workers in Canada." Newspaper reports carried photographs of LeBlanc chatting amiably—though separately—with Carter and Cashin. All around, it seemed to be accepted that the conference had established the basis for a policy, and that the policy involved a "tilt towards the inshore fishery." Before the month was out, however, the controversy was raging again, as heated as ever.

At the end of December it was announced that the West German company that had been involved in the 1977 joint venture, catching northern cod, wanted to buy a fifty-one per cent interest in the fish plant operated by Ocean Harvesters Ltd. at Harbour Grace. The German firm, Nordzee, was one of the largest fishing companies in the world, with a fleet of thirty-seven vessels, many of which were like the ten ships that had participated in the Newfoundland joint venture: large, ice-reinforced factory trawlers, each with a crew of fifty-five. Their onshore installations in the German cities of Coxhaven and Bremerhaven employed about nine thousand people. The Germans were facing some problems of their own, having recently been excluded from Icelandic and Norwegian waters. In turn, Nordzee was a subsidiary of the giant multinational Unilever Corporation with head offices in Rotterdam.

Harbour Grace and Unilever had been introduced to one another before. Back in the mid-1960s, the multinational's British marketing subsidiary, Birdseye Foods, had bought the fish plant there from Northeast Fish Industries Ltd., owned by members of Premier Frank Moores's family. The plant was then a seasonal operation, processing inshore fish. With government assistance, Birdseye renovated the plant, brought in a fleet of trawlers, and began to operate it year-round. After a few bad years, Birdseye sold the trawlers to Bonavista Cold Storage and pulled out. The renovated plant passed through government hands and was sold again—at a considerably lower price, it is said, than Birdseye originally paid for it—to members of the Moores family. When Nordzee made its offer, the plant was operating again on a seasonal basis, managed by its principal shareholder, Alex Moores. The German company proposed to use its big trawlers to put it back into year-round operation.

The catch, of course, was that the deal depended upon the federal government. The take-over would have to be approved by FIRA—the Foreign Investment Review Agency—and trawler licences would have to be assigned by the federal Department of Fisheries presided over by Romeo LeBlanc. The provincial government did not immediately give public endorsement to the plan, but it was clear that they liked it. Walter Carter said that he was not trying to "defend" the proposal, but felt that it had "some excellent points." Canadians, he said, were not investing in the fishery. "So what [should] Newfoundland do? Suck its thumb and wait . . . ?" The federal minister responsible for FIRA told the press that Premier Frank Moores had already called on him back in November to alert him to a proposal involving West Germany that would be coming up, and to argue for leniency for investment plans in the Newfoundland fishery.

Within a few days, the provincial government's support for the Nordzee proposal was made clear in statements by the premier and Development Minister John Lundrigan, the man who, as an MP, had inspired Prime Minister Trudeau to use in the House of Commons the words that he later translated for the public as "fuddle duddle." Their comments were strongly seconded by John Crosbie who had, by this time, resigned his provincial seat and been elected to the House of Commons in Cashin's old riding of St. John's West. The union held an emergency meeting and, to no one's surprise, came out forcibly against the take-over. Their statement referred to the province's history of experience with foreign investment all of which, they said, had been undertaken "in the name of jobs and of making Newfoundland a better place to live in. All that they have done has further held us up to ridicule in the world and . . . further undermined our confidence in ourselves." The responsibility for this, the union statement said, rested with "political leaders . . . who have been the handmaidens of our economic exploiters...who betray us and sell out our resources."

The war over fisheries policy was in full swing again, and the union was in the vanguard of battle.

The NFFAWU position was not quite unanimous. The plant workers' committee in Harbour Grace favoured the take-over, a position that the union executive described as "regrettable but understandable." Like most other areas of Newfoundland, Harbour Grace was desperately short of employment, and various promoters of the scheme were predicting that it would create jobs—some claimed as many as twenty-five thousand, including those created indirectly. Recognizing the appeal of such expectations, the union mailed out a position paper to town councils, chambers of commerce, citizens' groups, and unions, offering arguments in contradiction of the claims being made by proponents of the take-over. They also put their objections directly to FIRA and to Romeo LeBlanc. Presumably, they also put them to Don Jamieson, who came out with a position paper that, while not referring specifically to the Nordzee proposal, made clear his opposition to foreign take-overs in the fishery. At the end of January, a month after the scheme was first made public, the union took the unprecedented step of buying thirty minutes of time on the privately-owned television network for Cashin to deliver its message. The presentation was in marked contrast to the pugnacity and the savage one-liners that had characterized so many of his previous appearances in the media during conflicts with government and fish companies. Cashin was calm and almost professorial as he led his listeners through a review of the history of Newfoundland development efforts, explained the problems of fisheries management, and drew conclusions that showed the Nordzee proposal to be a crucial point in the development of fisheries policy. His air was much more that of the statesman than the union leader as he appealed to Newfoundlanders to take the opportunity "for once, to become masters of our own destiny."

In past conflicts the union had commonly been accused of drumming up emotional responses around matters that government and companies characterized as needing sober, practical judgement, and several times during the Nordzee controversy the premier had made the same accusation. With Cashin's half-hour television address, however, the position was neatly reversed. *The Evening Telegram*, never an enthusiastic backer of the union, remarked editorially that among all the many opinions offered on the subject the union president's "stands out as a rational and logical statement based on knowledge and fact." In contrast, it was those who favoured the proposal who appeared emotional and ill-informed.

After the broadcast the arguments continued, but they had a somewhat different tone. The proponents of the Nordzee scheme were on the defensive. The federal agencies deferred decision, asked for more information, pondered further. Finally, in August, nearly eight months after the plan had first been made public, Nordzee announced that they were giving it up. By that time the announcement was an anticlimax, and the union was neck-deep in another controversy, this time involving some joint ventures of its own.

The new dispute had its beginnings late in 1977 when some Polish trade officials approached the union with a proposal for buying fish directly from Newfoundland fishermen. The Poles had operated an arrangement of this kind in Nova Scotia that year, buying herring through a fishermen's co-operative in the Bay of Fundy: they were pleased with the results and interested in expanding the operation to other areas and other species. Cashin says that he felt that such an arrangement would be best handled through the fish companies, though with union participation, so he referred the Poles to the Fisheries Association, who apparently turned it down. In March of 1978, a Bulgarian trade representative came to the union with a similar proposal, and this time the union decided to pursue it on their own.

The Bulgarians were interested primarily in mackerel and to a lesser extent in squid, both species that were not greatly in demand by Newfoundland fish plants. The union negotiated a contract under which the Bulgarian fish company, Ribno Stopanstvo, would send five large factory trawlers into selected Newfoundland bays to take the fish from the fishermen directly over the side of the ship—hence the term by which the arrangement came to be called: over-the-side sales. The union would provide weighmasters to oversee the transfer of fish, would receive payment from the Bulgarians, and would pay the fishermen, keeping back a portion of the price for overhead costs. In short, the union was proposing to go into the fish business, and on a considerable scale—the contract was for twenty-two million pounds of mackerel and three million pounds of squid.

The contract was submitted to the federal Department of Fisheries and Oceans for approval in April. In addition, the union asked that the department agree to act as arbitrator if disputes should arise, and to underwrite any losses due to short-falls in landings. Within a very short time, the federal department gave its approval. Shortly after that, the union concluded a similar arrangement with a Swedish company, Joint Trawlers Ltd., that was acting on behalf of a fish company in the USSR: this contract was also given federal approval.

Suddenly, the union was plunged into a scramble of activity, all of it unfamiliar. Bill Short travelled to Nova Scotia and to Scotland to inspect vessels engaged in over-the-side sales in those places, and Max Short—the union's northern business agent, and no relation—canvassed the outports for the best locations. On July 25 the first Bulgarian vessel arrived and was assigned first to York Harbour on the West Coast, and then, when catches were unsatisfactory, to Virgin Arm on New World Island in the northeast. Everyone involved had a lot to learn, and it had to be learned quickly. Bill Short remembers the confusion of the first transfers of fish:

> They only had the one weighing machine, and it had a little dial on it like the face of an alarm clock. They'd haul up a load of squid, and that little dial would be up there hangin' at the end of this boom, and we'd be peerin' up at it to read it.
>
> Not only that, but it was in kilograms. The boys in the boats didn't know what in the name of God was a kilo—they was sellin' in pounds. So some fisherman would come in with a load of fish and it would weigh up to about half what he thought he had, and he'd figure he was bein' cheated.
>
> And there was Max, tryin' to keep track of it all with a pencil on a bit of brown paper . . . after that he got a school exercise book, but it was pourin' down with rain and there was no shelter on the deck. That exercise book swole up to twice the size it was when he started, and the pages all stuck together . . .

As more ships arrived, Bulgarian and Russian, the confusion was sorted out. The union hired Kevin Carroll, an ex-school teacher who had been a member of the town council in Marystown during the trawler strike in 1975, to oversee the operation. Checkers and weighmasters were placed aboard the ships and a proper receipting system was instituted. During the year the union sold fish to nine foreign vessels. Carroll issued seventy-eight hundred separate cheques to twenty-three hundred fishermen. The Bulgarians were paying 10.2 cents a pound for squid and 8.2 cents for mackerel; the Swedes paid 14.5 cents a pound for both. The union paid the fishermen 9 cents for squid and 6 cents for mackerel. Both prices were slightly above what the fish plants were paying, but the main advantage of the scheme was that it gave fishermen a chance to sell fish that they would not otherwise be able to sell:

the fish plants would take only small quantities of squid, and in past years most of the mackerel caught was funnnelled into offal machines for fish meal, and brought the fishermen only 1 1/2 cents a pound. The part of the price that the union retained was to pay for the costs of administration, and the disposition of any surplus was to be decided later by the fishermen at the union convention.

The fish companies were vociferous in their outrage. A delegation went to Ottawa to complain to Romeo LeBlanc and returned to say that LeBlanc had "aligned himself with the union" and "treated the industry with contempt." Among other things, they charged that the minister had waived for the union a number of regulations that bound the companies in their own joint ventures. LeBlanc defended his position coolly, saying that the sales to foreign vessels would not harm the companies because they involved fish that the plants would not buy anyway: "Since Newfoundland fishermen are without obvious markets for squid and mackerel, I intend to authorize these deals." Some plant operators charged that they could not get squid or mackerel from the fishermen when they wanted them, but this was put down to localized action by fishermen expressing their resentment of past treatment at the plants. There was enough of both species for all, and in most areas fishermen happily sold their catch to plant or foreign vessel impartially when they could.

Cashin, for once on neither the attack nor the defensive, fielded company criticisms not exactly with detachment, but with a rather lofty air. "For years they've accused me of being a socialist," he said. "Now we're engaging in a little free enterprise and they scream bloody murder." When the companies charged that the deals would interfere with traditional squid markets—mostly in Japan—he replied that the union's contract with the Europeans included an agreement that the squid would not be allowed to enter those markets, and then drew attention to a little-publicized joint venture between the companies and Japanese interests for the catching of twenty thousand metric tons of squid offshore. When the companies complained that the NFFAWU was making a profit, he blandly said that the union would open its books on the squid and mackerel deal if the companies would do the same, suggesting that the latter were making windfall profits from their venture without putting money into the hands of Newfoundland workers.

The provincial government took no great part in the debate, but the NFFAWU crossed verbal swords with John Crosbie, whose affection for the union's president had not been increased by the fact that Cashin had supported his NDP opponent, Tom Mayo, during the campaign in St. John's West. Crosbie questioned why the federal government would allow the union to deal with communist countries but had turned down the West German proposal. Cashin, still turning the tables, branded Crosbie as "hysterical" and in an open letter to him took a superior and almost patronizing tone, telling him to check his facts and do his homework before commenting. Crosbie retaliated by calling LeBlanc Cashin's "puppet" and in a letter of his own challenging Cashin to reveal his true political colours, slyly referring to him and the federal minister as "comrades." Overall, the controversy served to solidify the general impression of an alliance between the union and the federal Liberal government against the Conservatives and the province.

Over-the-side sales of squid and mackerel were continued in 1979, and altogether put about six million dollars into the hands of the fishermen and nearly a million into the coffers of the NFFAWU. The union's share was used to set up a health and welfare fund for inshore fishermen, providing them benefits similar to those embodied in collective agreements for plant workers and trawlermen. Each year since then the union has engaged in over-the-side sales to foreign buyers, though not on the scale of those first years.

While arguments over the union's entry into the fish business were going on, the government began issuing the first portions of a six-volume, thousand-page report entitled *Setting a Course: A Regional Strategy for Development of the Newfoundland Fishing Industry*, the product of a

$680,000 study by a mainland consulting firm.

The early volumes noted that there had been a general improvement in the industry since the crisis of 1974, in both landings and values, and that between 1976 and 1978 people "with limited access to employment opportunities in other sectors of the economy" had been entering the inshore fishery in increasing numbers. It also noted that much of the involvement of both levels of government in the industry had not been the result of long-range planning, but rather of *ad hoc* intervention at times of crisis, resulting in a confusing jumble of programmes by different levels and departments, and no clear line of development. The culmination of the study, of course, was to be a coherent strategy, laying out plans for the coming five to six years.

In November, Fisheries Minister Carter held another conference in St. John's to introduce the final two volumes of the report, detailing the government's plan. The slogan, "Fish is the Future," echoed that of the 1977 gathering. Households around the province received a glossy, twenty-page brochure with that title, produced by a public relations firm, in which the highlights of the plan were described in enthusiastic prose and generously illustrated with colour photographs. Its introductory message from the minister, accompanied by his picture, ended with a one-sentence paragraph: "The future is ours at last." Those words were repeated on the final page of the brochure over a full-page photograph of a golden-haired child watching a group of fishermen hauling a cod trap.

The conference was attended by a hundred selected fishermen and sixty-odd observers from government and fish companies. With both federal and provincial elections in the offing, political undertones and overtones were very much in evidence. Some of the fishermen complained that the NFFAWU had not been consulted in the process, and that the government had hand-picked the delegates. Even so, when Premier Frank Moores addressed the conference and gave the union credit for the improved conditions of the fishermen, he was roundly applauded. The delegates also complained that they had not been given time to consider the plan: they had not seen the two bulky final volumes of the report until the evening of the conference.

Evening Telegram columnist Wick Collins was even more pointed in his criticism, saying that the fishermen-delegates had been presented with "a complicated program which has already had cabinet approval," rendering any consultation meaningless. As a conference, he said, the gathering was "very much a washout," but he had a more damning indictment than that to offer. He pointed out that although the workshop sessions with the fishermen were closed to the press, a team from a mainland public relations company was circulating with cameras, filming material for use by the Progressive Conservative party in upcoming elections, an action he described as "one of the dirtiest tricks pulled by the PCs in their six years in office."

The development plan itself was sweeping. This time there was stress on a balance between offshore and inshore, but the emphasis was still very much on expansion. The numbers of all types of catching vessels were to be increased and many existing vessels replaced: among other things this would call for the building of over four hundred new longliners by 1985. There was to be gear and boat insurance, service centre improvement, research, and training. The centrepiece of the plan was to be a "primary landing and distribution centre" at Harbour Grace, a vast installation costing $61 million from which a fleet of new conventional and freezer trawlers would range out all year round, bringing back fish that would be distributed by trucks to plants that had been operating on a seasonal basis. The centre, quickly dubbed the "superport," would also include facilities for processing 160,000 tons of caplin annually.

As might be expected, much emphasis was laid on the jobs that would be created to ease the province's chronic unemployment problem. The Harbour Grace development was to create 2,200 of them directly and a similar number indirectly. The improved processing facilities, along with boat loans, grants, and training programmes, were to increase the number of full-time fishermen from 12,000 to 30,000 by 1985.

In total, the plan was to involve $250 million in public funds and a matching amount from the private sector. Although there was to be a provincially-owned Fisheries Development Corporation, the objective was to "create an environment where private enterprise can thrive."

In the early announcements, Carter was quoted as saying that the plan was not dependent on Ottawa: he would not be going to the federal government for new money, and part of the purpose of the plan was to achieve greater autonomy for the province in the fisheries management. Later, he indicated that Ottawa would be asked to participate in the establishment of the superport.

The overall plan was never implemented. The provincial government was already engaged in expansion-oriented programmes providing easy-access loans to encourage new entrants to the inshore fishery and to enable existing fishermen to move up to larger vessels: at the end of the year the minister announced a 260 per cent increase in the value of such loans over 1977. These programmes and others to encourage the building and expansion of processing facilities were continued in 1979. The "superport," the last of the mega-projects of the Smallwood–Moores era, was never begun. The corporation that was to run it was established, at least on paper, and land was acquired on the Harbour Grace waterfront, but by that time the political scene was undergoing some drastic changes, and the fishery was building toward another crisis.

In January of 1979, Premier Moores announced his intention to resign, and in March the minister of mines and energy, Brian Peckford, became leader of the Progressive Conservative party and premier of the province. In May, a federal election placed in office a shaky Conservative Government under Prime Minister Joe Clark. Within a week, Premier Peckford called a provincial election. Several key cabinet ministers of the Moores administration chose not to run, and on June 18 Newfoundland elected a Progressive Conservative government with a set of priorities and attitudes to resource development somewhat different from its predecessor. In both Ottawa and St. John's, fisheries policy was again—or still—open for formulation.

Things were not, however, quite as they had always been. Over the preceding five years, the NFFAWU had emerged as a major player in the policy-making arena.

Chapter 11

When it was first formed, the NFFAWU was quickly labelled in the press and in everyday speech as "the fishermen's union", and it continued to be known by that name. Its development, however, was very different from what had been envisaged by the little group of Father McGrath's parishioners who took the first tentative steps back in Port au Choix. They had set out to found an organization of inshore fishermen: the NFFAWU became a comprehensive union of fishery workers. After the initial campaign to win collective bargaining rights for inshoremen, the major battles had been fought in the plants and on the offshore trawlers. This order of events was dictated by circumstances and perhaps by the fact that industrial settings, where groups of workers sell their labour directly to companies that own the machinery of production, are the more conventional location of union activity. Contracts, wage rates and fringe benefits fall into well-established patterns in such settings. For independent fishermen owning their own boats and gear, the patterns have to be worked out.

This is not to say that the inshore fishermen had been neglected: far from it. Even before their actual membership warranted it they had equal representation in the union structure with plant workers. Much of the union's involvement in the policy dispute over northern cod stocks was on their behalf, and the over-the-side sales had put money directly into their pockets. In 1972, as the first inshore bargaining units were being formed, fishermen were receiving average prices of about six cents a pound for cod: five years later, including the two-cent federal subsidy won in 1975 and a half-cent provincial subsidy, they were getting nearly triple that amount.

However, the "fishermen's union" had not yet faced a major challenge to its strength among the people who gave it its colloquial name: the single inshore strike, at Port au Choix in 1974, had been quickly overtaken and overshadowed by the trawler dispute. To be sure, as the NFFAWU approached the end of its first decade, it was negotiating with the association of fish companies for contracts that were applied in all areas where the companies bought fish—and that meant for most of the industry. But the question of how much actual power there was among inshore fishermen—of how successfully they could resist an attempt by the companies to break their organization—had not yet been put to test.

The test came in 1980, in the biggest confrontation yet: a battle that would shut down most of the industry for most of a summer.

In the period leading up to the confrontation and all during it, government, companies, and union engaged in a complicated war of words over the state of the industry and the underlying causes of the dispute. To the uninitiated observer, the statements and counter-statements, full of numbers and estimates, were baffling. Even from the perspective of several years it is difficult to sort out details, for the fishery had undergone a series of rapid changes that made it a very different industry from the one into which the union had been born: changes that were to result in its virtual collapse. Some explanation of this background is necessary.

In previous chapters, mention has been made of estimated numbers of inshore fishermen, and of the distinction within that designation between those who operate the larger, more mobile, three- and four-man vessels called longliners, and those who fish from smaller, open boats near their home ports. The references are accurate enough, but they mask a vastly more complex reality.

The inshore fishery is really several fisheries, involving a wide variety of boats, gear, and marine species. Invertebrates—scallop, lobster, and crab—are taken with specialized gear in designated areas. Salmon are caught in gill-nets during strictly limited periods. In some areas, longliners specialize in herring. Traps and seines are used for mackerel and squid. But the major product—the species that in good years keeps the plants operating and gives work to the processors—is cod. They may be taken on jiggers or on baited hooks, but the highest volume of production comes from gill-nets and traps.

Most of the inshore fishery is prosecuted during the summer months, when the bait-fish come to the inner waters and the cod follow, reaching a peak in July or August. The fisherman's activities are governed by the seasonal movement of the fish: to make money he must produce at the highest possible volume when the fish are available. In good years, this leads to the problem of "glut"—fishermen bring in more fish than the plants can handle; fish deteriorate in quality while waiting to be processed; loads of fish must be dumped when the plants are blocked.

The highly seasonal nature of much of the resource, and adverse winter conditions of weather and ice for much of the province mean that most inshore fishermen cannot work the year round. The larger and more mobile longliners can move from area to area and from one fishery to another as the seasons change—indeed, many must do so in order to justify the capital involved in boat and gear. Others, especially the small-boat operators, may work for only a few months, through the periods of peak productivity. Thus, when estimates are given of the numbers of inshore fishermen, they include some who fish for ten months or more, in a year-round operation, many more who fish for four or five months, and others who fish only during the peak periods of the summer. Unemployment insurance arrangements reflect these patterns: inshore fishermen may draw benefits only from November 5 to May 15.

Obviously, too, these very different sorts of fishing enterprises involve very different levels of investment. The larger longliners might cost a half a million to a million dollars. They may employ sophisticated electronic and navigation and fish-finding equipment, and use extremely large numbers of expensive crab-pots, or gill-nets. Such vessels must produce continuous high volumes of fish to repay their investment and provide a return for their owners and the sharemen who operate them. The smaller vessels represent correspondingly smaller capital investment, down to the home-built open boat with an outboard motor using gear largely made up by the fisherman himself. Thus, the generic term "inshore fisherman" covers a range from quite large business enterprises to individuals with only a few thousand—or even a few hundred—dollars worth of equipment who work at it for a brief period in midsummer.

From quite early on, governments have tried to protect some marine resources by such measures as catch quotas, closed seasons, and limits on types and amounts of gear. In 1967, the federal government also began to limit access to certain species—notably lobster, salmon, and later herring—by regulating the numbers of people or vessels allowed to participate. The main inshore ground-fishery in Newfoundland, however, was traditionally open to anyone who chose to engage in it: the only restriction was a long-standing set of arrangements through which fishermen in local areas annually drew lots for specified locations, called "berths" to set cod-traps or salmon nets. The fish were a "common property resource" available to all. Thus it was that the numbers of people engaged in the fishery waxed and waned in inverse proportion to employment opportunities in other sectors. For some fishermen it was a full-time occupation, pursued through good years and bad. For some it was an occupation to fall back upon when other jobs were scarce or to take advantage of when conditions were especially propitious. For others, a period of summer fishing was one part of a complicated seasonal round by which they pieced together a year's work and income—a round that could include small-scale agriculture, work at pulp-wood cutting, periods of wage-work away from the home community, spring-time seal-hunting, unemployment insurance, or any of several other possibilities. For yet others, the inshore fishery provided a supplement to income from full-time employment as, for example, a teacher or civil servant: a means of earning extra money during time off from a regular job.

In 1973, when the federal government announced its intention to adopt a licensing and limited-entry policy for the Atlantic coast fisheries, it occasioned a considerable amount of comment and some alarm. Fears were expressed that such a policy would take away what some described as their birthright—free access to ocean resources. As it was implemented, however, the licensing programme imposed limits on entry only to the large-scale offshore ground-fishery and to some of the specialized species. For inshore fishermen it was mainly a system of registration, and imposed no limits on their numbers. Almost anyone who wanted a license could have one.

As has been noted in earlier chapters, during the early years of the NFFAWU, fish stocks—especially cod—were declining off the Newfoundland coast because of over-fishing by the large foreign vessels. In 1974, by international agreement, tighter catch restrictions began to be placed on the foreign fleets, and stocks began to rebuild, making more fish available inshore. With improvements in U.S. markets and the efforts of the union, prices paid to the fishermen also increased dramatically.

Improving prospects in the fishery, coinciding with a period of narrowing opportunity in other sectors and rising rates of unemployment, led to the expansion-oriented programmes mentioned in the previous chapter. From 1971 to 1976, the numbers of people engaging in the inshore fishery hovered around the fifteen thousand mark. In 1977, the year of Walter Carter's first "Fish is the Future" conference, twenty thousand held licences. In 1979, the figure had grown to thirty-two thousand, and by 1980 it had reached thirty-five thousand.

These figures do not reflect the actual number of people engaged in fishing, and still less the number making a living at it, since even the most occasional fisherman—and some who did not fish at all—took out licences. They do, however, indicate that a dramatic increase was taking place.

They also provide the base for widely varying estimates of the "actual" numbers of fishermen. Depending on the purposes of the person doing the estimating, these could range, in descending order, from the full number of licence holders, to the numbers who actually engaged in fishing—no matter how briefly—during a given year, to the number of those who made a substantial part of their living from the inshore fishery, to the number of those who fished full-time, all year round. The union could cite the total number of fishermen paying dues, whether or not they were in the union, or the total number of card-carrying union members; in either case, they could choose a peak figure reached at the height of the season or a "weighted average" for the full twelve months. All the figures were different, and all could be used to make a point in the acrimonious disputes among government, union, and companies over who should be able to fish and for what return.

A perennial thorny problem was the question of who, among all those variously involved in fishing, should be regarded as *bona fide* fishermen. Many of the parties to the general argument agreed that professional fishermen should receive preferential access to licences and to plants, but how were such fishermen to be identified? Given the diversity of conditions around the province, it was impossible to establish a definition based on such criteria such as length of time spent fishing during the year, earnings, capital investment or even the proportion of livelihood gained from the fishery, though all of these could have some bearing. Professional status seemed to have more to do with attitude—with commitment to fishing as a way of life: with having served the informal but rigorous apprenticeship demanded by the job. A committee investigating the proposed licensing programme in 1973 was told by one hard-handed veteran than the quickest way to tell if a man was a real fisherman would be to see whether he could straighten out his fingers.

After much impassioned discussion, both outside the union and within it, the conclusion was reached that no province-wide definition was possible, but that fishermen in each area could decide. In 1980, under NFFAWU's auspices, local fishermen's committees drew up lists of *bona fide* fishermen. An appeal procedure was provided for those who felt they had been unfairly omitted. Many related questions, of course, having to do with the new entry, re-entry, disposition of licences, and so on, have yet to be resolved.

By the union's reckoning, in 1977, when twenty thousand licences were issued, there were about eight thousand *bona fide* fishermen. By 1980, there had been a seventy per cent increase in the number of licences and a fifty per cent increase in *bona fide* fishermen, for a total of about twelve thousand. At the time, the union was claiming about ten thousand inshore fishermen as members.

The processing sector also expanded in those years. With the help of government grants, loans and subsidies, existing plants were enlarged and new plants opened. In 1977, the provincial Department of Fisheries issued 150 licences to processors; in 1980, they issued 208. The new Peckford government, in keeping with its campaign to lay claim to Newfoundland's "birthright" of resources, such as offshore oil and Churchill Falls power, argued vociferously for exclusive control of the northern cod stocks. The NFFAWU, to some people's surprise, argued as vociferously against such a policy. If Newfoundland gained control of the northern cod, the union said, the other Atlantic provinces would undoubtedly want similar rights over the fish of the Gulf of St. Lawrence, which would jeopardize the livelihood of Newfoundland fishermen in the west and south, who, in fact, were catching more fish in "Maritime waters" than Maritimers were catching in what the Newfoundland government wanted to claim as Newfoundland waters.

In any case, the union argued, the provincial government had been collaborating with the large processing companies in pushing for joint ventures with European offshore catchers and for the large-vessel building programmes to supply what they termed the "resource-short" plants in the northern part of the province—plants that were operating only on a seasonal basis—in order to make them year-round operations and create more jobs on shore. This policy, the union said, would undercut the inshore fishermen, and, since there were a hundred "resource-short" plants in operation, could jeopardize existing year-round operations in the south.

While the arguments went on, large Nova Scotia-based companies—Nickerson's and National Sea Products—moved in and took over Newfoundland plants to gain easier access to the northern cod, and pressed for licences to build large factory freezer-trawlers.

In short, in spite of all the policy arguments, the regulation, and the legislation, the fishery was no more under control than it had ever been, and was drifting, almost rudderless, toward another crisis. And in the midst of it all, the inshore fisherman were about to make a stand.

As has been noted before in these pages, the early moves toward collective bargaining for inshoremen were slow and beset with difficulty. Of necessity, the process of certifying fishermen for union representation was different from that for plant workers. It began with the union signing up members among the fishermen in a particular area who were selling to a particular buyer or group of buyers. When application was made to the Department of Labour, the union and the company or companies involved each drew up a list of fishermen in the area. If a company wished to resist the process, it was in their interest to inflate their list, including as many people as possible: the union concentrated the most active and fully-committed. With provincial officials as referee, the two lists were reduced to one agreeable to both parties, which was the basis for a certification vote. In an industrial setting, a union must win such a vote by a majority of persons in what will become the bargaining unit: in effect, votes not cast are counted as negative. For the fishermen, it was required that a majority on the agreed list actually cast ballots; those who did not were ignored, and a majority of votes cast won the day. In spite of this advantage, in areas with large numbers of fishermen the process could take a lot of time and effort.

When the first inshore strike was called in 1974 at Port au Choix the NFFAWU had only five certified inshore bargaining units, covering about two thousand fishermen. In 1975, two more were added, and one in 1976. The breakthrough came in 1977. In that year six more units, covering about a thousand fishermen, were certified. Even more important, the association of fish companies agreed to have the full union contract, including the deduction of union dues, apply to all areas of the province, whether certified or not, where the union had been active and the companies bought fish. In effect, this amounted to voluntary recognition of the NFFAWU as bargaining agent even in areas where the formal certification procedure had not been completed. The contract also included a clause that would give "*bona fide* fishermen" first rights of sale during glut periods, though resolution of the problem of definition had not yet been achieved. The breakthrough on union recognition was accompanied by a record increase in fish prices.

Further increases were negotiated in 1978, bringing the price of trap-caught cod to about seventeen cents a pound. Of this figure, the companies paid fourteen and a half: two cents of it was the federal subsidy won through union efforts in 1974-75, and a half a cent was a provincial gear-replacement subsidy.

These steady and impressive gains were not to last. At the end of the 1978 season, the federal subsidy programme came to an end. Thus, in 1979, the union asked the companies to add another two cents to their price, to keep the amount received by the fishermen at least at the 1978 level. The companies offered one cent. Negotiations were protracted, and by June the union began to take a strike vote at a series of meetings in the certified areas. The strike deadline was to be August 5.

If it came, the strike would be over more than the one-cent-a-pound difference between demand and offer. Since early on, the union had been advocating a radically different way of negotiating fish prices, similar in some respects to Scandinavian practices. Their proposed system would involve three-cornered negotiations among union, companies, and government. Fishermen and companies would be required to make full, open-book disclosure of their financial position, the former to demonstrate what they needed to cover costs and make an adequate return, and the latter to demonstrate their ability to pay. The government would assess the two positions and decide whether subsidy was needed to make up differences.

Under the existing system, the union said, the companies disclosed nothing of their financial situation. It was therefore assumed that they calculated their offers in such a way as to guarantee a profit for the least efficient operations, and thus a much higher level of profit for the others. The union conceded that there might be sound social reasons for keeping less-efficient plants in operation, but argued that this should be done only after full disclosure, and that the fishermen should not be required to bear the full burden of the cost. There could be years, the union said, when the fishermen would have to forego price increases, but they should not be asked to do so unless the need for it was fully demonstrated.

While the strike vote was being taken, the companies implemented their offer of one cent, and negotiations broke off. The provincial government intervened with a suggestion that the question of how prices were to be set be put aside for study by a committee, and that prices for 1979 be settled. In July, companies and union agreed on a raise of a cent and three-quarters, and the strike was averted. Cashin predicted that it was only a temporary truce. The companies, he said, had not thought that the fishermen would vote for a strike: when they did so by an over eighty per cent majority, the companies gave in. Next year, he suggested, it might take an actual strike to convince them.

That agreement expired in April of 1980. Negotiations for a new one went on for two months before going to conciliation, and finally broke off in May, unresolved. This year the provincial government's gear subsidy was withdrawn, and the companies, while offering increases for some specialized species, proposed a price structure that would give the fishermen a cent and a quarter less for trap fish than they had received under the previous contract. The combined effect would put the prices to fishermen back to 1978 levels, and in some cases to 1977. The company proposal also included a drop of four cents a pound for crab.

The union rejected the company offer outright, pointing to the plant expansions and new plants as evidence that the companies could afford more. In June, the companies implemented their proposed price structure and served notice that they intended to stop collecting union dues from fishermen. The union began another series of meetings among the fishermen's committees, asking for a mandate for a strike.

Battle lines were being drawn for the biggest confrontation yet between the NFFAWU and the fish companies. The companies, still smarting from the union's interventions in the policy arena and the over-the-side sales, were prepared to take a hard line. The position of the fishery workers, in spite of the union's previous successes, was deteriorating. Back in 1977, the summer characterized by the NFFAWU newsletter as "probably the closest fishermen have ever come to being satisfied with the price of fish," the union said that the average earned income of fishermen who collected unemployment insurance was sixty-five hundred dollars. Since then general inflation had increased by about thirty per cent and costs of fuel, boats, and gear had gone up even more. In 1978 and 1979, according to the union, the only thing that had kept fishermen's incomes up to the 1977 level was the boom in both prices and markets for squid. Now, in 1980, they were being offered 1977-level fish prices; squid had dropped to less than half the 1979 price, and the companies had indicated that they would be buying far less of it.

The plant workers also had their problems. After their major breakthrough in 1973 they had made steady progress, but gains were counterbalanced by general inflation. For 1977, they had negotiated a three-year contract that allowed them some gains slightly above the guidelines of the federal government's Anti-inflation Board that came into force that year. When the anti-inflation measures were extended into 1979, however, the plant workers did not receive the increases they expected for the last year of the contract. By the end of 1979 and the beginning of 1980, contracts with practically all the fish plants in the province were up for re-negotiation. The plant workers hoped to make up some of the lost ground, and the companies intended to hold wage increases to a minimum.

Thus 1980 began, and half of it passed, with the union involved on several fronts in some of the toughest bargaining it had ever faced. Both leaders and membership were apprehensive about what might happen, according to Cashin, but could see no other course than to meet the challenge head-on.

The battle began with the plant workers. In June, negotiations with Fishery Products Ltd. for a contract covering nine plants had gone to conciliation. Also in conciliation was a contract with what had become the Lake Group Ltd., covering another five plants, but this one had an added complication: the union wanted a master contract for all five, as they had with Fishery Products, but the Lake Group insisted on separate negotiations for each. Bargaining was going only a little better with National Sea Products, with which the union still had its best contracts, for four more plants: their offer was better than Fishery Products', but still not satisfactory to the union. By the end of June, conciliation with Fishery Products had failed, a strike vote was taken, and the company was served notice that workers at Marystown, Harbour Breton, Burin, Trepassey, and Catalina would walk off the job in ten days. The union leadership hoped to do as they had in the past—force a settlement with Fishery Products that would be accepted by the others.

On July 2, the 250 workers at the National Sea Products plant in St. John's, impatient with the delays in their own contract negotiations and unwilling to await the outcome of the Fishery Products strike, walked off the job without notice. After three days of sometimes raucous meetings the union leaders talked them into going back to work, but once they had processed the fish remaining in the plant the company withdrew the contract offers it had been making and closed its doors, saying that the walk-out and the comments made during it by the union's plant committee chairman served as notice of a strike. The union insisted that there was no strike and that the company's action constituted a lock-out, but the plant remained closed.

On July 9, workers at the five Fishery Products plants—twenty-three hundred of them—went ahead with their legal walk-out. The thirty-eight trawlers serving the plants tied up, and their five hundred-odd crewmen, although not on strike, were also out of work.

The industry, therefore, was already in a turmoil while the inshore fishermen took their strike votes. On July 13, about fifty representatives of fishermen's committees around the province met in the Airport Inn in St. John's and voted by an eighty-eight per cent majority to exercise the strike mandate the committees had voted for.

The first actions were to be selective. Fishermen would immediately stop selling crab to plants at Bareneed, Port de Grave, Bay de Verde, and Hants Harbour; and on Monday, July 21, they would stop selling all species—which at this time of year meant mainly cod—to the seasonal plants of Fishery Products Ltd. in Port au Choix and St. Anthony. The tactic was obviously carefully planned. The crab fishermen were a relatively small and cleary-defined group, each of whom had a heavy investment in boats and specialized gear: they were also highly motivated, having been offered a fifteen per cent price cut, from twenty-seven to twenty-three cents per pound for their product. For the second part of the action, the union had turned again to the fishermen of the northwest coast: the men who had started the union in the first place, ten years before, and who had taken the first inshore strike in 1974.

The Fisheries Association of Newfoundland and Labrador was quick to respond. Bill Wells, who had been the association's lawyer in 1974-75 and was now its president, announced that if the union proceeded with its plans, the twenty-one member companies of FANL would shut down all the major fish plants in the province.

The announcements prompted the usual flurry of news media stories featuring inshore fishermen who disagreed with the strike action, predicted that it would fail, and questioned the representativeness of the process by which the strike vote had been taken. The union proceeded as planned, however, and by July 21, all of the seventy-seven plants operated by FANL members were closed, leaving only eighteen smaller plants belonging to the Newfoundland Association of Independent Fish Operators still processing fish.

With the vast majority of fishery workers off the job, the question arose of which of them were entitled to unemployment insurance benefits, strike pay, or social assistance. They were not all out of work for the same reason. The twenty-three hundred workers at the five Fishery Products plants who had walked out early in July were clearly on strike: the union provided them with fifty dollars a week in strike pay. But what of the workers at National Sea Products in St. John's? The company insisted that they were on strike, too, while the union insisted that they were locked out. The trawlermen, who had their own collective agreement, were out of work because the plants were closed, but were not on strike. As for the inshoremen, according to the union, only two small groups were on strike: the crab fishermen on the Avalon Peninsula and the ground fishermen supplying the plants at Port au Choix and St. Anthony. The rest of the fishermen—the vast majority—were not on strike, but locked out. No strike pay was available for them, but the union indicated that help might be provided in cases of special hardship.

Either way, the inshore fishermen faced a severe problem. They could not draw unemployment insurance in any case, since they were eligible only between November 1 and May 15, but for many of them—

especially the small operators—the winter UI benefits were a crucial part of their annual income. This is one of the reasons the union initially pursued the tactic of striking only a few plants and contemplated a series of rotating strikes if the dispute continued. Now, however, with practically all the plants shut down, the fishermen were threatened with the prospect of being unable to earn enough UI stamps to qualify for the next winter's benefits. Workers in the seasonal plants faced a similar problem. That threat, of course, was undoubtedly one of the reasons why the fish companies had chosen to shut down the industry.

For many inshore fishermen and their families there was a more immediate problem. Unable to fish, and without alternative sources of income, they had no choice but to apply for social assistance—and the government turned them down. The minister responsible, Tom Hickey, explained the action as an application of the same policy that had been enforced during the trawler strike of 1974-75. In the process, he made an odd, backhanded argument for the NFFAWU's influence and coverage. "I am not aware of any fishermen who are not members of the . . . union," Hickey said, and went on to note that all the fishermen, no matter where they lived, benefitted from the union's negotiations:

> We have refused these people, like others, social assistance because they have stopped fishing . . . They've absented themselves from their place of employment—their boats—and therefore, from their rights to social assistance because they are able to work.

The labour movement condemned the government action as a blatant intervention on behalf of the fish companies. Austin Thorne, secretary-treasurer of the Federation of Labour, charged that in many rural areas even the most occasional fishermen who were not members of the union, including even some long-term welfare recipients, were being denied assistance. In at least one community, Thorne said, a social worker was requiring anyone with the most remote connection with the fishery to turn in the cards that qualified them for a prescription drug subsidy. "The government," said Thorne, "is using these innocent bystanders as hostages in a dispute in which they have no part." A woman from Belleoram, in Fortune Bay, which had been affected since early July by the plant workers' strike, was quoted as saying, "Babies are pretty well dying here. There's no milk, no tea, no sugar, no nothing. All we have is fish and water."

The government, of course, rejected any suggestion that the policy constituted intervention in the labour dispute. In a strangely contradictory statement, Hickey was quoted as saying that his department would not " . . . turn a deaf ear to any individual application because of union affiliation or otherwise." The department would, however, "thoroughly investigate each case that comes to our attention," and that investigation, he indicated, would, in part, require the applicant to show that he or she was not a member of the union. Fishermen, Hickey said, would have to try everything in their power—salting, selling door-to-door, or whatever else they could do—to earn money. In response to the argument that most of the fishermen had not withdrawn their labour, but had been locked out, he observed, "You can't lock the sea."

On the day after the industry shut down, Premier Peckford called an emergency meeting of his cabinet, and on the day after that, publicly asked for a thirty-day "cooling-off period" during which everyone would return to work, and the union and companies would return to the bargaining table. The management side quickly agreed. On behalf of the union, Cashin indicated that they might be willing to accept, but only if certain conditions and safeguards were agreed to. Peckford replied that the proposed truce was in order to get negotiations going again—they would not bargain before it. Cashin expressed the union's willingness to re-open negotiations, but insisted that the strikes at the crab plants and on the northwest coast would have to continue. It was already July 23, and in thirty days the inshore fishery's main season would be nearly over. To ask the union to give up its strike action for a month, Cashin said, "is to ask us to relinquish our bargaining power."

A few days later the fish companies made a proposal for a seven-day truce during which a mechanism for ending the strike/lock-out could be discussed. The plants would re-open, the companies would begin collecting union dues again, and the striking fishermen would go back to work. This time Earle McCurdy, the union's new secretary-treasurer, replied for the NFFAWU, saying that it is customary in labour disputes to negotiate while a strike or lock-out is going on. Most of the fishermen, he said, had their gear out of the water. It would take them several days and cost them a lot of money to begin fishing, and they might have to stop again after seven days if negotiations were unsuccessful. It would be better, McCurdy said, simply to negotiate right away.

As in previous disputes, the two sides battled for public opinion. Both took out full-page advertisements in daily and weekly newspapers, and both bought half-hour segments of television time to put their case before the public. The FANL publicity showed the increases that fishermen had enjoyed since 1976, and pointed out that in 1980 both prices and volumes were down in the U.S. market. The prices to fishermen, they argued, must reflect conditions on the export market.

The union argued that the companies had benefitted from three very profitable years during which plant workers' wages were held down by government anti-inflation measures, and pointed to plant building and expansion as evidence of profitability. Even during the strike, government loans and investments in the processing sector were being announced. As for the price on the U.S. market, Cashin pointed out that about seventy-five per cent of the fish was being handled by four large companies—Fishery Products, The Lake Group, Nickerson's, and National Sea Products—that were vertically integrated, having their own companies to receive the fish in the United States. In effect, he said, they were selling fish to themselves at a price set by themselves. Union spokesmen called for nationalization of the industry. Talks between the two sides re-opened briefly, then broke off again.

In the third week of the strike, there were reports of a weakening of union solidarity at the Fishery Products plant in St. Anthony. Plant workers were said to be disgruntled by the fact that some fishermen were picketing for part of the day, then going fishing and selling their catch to a buyer for the Saltfish Corporation. The plant workers were said to have escorted a truckload of ice out of the plant for the fish buyer, and escorted a truckload of fish back in, through the fishermen's lines. The union discounted the reports, saying that the fish buyer had been induced to sell a load of fish to the plant and some moonlighters and part-time fishermen, along with a handful of union fishermen who had been "misled", had gone along. The latter group had seen the error of their ways, the union said, and would not be doing it again. Nevertheless, the St. Anthony plant continued to operate on a limited basis.

The processors apparently felt that the time was ripe to break the strike. The minister of finance, Dr. John Collins, had said that the dispute was costing the province a million dollars a day. Fishermen were losing crucial income and unemployment stamps, and were still being refused social assistance. Bill Wells announced that on Monday, August 11, the FANL plants would be open for business. The independent plant operators, who had just decided to join the lock-out, reversed their decision and decided to stay open.

Representatives of the NFFAWU's fishermen's committees from around the province, hastily assembled in St. John's for a strategy session, mulled over a difficult set of problems. Since the beginning, the union had been repeating that fishermen were on strike only at the four crab plants and the two northwest coast fish plants. They were not refusing to sell to the others, thus it was FANL, not the union, that had closed down the industry. However, if fishermen around the province went back to work when the plants re-opened, much of the momentum that had built up would be lost—which was clearly what FANL hoped would happen. Wells had announced that if fishermen refused to sell to any of the plants, they would all close again, but the union strategists interpreted the statement broadly. If the processors could force a breach of union solidarity they could gain the upper hand.

There was, however, another weapon in the union arsenal that had not yet been used. Although they had stated that fishermen would continue to sell to plants other than the six where they were on strike, the union had also said that the other plants might be subjected to rotating strikes. Union leaders reiterated this policy for the news media as the fishermen's representatives fanned out again from St. John's back to their home areas.

On Monday, August 11, the plants re-opened. In some areas, the weather was bad, and nothing happened. In Bonavista, Old Perlican, Bay de Verde, Harbour Grace, and Carbonear, fishermen picketed. Only a small trickle of fish found its way to a few of the cutting lines. On the following day, more picket lines went up. Harold Parsons, the NFFAWU representative at Carbonear, was quoted as saying that there would be no more inshore fishing that year. It was the fishermen's own decision, he said: " . . . this is a fishermen's union, not Mr. Cashin's union as some people have been led to believe." On Wednesday, August 13, Bill Wells announced that the association's plants would close again, and called for a Royal Commission or some other form of general inquiry to determine the needs of the fishermen and the ability of the companies to pay.

Of all the FANL plants only St. Anthony, one of the six where the fishermen were officially on strike, continued to process a small amount of fish. On Wednesday, August 14, about three hundred fishermen attended a rally in the town and went from the rally to the fish plant. The management reported that they were "rowdy and threatening"; Reg Anstey, the NFFAWU business agent who led them, claimed they were disciplined and well-behaved. Whatever they did and however they did it, the plant closed, and stayed closed. Over the next few days there were scattered incidents of picketing and demonstrating at the handful of independent plants still operating, and the full cabinet held a series of meetings to discuss the issue. The union laid plans for a major rally in St. John's.

On August 18, the government announced the establishment of a Royal Commission of inquiry that would be charged with establishing fish prices for the year, with investigating the whole process by which inshore prices were arrived at, and pursuing a variety of other questions relating to the fishery. It was to be chaired by the Dean of Memorial University's Faculty of Education, Brose Paddock, and to include Aidan Maloney, the chairman of the federal Fisheries Prices Support Board, and David Howley, a former provincial auditor-general. Premier Peckford urged the fishermen to go back to work, saying that any increases achieved through the commission would be retroactive, but the NFFAWU remained adamant that there would be no end to the strike until a settlement was reached. They had not been consulted on the establishment of the commission, they said, and would not go back to work without guarantees. However, representatives of the union and FANL began to meet at provincial Department of Labour offices.

On Friday, August 21, between one and two thousand people gathered on the shore of Quidi Vidi Lake in St. John's, waving signs and placards. Besides Cashin and Father McGrath, they were addressed by Dennis McDermot, president of the Canadian Labour Congress, and Ed Johnson, who had helped to bring the NFFAWU together ten years before; Tom Mayo, president of the Newfoundland and Labrador Federation of Labour, and Austin Thorne, its secretary-treasurer; fishermen Sam Anthony and Kevin Condon, each a veteran of thirty years in the boats. Jim Payne, a local folksinger, led the crowd in labour songs.

Cashin was in rare form as he recounted the events of the strike, drawing bursts of laughter and applause from the enthusiastic crowd. He ridiculed company officials, saying that they were afraid that if they gave the fishermen a few cents more they would have to forego a bottle of wine at dinner, or perhaps fly to Florida for their winter vacations by economy instead of first class. He twitted the news media for their coverage of the strike and lack of understanding of the issues. Mimicking a CBC reporter, he held out an imaginary microphone to an imaginary fisherman, asking if he wasn't tired of being on strike, and then, changing to the role of the fisherman, bellowed, "Of course we're tired of it!" To illustrate the anti-union sentiment of the government and industry, he depicted them as occupying a luxurious boat while ordinary workers struggled in the water. "If they see a hand coming over the gunwale," he said, "What do they do?" Bringing his foot down on the stage for emphasis, he answered his own question: "They *stamp* on it!" he shouted.

Turning serious and sombre, Cashin told the crowd of an ageing, diabetic working man who spent most of each year on social assistance, except for a few weeks of the summer when he worked at the only trade available to him, as an inshore fisherman, and this year was denied his social assistance. "I shall never forget that if I live a thousand years," he told the crowd in a voice full of emotion, " . . . What the government did to that innocent man was an act of inhumanity that shall never be forgiven!"

This last was a declaration of hostility toward the Conservative government, and particularly toward Premier Brian Peckford, that had begun early in Peckford's tenure and was to intensify over the years to follow, with savage attacks on Peckford becoming a regular feature of Cashin's public statements. "There is a cast of mind there," Cashin said, "that will have to be dealt with, but that is a fight for another day."

Returning to the main theme, Cashin reminded the crowd that the plant workers' strike, going on since early July, was still to be settled. As for fish prices, he suggested, they could expect a breakthrough soon. Picking up another of his familiar themes, he told the crowd that one of the weaknesses of Newfoundlanders is that they confuse talking with action—"talk is the orgasm," as he frequently phrased it. People paid too much attention to the media battle, but the reality is the actual negotiation, and that was going on. It might take another twenty-four hours, or forty-eight, or even a couple of weeks, he said, "But either way, we've got 'er won!"

The excited crowd finished the rally with a motorcade to the offices of Fishery Products and of FANL, a few doors away, where they piled placards and picket signs on the lawn. Before dawn the next morning, an interim agreement was reached, pending the report of the Royal Commission, and the five-week strike *cum* lock-out was effectively over. The speech had been vintage Cashin, and the union had indeed "got 'er won," but the settlement was not what the fishermen and the union leadership had hoped for at the beginning.

Settlement of the plant workers' strike against the five Fishery Products plants took another month. Although they had been out since early July, morale among the strikers remained high. Their counterparts at plants that went back to work with the end of the lock-out voluntarily paid extra dues to supplement strike pay, and in September the strikers were jauntily signalling their willingness to stay out all winter if necessary by displaying signs reading, "No picket duty on Christmas Day, Boxing Day, and New Year's." The contract signed at the end of September was a good one, giving raises of $2.00 to $2.50 over thirty-two months, and improving holidays and overtime provisions. The lock-out at the National Sea Products plant in St. John's took another few weeks to settle.

After it was all over, the union leadership hailed the 1980 strike as a victory on a par with Burgeo and the trawler dispute of 1974-75. The claim had some validity. As on the other occasions, the very existence of the NFFAWU—at least as a union of fishermen—had been at stake, and the union had survived. If the companies had succeeded in their tactic of unilaterally setting fish prices and refusing to collect dues from fishermen, there would have been little left to show for ten years of union organizing. However, whereas the other major strikes had produced significant immediate gains, the victory in this one had been primarily defensive. The plant workers had made respectable gains, but the interim settlement of fish prices, amounting to about a half a cent a pound above the company offer, was decidely disappointing.

At the union convention in November, Cashin also presented this as a victory of sorts: it had come, he said, after the companies had spent the summer maintaining that they could not afford "another nickel," and the negotiated increase represented about "forty million nickels" to the fishermen. He did not, however, complete the arithmetic by working it out on a *per capita* basis, and the union newsletter later described it as "admittedly a token increase." Although Cashin stressed that it was an interim agreement and that the fishermen could still strike again if they did not like what came out of the Royal Commission, throughout his speech there were ominous hints that it might be some time before the fishermen would regain the sort of prices they had had in 1978. The Commission might reveal that between fishermen's needs and the ability of fish companies to pay there existed a gap too great for government to bridge. Even if that should happen, however, he said, the union would still have won a point of principle of great significance for the future.

The report of the Paddock Commission did not provide a "Magna Carta" for inshore fishermen as the Harris report had done for the trawlermen. Its first phase, at the end of 1980, concluded that the companies could not pay more for fish. The second two phases, published in the fall of 1981, confirmed some of the union's claims that fishermen, even in the bumper year of 1979, had been in a precarious financial position, but it offered little in the way of solutions to their problems.

In any case, by that time the issues it was addressing were increasingly in the realm of the academic, for the whole Canadian east-coast fishery was in a state of near-collapse. A combination of the effects of overextension during the expansion period, heavy indebtedness, poor U.S. markets, and high interest rates led to bankruptcies, plant closures, and bank foreclosures. Inshore fishermen who had received government grants and loans and sunk their own capital into larger vessels could not catch or sell enough fish to keep up their payments. While the grants and loans were being issued—as Cashin had warned in a speech to the St. John's Rotary Club in 1980—no one had been calculating how much fish the boats would have to produce, and at what price, in order to make them pay. In 1981, they were finding out the hard way.

The continuation of that sequence of events—the collapse, the federal Royal Commission that investigated it, the enforced re-structuring of the processing industry and its aftermath—is material for another book of a different sort. The purpose of this one has been to tell the story of the building of the NFFAWU, and the strike of 1980 marks the culmination of a phase in its history.

A signal of a new phase—and a continuation—came in the fall of 1981, when amid the confusion of the growing fishery crisis it was announced that the Newfoundland fishermen's union was to incorporate its first members outside of the province. Ten years before, its international parents had played a part in thwarting the efforts of the UFAWU of British Columbia to represent the trawler crews at Petit de Grat in Nova Scotia. In September of 1981 the Petit de Grat trawlermen and plant workers became part of the Newfoundland union. Other mainland fishery workers were to follow. Father McGrath had taken leave from his parish duties to work full-time with the union for what turned out to be a three-year stint, and for a time he and Cashin were on the road again, this time with a lot of people and a large and powerful organization behind them on the other side of the Cabot Strait. Helping with the organizing in Nova Scotia was a young fisherman who had been an altar-boy serving at McGrath's Masses back in Port au Choix in 1969.

Chapter 12

The story of the NFFAWU has been described by one academic authority as "nothing short of amazing." In a decade, it grew from unprepossessing beginnings as a parish organization to one of the largest, most comprehensive unions of fishery workers in the world. By contrast, its nearest analogue in Canada, the UFAWU of British Columbia, was the end product of nearly fifty years of struggle. In the Maritime provinces, in spite of militant and politically-informed efforts at organization going back to the 1920s and 30s, no comparable union has emerged, and it seems likely that when comprehensive union organization comes to the fishery in the Maritimes it will come through the expansion of the NFFAWU.

There was little in the situation of the Newfoundland fishery in 1969 that would have led anyone to predict such success. By most measures, the industry was among the most backward in the country. The labour force was scattered, poor, politically conservative, and virtually captive, since there was no alternative employment in most of the fishing communities. There was also practically no tradition of democratic local organization, and little history of organized resistance to established order to draw upon—apart from the ambiguous lessons to be learned from the Coaker movement. It could be said that the NFFAWU was built from scratch, and its building blocks would not have been judged the most likely for the purpose. Besides being widely scattered, and representing at least three distinct interest groups in the industry, its constituents were divided by community, regional, and religious boundaries, their outstanding characteristic a hardy individualism and self-sufficiency.

Explanation of the growth of social movements has traditionally focused on two main themes: on the dissatisfaction that people have felt that leads them to question their existing situation in the first place, and on the process by which their individual dissatisfactions are mobilized and given collective expression. There is little need to stress the dissatisfaction of Newfoundland fishery workers in 1969. They had been dissatisfied in 1908 when they rallied to Coaker's banner, and after all the social, political and technological change of the sixty years that followed they were still at the bottom of the pyramid. Whereas in Coaker's day the fishery, however harsh and demanding, was the centre of a way of life, it had become ever more peripheral, at the mercy of forces that were difficult to understand and apparently impossible to control.

That there was dissatisfaction is obvious, but is equally obvious that disssatisfaction does not by itself produce a movement for social change—if it did, the history of labour organization would be very different. The success of the NFFAWU must be explained by the coming together of a number of key factors; a conjunction that was partly fortuitous and partly the result of skilful management, partly the product of the same social forces that have led to union organization in other industries in other places, and partly the product of particular features of Newfoundland society and culture.

To begin with, the union was born in a larger social climate favourable to the emergence of challenges to existing order. Newfoundland had passed through thirty years of social change during which an isolated, traditional society had been exposed with increasing intensity to influences and examples of other, more affluent places. For twenty of those years, since confederation with Canada, her people had undergone a "revolution of rising expectations" fed by mass communication media and their own political leaders. And Newfoundland, though on the periphery, was after all a part of the industrial western world. While the cumulative effects of her own recent history were reaching a peak she was also experiencing the broader social upheavals of the 1960s. In the latter part of that decade, and in the early 1970s, as one newspaper columnist put it, Newfoundland entered "the age of protest." From the stream of transient youth in beards and backpacks who hitch-hiked across the continent, a trickle found its way across the Gulf of St. Lawrence. A handful of young American war-resisters found in Newfoundland a field of social action on a scale more manageable than the one they had left behind. In a bureaucratized Canadian version of China's cultural revolution, the federal government provided funds for groups to attack established institutions, perhaps in the hope that most of the institutions attacked would be at a different governmental level. In St. John's, talented young writers produced a radical/populist monthly newspaper, the *Alternate Press*, and talented young actors formed the

Mummers' Troupe, the first of several socially-critical theatre groups. In scores of rural communities, field workers from the Company of Young Canadians, Frontier College, and most particularly from Memorial University's Extension Division, fostered community action to demand—and sometimes to resist—social change. On the Great Northern Peninsula, before Father McGrath was posted there, the Northern Regional Development Association had begun its work, and on Fogo Island communities threatened with resettlement started a fishing and boatbuilding co-operative that is still flourishing—outside the NFFAWU.

At the outset, then, the Northern Fishermen's Union was merely one of many organizations of protest, and its early growth was fuelled in part by the general atmosphere of social action. In its transition from local protest movement to province-wide organization, a factor of great significance was the financial backing of the Amalgamated Meat Cutters and Butcher Workmen. The wide dispersal of the potential membership in small communities, many of them accessible only by difficult roads or not accessible by road at all, meant that organizing was time-consuming and costly. Earlier efforts had been hampered by a lack of resources to overcome this obstacle. The initial formation of the Federation of Fishermen had been possible only because the provincial government paid for the first convention, and its continuation was made possible only by the annual government grant. The early independent unions of plant workers were too small to generate enough money for much expansion or for backing protracted strikes; what common contact they had was through central labour bodies that themselves operated with severely limited resources. Even when the meat union first began its organizing drive among Newfoundland fish plant workers in 1968 the funds allocated for the purpose were not sufficient to support a major effort, and much of the money generated by the local unions was spent in maintaining their own structures.

McGrath and Cashin began organizing for the Northern Fishermen's Union without salaries, and the union members, recognizing the problem of inadequate funding, set themselves dues at a surprisingly high rate. Even so, as the organization spread beyond McGrath's parish, in the absence of any means of instituting a check-off system the collection of dues presented an almost insuperable problem. In any case, when the campaign to gain and then to implement collective bargaining rights developed into such a lengthy struggle, it is questionable whether enough fishermen would have been willing to continue paying dues without receiving the usual demonstrable benefits of union membership. McGrath, Cashin, and the union's leaders in Port au Choix were well aware of the problem, and were able to convince the headquarters of the international of the need for heavy initial subsidization. The successively renewed fifty thousand dollar grants, the supplying of mainland personnel for assistance in organizing, and the provision of strike pay—especially during the crucial strikes at Burgeo, Marystown, and Bonavista—constituted an essential base for the organization. Even after all this expenditure, and after five years of the union's life, the NFFAWU was in extremely precarious financial condition during the trawler strike of 1974-75. In short, it had to win its major battles before it could become a self-supporting institution, and it seems most unlikely that it could have won them if it had been dependent solely upon the money that could be generated locally.

This heavy outlay of money by the international was almost unprecedented, and it seems to have been motivated by two main factors. Part of the motivation was undoubtedly a desire to contain and forestall the efforts of the UFAWU of British Columbia in Nova Scotia. In spite of the BC union's exclusion from the CLC, it had some powerful support among elements in the labour movement in the Atlantic provinces. The Northern Fishermen's Union, if it was to expand, had clearly to seek outside support, but it had rebuffed an overture from the Meat Cutters' international representative in Newfoundland and had offered moral support to the strikers in the Strait of Canso. If a link were to be made between the NFU and the UFAWU, and particularly if the NFU were to turn its attention to trawlermen as well as inshore fishermen, the BC union's hand might have been greatly strengthened. It was therefore very much in the interest of both the Meat Cutters and the CLC to offer the NFU an attractive proposal for a merger, even over the opposition of the international union's own local representative.

In taking this action, however, the international needed to have some assurance that the union they were backing had a reasonable chance of success. This they found in their assessment of the leadership potential of Cashin and McGrath, and subsequent events have proven that assessment correct. Even though the NFFAWU is a branch of an international union, and even though it frequently has presented as much a threat to the local establishment as did the IWA in 1959, there is a crucial difference: the central figures in its leadership are Newfoundlanders, with roots as deeply embedded in the society as those of any of their opponents. In spite of efforts like Spencer Lake's to identify the union with external forces, the NFFAWU has maintained an image as a quintessentially Newfoundland organization. Its success rests as heavily upon respected local leaders—its business agents and local officers—as it does upon the two central figures of its early development, but it was the charismatic appeal of McGrath and Cashin that was able to pull those local leaders together in the first place, and the two have continued to provide a central identification for both union members and general public. Their leadership is powerfully symbolic: representatives of two of the over-arching institutions of Newfoundland society—religion and politics—doing battle with the third—the merchants—on behalf of the common people.

Every union leader must become skilled at the practical exercise of institutional politics, but few have Cashin's experience of holding elected office, and fewer still combine this with legal training. He has been able to exercise his skills on behalf of the union in the wider political arena in a manner that no other labour leader in Newfoundland—and perhaps in Canada—can match. While keeping observers guessing about his intentions, he did not allow his political contacts to lapse, and they gave him access to channels of communication that a union leader rising from the ranks would have no opportunity to develop. Similarly, McGrath's clerical position in a society that maintains a strong respect for religion allowed him to speak and act at crucial times in the union's history with a moral authority beyond that of the ordinary labour representative.

Their leadership in both its symbolic and practical dimensions, combined with the financial backing of the international, allowed the NFFAWU to develop a style and tactics that were ideally suited to its social milieu. In many industries, emotional involvement with a strike is confined mainly to those directly affected and a few politically active people who see it as part of a larger sequence. Unless there is violence or the stopping of a public service, most people can remain aloof, paying little attention beyond an occasional grumble about unions "getting too powerful" or management being "too greedy," depending on the speaker's point of view. In this, the Newfoundland public is much like any other in the country, but its response to the NFFAWU was not in the conventional mode. The union did, in fact, carry through some disputes—and even strikes—that were given little public notice, but its major struggles captured the attention of the entire society, leaving few who could be unconcerned or neutral. In part this was because of the confrontational style the union adopted, but it was also because of the place of the fishery in Newfoundland society.

By the time the NFFAWU began, the fishing industry had long since lost its role as the centrepiece of the economy. It contributed only eighteen per cent of the value of export production, accounted for only six per cent of the gross domestic product, and employed only fifteen per cent of the labour force. It retained, however, a central place in the consciousness of the people—in their collective, historic sense of what Newfoundland was, and meant. For the fishing and plant-working families, the struggle for recognition and contracts were bread-and-butter issues of work and wages, but those struggles struck deep and powerful chords in the whole society. They took on an aura of mythic drama; a cultural significance far beyond their purely economic meaning.

This sense of profound significance was present on both sides, among those who supported the union and those who inveighed against it in newspaper columns and from boardrooms. Similarly, the image of the fishery workers as underdogs was validly usable by both sides: the union could be represented either as a vehicle by which they would free themselves from historic bondage or as a means by which cynical forces could exploit them for other ends. If the NFFAWU could have been convincingly displayed in the latter light, the way Spencer Lake and Peter Simple saw it, as the work of outside-influenced agitators and local malcontents bent on destroying the harmony of a valued rural way of life, its history would have been very different. The actions of governments headed by three successive premiers indicate that they were not averse to intervening on the side of the fish companies. The weight of public opinion was an important moderating factor: the parallels with the IWA that were frequently drawn were not merely empty rhetoric.

One of the reasons that the union won this battle of images has already been mentioned—the fact that its leaders were Newfoundlanders—but this is not sufficient by itself. Both Cashin and McGrath were vulnerable to being impugned, Cashin as an ambitious politician on the make, and McGrath as a naive and unworldly cleric. The public imagination was captured not by the mere fact of union organization, but also by its style. Perhaps because of its history of being peripheral and relatively powerless, Newfoundland has developed a partiality for high drama in its political life. The admired characteristics are audacity and recklessness—a willingness to risk everything on a single throw, to dive headlong into battle and emerge triumphant or go down fighting. This was the early Coaker, and the early Smallwood, and the early Peckford: cocky, brave little Davids slinging rocks at some lumbering Goliath. In the interval between Smallwood and Peckford, Frank Moores achieved something similar on the personal, rather than the political level: he had a reputation for devil-may-care rambunctiousness in his private life.

To some extent, the NFFAWU had its style thrust upon it. The initial effort to win collective bargaining rights for inshore fishermen was, by its very nature, less a conventional union struggle for recognition than a political campaign. This was followed almost immediately by the challenge of Burgeo and even if the union's leaders had wanted to pursue a different set of tactics, Spencer Lake would not have let them. In his own view, and the view he tried to project to the public, *he* was the bold champion of rural Newfoundlanders, resisting their seduction by powerful external forces—"the priests, lawyers, and gangsters from Chicago." The union had to fight for its life, and those were the terms it had to fight upon.

In the Burgeo fight, two other features that contributed to the union's ultimate success were established. Lake, like other fish company representatives who followed him, concentrated his attack on the union's leaders who were, he said, misleading and deluding its membership. Although Cashin and McGrath inevitably played a central role, strong leadership within the community and the support of the Reverend Joe Burke validated the idea that this was a people's revolt against a feudal master. Cashin has continued to be a strong central leader, but attempts from both within and without to brand him as an old-style union "boss" and the NFFAWU as "Cashin's union" have been largely ineffective.

The Burgeo strike was also important in validating a fundamental part of the union's ideology: that plant workers, trawlermen, longliner operators and their sharemen, and inshore fishermen in small open boats all belonged in the same organization. The differences of interest among those groups stressed by Fred Locking and the editorial writers are undeniably real. The rewards for their work all come from the same pot, and a work stoppage by one group deprives others of income. But in Burgeo the feudal position of the Lake family underscored their common interests: in relation to the Lakes, they were all in the same boat.

In fact, there were few other places in the province where this point could have been made so thoroughly and dramatically. The fish companies everywhere controlled people's lives and work, certainly, but the control had in many places become more modern, more diffuse, and less clearly identifiable with a single individual or family. When workers in a Fishery Products plant became dissatisfied, local managers could be replaced or delegations from the head office could descend to set things right. In Burgeo, the entire fishery was represented in microcosm. The totality of the Lake family's control, combined with their baronial style of life, made obvious the continuity between the modern fishery and the old, paternalistic system that for twenty years J.R. Smallwood had been telling people they had overcome. Disputes over differing interests within the union have not been—and could not be—completely avoided, but the Burgeo experience laid a firm foundation for the recognition of joint interests and of the value of joint collective action.

The NFFAWU has been remarkable not only for its rapid and successful growth, but also for the unique place it has held in the political consciousness of the province. From the time that it first came to public attention as the NFU it has been identified not merely as a labour organization, but also as a political phenomenon. It is this, more than anything, that has justified its description as "more than just a union." No other organization since the FPU has had its activities so closely watched, so widely commented upon and speculated about.

Many of the factors discussed immediately above as contributing to its success as a union also contributed to its peculiar political role. It was born as an organization of protest in a time of social ferment. Because of the diverse and dispersed nature of its constituency, it had to conduct its early organizing efforts in the manner of a political party soliciting support. Its main initial objective, to force a change in provincial legislation, required an overtly political campaign. The Burgeo strike, crucial to the union's survival, coincided with a pair of elections that marked a turning-point in the province's political history. And, of course, the man who came to be the NFFAWU's primary public figure was known, first and last, as a politician.

The union's leadership did not question its political dimension, but were cautious about giving it specific definition. In January of 1971, three months before the founding convention, Richard Cashin told students at Memorial University that "undoubtedly, the union will have to use some sort of political power," but he rejected any possibility that it might do so in the manner of the FPU. He did, however, suggest that it "would likely back some political party." The second issue of the *Union Forum*, published two months later, withdrew the latter suggestion. In an article answering queries that fishermen might have about the NFFAWU, it addressed the question, "Is this union mixed up in politics in any way?"

> The union is mixed up in politics only so far as any group of ordinary citizens are mixed up in politics—that's what makes our society work.
>
> If you mean *party* politics; if you mean, is the union backing any political party, the answer is no. Union members are as free as anyone else to choose their own brand of partisan politics.

By the time the third issue of the *Forum* was published, in August of 1971, the Burgeo strike was in full swing. An editorial reiterated the earlier position:

> We do not believe in getting . . . involved in partisan politics to the extent that we are going to field our own slate of candidates, and form another Fishermen's Union Party. Nor is it very likely that we will be coming out publicly for any political party or individual politician, as a matter of policy.

However, with the union engaged in a battle for its very life and with a provincial election in the offing, the matter could not be left at that. After a somewhat rambling discussion suggesting that the NFFAWU would oppose or support politicians in the measure that they represented policies beneficial to its membership, the editorial concluded,

> . . . at this particular moment we are engaged in a battle with one of this province's most powerful industrialists, Spencer Lake of Burgeo Fish Industries. Mr. Lake is a staunch Liberal. (His brother Harold, also a part of the same company, is incidentally a strong Tory.) He was appointed by the Liberal government in Ottawa to the board of directors of the Bank of Canada, and has received millions of dollars, in loans and subsidies, from both the federal and provincial governments.
>
> What are the political implications of the union in this situation? Obviously the union cannot support any party that supports a man like Spencer Lake who is violating civil liberties.

It is significant that the article ends there. In a union publication almost anywhere else in Canada, the paragraphs quoted would have led to a rousing condemnation of both Liberal and Conservative houses and a pitch for the NDP. In Newfoundland in 1972, however, this was not possible. It was not merely that the NDP was small, struggling, able to capture only a tiny percentage of the popular vote, and confined mainly to a few urban and industrial areas. More important was the fact that most of the constituency to which the NFFAWU had to appeal was also the solid back-bone of support for Smallwood's Liberal Party. According to an academic analysis of the day, based on statistics from elections since 1949, it had been the fishermen's votes that installed Smallwood in power and kept him there. The union had to put Smallwood on the spot, but it could not risk alienating its own members and potential members. In any case, there was little reason to expect better treatment from a Conservative government, should one take office. The *Forum* editorial, then, was not so much an appeal for the membership to abandon their traditional political allegiances as an appeal to the two major parties to abandon Spencer Lake.

The election of 1971, of course, did eventually lead to the un-seating of the Smallwood Liberals. Several academic analyses of the vote, however, underscore the ambiguous position of the union by showing that in spite of the furore surrounding Burgeo, districts with higher percentages of fishermen continued to be Liberal strongholds. The change in popular vote, these analyses suggest, had to do less with shifts in party allegiance than with changes in the voting public. There were increased numbers of young, better educated, more urbanized voters, and they tended to vote Conservative. One article stated that the election of 1971 " . . . has no more claim to be a 'critical election' than do the three previous provincial elections," in that there had been a fairly steady erosion of the Liberal vote going on since 1949 anyway: it just had a long way to erode—from highs of eighty to ninety percent in some areas. The union probably was a factor in the defeat of the Liberal candidate in St. Barbe South, and possibly in one or two other districts, but if so, it was only one of several factors—there was no evidence of any great union-backed swing behind the un-seating of the government.

The statistical analyses, however, do not—and cannot—take account of the impact of the NFFAWU on the society at large. The opinion has already been offered above that for Newfoundlanders in general the fishery had a cultural significance above and beyond its economic importance. This is not to say that the industry was economically unimportant: even though it had lost its central place, it was still the main—or the only—base for hundreds of rural communities. But in addition to that, even in the most urbanized segments of the society, the historic sense of Newfoundland as a fishing nation was a focal point of cultural identity. A powerful illustration of this contention is provided by the intensity of the popular reaction in the late 1970s to international criticism of the seal-hunt—the outrage and anger that was expressed even by people who had never been remotely associated with sealing. The fishermen/sealers were more than just a group of workers threatened with loss of income—they were symbols of Newfoundlanders in general as historic underdogs. It is also important to recall here that the NFFAWU never lost its popular designation as "the fishermen's union," in spite of the central role of plant workers in its structure. It is the fisherman who triggers the public imagination.

Thus, a social movement among fishermen had a ready-made cultural significance. In addition, memories of the FPU gave that significance a ready-made political aspect. The NFFAWU was spoken of and written of as a potential "third force" in provincial politics as though it were directly comparable to the FPU, in spite of the fact that since Coaker's day the total population had more than doubled and the number of fishermen had declined to less than half. For many people of all political stripes, organization of fishermen symbolized a social revolution. Many people who were young and urban at the time speak of the excitement they felt at the idea of the union and the eagerness with which they followed the story of Burgeo. If the fishermen could band together to fight the merchants then, surely, other sorts of social change were also possible.

The elections of 1971 and 1972 may have marked, as the statistical analysts say, merely the point where the balance tipped after long and steady erosion of Liberal support. However, the Liberal share of the popular vote did drop from sixty-two percent in 1966 to forty-five per cent in 1971 and to thirty-eight percent in 1972. Those young, educated, urban voters were not voting against the Liberals simply because they were young, educated and urban. Although it may seem paradoxical to people who did not live through the period, many of them voted for an at least nominally Conservative Party and against an at least nominally Liberal one as an expression of a desire for something new and progressive and hopeful, and the NFFAWU played no small part in creating the climate in which they made their electoral choice.

If this is so, then it involves another paradox—the perception of the NFFAWU as a potential political force may well have had more effect outside the union than it had within it.

In the years following, the union clashed repeatedly with Conservative provincial governments under Frank Moores and Brian Peckford, and occasionally with the federal Liberal government. Many fishery workers kept their traditional Liberal allegiances, and many others supported the PCs, but both seemed content for their union, through its leader, to act as a kind of extra-parliamentary opposition to either Ottawa or St. John's as occasion demanded. Through it all, its role was strengthened and its effectiveness enhanced by its continuing perception as a latent force which, if it were ever to be mobilized, could profoundly affect the political scene.

Cashin, in public pronouncements and at biennial conventions, continued to foster the image of the NFFAWU as "more than just a union." In a thoughful interview in 1975 he was quoted as saying, "One of the things we've been doing is encouraging some of our people to go into municipal politics . . . We need more of our people on school boards as well. It's at this level we have to work. It'll take a long time—perhaps a generation." In 1978 he told fishery workers that the union "has to go beyond the collective agreement, beyond the price of fish. It has to deal with the type of society we have. You can start with the collective agreement, but it has to go beyond that." What was never very clear was just how this was to be done.

After the strike of 1980, when Brian Peckford was building toward the peak of his popularity, Cashin's was one of the few voices raised against him. While other non-PC commentators grudgingly gave Peckford what they believed was his due, the union leader attacked the premier savagely and scathingly on every possible occasion. Cashin's detractors would say that there was more than a hint of personal jealousy in the attacks—that Peckford, with his populist appeal to Newfoundland nationalism, had pre-empted the position that Cashin had held for so long, as the man who could be premier. Even during Frank Moores's term of office, the argument goes, his tenure was widely regarded as an interregnum: the province was waiting for a new monarch, and Brian Peckford had seized the crown. Others, however, would argue that Cashin's anger arose from the frustration not of personal ambition, but of aspirations for Newfoundland—of hopes that it would develop the more liberal, open, and democratic society that he had so often spoken of so passionately. In this view, Cashin attacked Peckford not because he became premier, but because he became Smallwood.

Personalities aside, the Peckford years gave the NFFAWU much cause for frustration. In 1978, when Cashin spoke of "going beyond the collective agreement," he also looked forward to 1985 as "a time when fishermen and plant workers and ordinary people will have greater control of our industry." Instead, of course, the industry all but collapsed and was cobbled together again in a shaky new structure which retained many of thc weaknesses of the old, and the position of fishery workers deteriorated. The events of those years are too recent and too complex to be summarized here, but a final word on the union's role in politics is in order.

In December of 1984, after a summer during which it was widely and confidently predicted that Richard Cashin would be a candidate for leadership of the provincial Liberals, the NFFAWU and its president came out publicly in support of the New Democratic Party. In a provincial election in April of 1985, during which a good deal of media attention was given to the union's involvement, Brian Peckford and the Conservatives were returned to office with a reduced but still healthy majority. The lost seats went to the Liberals. The NDP did well, though not as well as its supporters had hoped—it kept the single seat it had gained in an earlier by-election, came very close to winning another, and quadrupled its popular vote. Its best showing was in urban and industrial areas: there was little to indicate that official backing by the fishermen's union had translated into very many fishery workers' votes. Again, it appeared that the union's influence had been strongest on people outside it.

It remains to be seen whether, by finally coming out in support of the NDP, the union has forfeited the role it played for so long as a potential political force. The decision was not universally accepted among the membership, and NFFAWU could fall into the position of many other Canadian unions, with the leadership backing the NDP and the rank-and-file passively resisting. Perhaps by 1984-85, with Conservative governments entrenched in Ottawa and St. John's and the Liberal Party in disarray on both provincial and federal levels, the role had played itself out in any case. On the other hand, the place of fishery workers in the popular consciousness is still strong. The fishermen's union may yet fulfill its long-imagined political potential.

On the most general level, the development of the NFFAWU was similar to that of unions anywhere—a process that one analyst has described as "a collective response to the personal experience of tradesmen whose status, skills, and bonds of community were being reduced and destroyed by the process of industrialization." Some form of unionization in the Newfoundland fishery, as Kevin Condon suggests in a statement quoted earlier in this book, was probably inevitable.

However, as Condon also suggests, the form that it took and the success that it achieved were not inevitable at all. They were the product of particular circumstances and particular forces at work in Newfoundland society at the time. The men and women who built the NFFAWU—those who are mentioned in this book and the many thousands who are not—did more than build a union. They wrote an important chapter in the history of Newfoundland, and of Canada.

Notes and References

In the notes below, numerals on the left refer to pages in the text. Sources are referred to by author and title for the first citation, and by author only for subsequent citations in the same chapter. Full publication data for sources other than newspapers are given in the Bibliography. The three periodicals most frequently cited are referred to by initials: ET — *The Evening Telegram* (St. John's); DN — *The Daily News* (St. John's); UF — *The Union Forum* (St. John's). The *Union Forum* is in two series: Volume 1 begins in 1970; Volume 1 (n.s.) begins in 1977.

Direct quotations and attributions not referenced here come from interviews conducted by the author.

PREFACE

7 Ron Crocker, ET May 26, 1970

CHAPTER 1

15 A brief history of the NFFAWU from 1971 to 1976 by Earl McCurdy, appeared in nine consecutive issues of the UF, between June, 1977 and May, 1978.

Descriptions of the St. Barbe Coast in the late 1960s and early 1970s are contained in a series of filmed interviews in the library of the Extension Division of Memorial University. See also Ray Guy, ET Sept. 28, 29, 1971; Wick Collins, ET Oct. 8 1971.

16 Northern Regional Development Association, *Report of the First Annual Conference.*

18 Scallop fishery: ET Sept. 26, 1969; Trawlers: ET Sept. 6, 1969.

19-20 Scallop price war: *Financial Post* Feb. 20, 1971.

20 Antigonish Movement: see, for example, Alexander F. Laidlaw, *The Man from Margaree.*

21 For a discussion of the crisis in the fishery in 1968, see a series of articles by Dave Butler, ET April 29 — May 3, 1968.

Reports on the 1968 tie-up: ET May 24, 29, 31; June 11, 12, 1968.

23 The ERCo case is discussed in more detail in Chapter 4.

24 Report of founding meeting: ET April 29, 1970.

25 NFF application: DN April 29, 1970; ET April 30, May 25, 1970.

Cashin interview: ET May 1, 1970.

26 Assistance to Labrador schoonermen: ET June 25, 1970.

27 UFAWU: See Harold Griffin, *A Ripple, A Wave.*

28 NFU strike: ET June 11, 1970.

29 Negotiations with Fishery Products: ET June 18, 19, 1970.

30 For a discussion of sectarian institutions, see S.J.R. Noel, *Politics in Newfoundland*, pp. 21-25.

31 Bonavista Bay meeting: ET July 6, 1970.

32 The description of McGrath's speech to the Federation of Labour is from eyewitness reports.

33 For an account of the UFAWU strike in Nova Scotia see Silver Donald Cameron, *The Education of Everett Richardson.*

NFU telegram: ET July 17, 1970.

UFAWU expulsion from CLC: Toronto *Globe and Mail* Aug. 22, 1953.

35 Rejection of UFAWU petition: ET May 18, 1970.

"Traditional enemies" quotation: *Alternate Press* (St. John's) Vol. 1, No. 1 (May, 1971).

36 For a history of the AMCBW, see David Brody, *The Butcher Workmen.* See also Hilton E. Hanna and Joseph Belsky, *The 'Pat' Gorman Story.*

37 UF Vol. 1, No 1 (November, 1970).

CHAPTER 2

39 Editorial comment: Wick Collins, ET April 30, June 25; also ET editorial June 3, 1971.

Giacomo Casanova, *History of My Life*, Vol. 1, p. 32.

The account of the history of the Newfoundland fishery depends mainly upon three papers and a book by David Alexander: "Development and Dependence in Newfoundland"; "The Political Economy of Fishing in Newfoundland"; "Newfoundland's Traditional Economy to 1934"; *The Decay of Trade.*

42 Newfoundlanders in Massachusetts: P.F. Nearly and S.J.R. Noel, "Continuity and Change in Newfoundland Politics," p. 5. The "one in six"

figure is an estimate that would not satisfy demographers. However, census figures show about 24,000 Newfoundlanders in the USA in 1930, and 26,000 in Canada in 1931. The population of Newfoundland in 1935 was 289, 588. (See Peter Neary "The Issue of Confederation in Newfoundland 1864-1949" and "Canadian Immigration Policy and the Newfoundlanders, 1912-1939.")

43 Economic dualism: See Ottar Brox, *Newfoundland Fishermen in the Age of Industry.*

Discussion of labour history is drawn mainly from William Gillespie, *A History of the Newfoundland Federation of Labour,* and Rolfe G. Hattenhauer, *A Brief Labour History of Newfoundland.*

44 Smallwood: See Richard Gwyn, *Smallwood, The Unlikely Revolutionary.*

Labour Federation oath: Gillespie pp. 61-62; Hattenhauer p. 61.

45 Gwyn p. 206.

46 Donald McDonald: quoted in Gillespie p. 108.

Smallwood labour legislation: Gillespie p. 127.

47 IWA: See Gwyn, Chapter 18; Gillespie p. 130 ff.

49 1832 fishermen's strike: Hattenhauer pp. 102-103. Sealers' strikes: Hattenhauer p. 99.

SUF: See L.L. Hodder, *A Brief History of the Society of United Fishermen.*

51 Quotation on economy from Thomas Lodge, *Dictatorship in Newfoundland,* pp. 49-50. Other sources on the political system: S.J.R. Noel, *Politics in Newfoundland;* and St. John Chadwick, *Newfoundland: Island into Province.*

1933 Commission: William Warrender Mackenzie, baron Amulree, *Newfoundland Royal Commission Report.*

52 Lodge p. 15. The present author is aware of the temptation to which Lodge refers.

Coaker and the FPU: See John Feltham, *The Development of the FPU in Newfoundland;* Ian McDonald, *W.F. Coaker and the Fishermen's Protective Union in Newfoundland Politics, 1908-1925;* J.R. Smallwood, *Coaker of Newfoundland;* W.F. Coaker, *A History of the Fishermen's Protective Union of Newfoundland from 1909 to 1929.*

55 The Coaker song exists in several versions. According to folklore authorities, none of them can be regarded as definitive. The lines quoted are a composite of several sources.

56 Coaker on Labour Party: Feltham p. 145. On Liberal party, Feltham p. 52.

57 Autocratic operation of FPU: Noel p. 148.

57-58 Change in FPU cash policy: Feltham pp. 135-136.

58 Smallwood on Coaker, p. 96.

59 Founding of NFF: J.W. Hutchings, *Proceedings of the Fishermen's Convention Held at the Gaiety Theatre, St. John's, April 2nd–April 9th, 1951*. Also ET, DN April 3-15, 1951.

Delegate's observation: ET April 6, 1951.

60 "Free of politics": ET April 7, 1951.

Smallwood: ET April 10, 1951.

Higgins: ET April 12, 1951.

Horwood: ET April 14, 1951.

61-62 Descriptions of NFF, including Smallwood quotation on p. 62 drawn from filmed interviews with J.R. Smallwood and Pat Antle, *The Federation of Fishermen, Part I* by Memorial University Extension Division.

62 Antle: See ET July 23, 1977; *Globe and Mail* May 20, 1971.

63 Labour organization in fishery: See Janet O'Brien, "Collective Bargaining in the Fishing Industry of Newfoundland."

Burin minute-books in possession of NFFAWU.

64 FPU not recognized: Maxwell Cohen, *Report of the Royal Commission on Labour Legislation in Newfoundland*, p. 85.

66 Royal Commission: Cohen pp. 95-98.

CHAPTER 3

72 Kevin Condon: ET FEB. 16, 1968.

77 Smallwood promise, Scandinavian visit: ET Jan. 6, 1971.

Norwegian system: ET Jan. 27, 1971; DN March 3, 1971.

78 Competition, NFF and NFFAUW: ET Sept. 4, 1970; DN March 3, 1971.

79 NFF Convention: ET April 12-15, 1971.

Taylor, Antle: ET April 14, 1971.

Demise of NFF: DN May 17, 1973.

NFFAWU: *Report of Founding Convention.*

80 Chesley Beck: NFFAUW *Founding Convention* pp. 40-42.

81 Cashin: NFFAWU *Founding Convention* p. 45.

81-83 Smallwood speech: NFFAWU *Founding Convention* p. 47 ff.; ET April 28, 1971.

CHAPTER 4

85 Collective bargaining legislation: ET May 21, June 2, 1971; DN June 2, 1971.

86 Letters in NFFAWU files.

87 ET May 1, 1970; Wick Collins, ET April 30, 1971; Ray Guy, ET June 10, 1971.

96 Newfoundland and Labrador Federation of Labour, *Now That We've Burned Our Boats...Report of the People's Commission on Unemployment.*

98 Cashin family: See Major Peter Cashin, *My Life and Times 1890-1919.*

99 Cashin p. 17.

100 Cashin and Lloyd: S.J.R. Noel, *Politics in Newfoundland* pp. 128-129.

101 Cashin and Squires: Noel pp. 198-199.

104 Public speaking contest: ET March 26, 1952.

105 William J Browne, *Eighty-four Years a Newfoundlander* (Memoirs, Vol. 1) and *Eighty-seven Years a Newfoundlander* (Memoirs, Vol. 2).

106 Browne made these charges in a letter to the editor, DN May 5, 1983, and expands on them in Volume 2 of his memoirs.

Election results: *Globe and Mail* Sept. 22, 1962.

Cashin maiden speech: undated clipping in ET files; later speech: ET April 15, 1964.

107 Parliamentary Assistant: ET Oct. 7, 1966.

Cabinet possibility: ET Sept. 13, 1967.

108-109 ERCo: ET Sept. 8, 9, 1969.

109 Solandt: ET Sept. 18, 1969.

110 Settlement: ET Nov. 27, 1969.

Cashin and NDP: ET Feb. 9, 19, May 1, 1970.

111 Cashin at Memorial University: ET Feb. 8, 1971; *The Muse* Feb. 12, 1971; ET Nov. 22, 1972. The line quoted does not appear in the newspaper reports, but was supplied by an eyewitness.

112 Cashin's union: ET Jan. 3, 1976; *Montreal Star* Sept. 22, 1971.

112-113 Speeches to union members, etc. from eyewitness accounts.

CHAPTER 5

115 Farley Mowat, *A Whale for the Killing.*

116 Spencer Lake: ET Nov. 6, 1970.

117 Fred G. Douglas, "A Brief History of the Town of Fortune."

118 Lake holdings data from Registry of Companies, Government of Newfoundland and Labrador.

119 General accounts of the Burgeo strike include *Alternate Press* Vol. 1, No. 4 (August 1971); Ron Crocker, ET July 2, 1971; Hugh Winsor, *Globe Magazine* July 31, 1971.

Lake quotations: ET Nov. 6, 9, 1970.

120 Text of telegrams: UF Vol. 1, No. 1 (November, 1970) p. 5.

121 Original letter in NFFAWU files; quoted in ET Aug. 6, 1971.

123 Lake: ET May 24, 1971.

124 Lake: ET June 7, 1971.

125 Cashin: ET June 9, 1971.

125-126 Strike incidents: *Alternate Press* Vol. 1, No. 4, p. 10; UF Vol 1, No. 3 (August, 1971) p. 5.

129 Burke: UF Vol. 1, No. 3 (Aug. 1971) pp. 11-12.

132 Gloucester incident: ET June 16-18, 1971.

136 Injunction: ET July 22, 1971.

137 Locking: John Joy and Brian O'Neill, "Locking and Cashin: Union Power Struggle" *Alternate Press* Vol. 2, No. 4 (June, 1972) p. 5.

139 Government assistance to Lake: ET Sept. 10, Nov. 6, 1954.

CHAPTER 6

144 Threats, bumper sticker: ET July 16, 1971.

145 ET July 16, 1971; Ron Crocker, ET July 2, 1971; ET Aug. 7, 1971; Hugh Winsor, *Globe Magazine* July 31, 1971.

146 Lake: ET Aug. 7, 1971.

Editorials: ET July 23, 26, 1971.

Sympathy actions: ET Aug. 26, 1971.

147 Federation of Labour: ET July 27, 28, 1971.

149 Richard Gwyn, *Smallwood, The Unlikely Revolutionary*, p. 289.

Cashin: ET June 9, 1969.

151 ET July 30, Aug. 3, 5, 7, 1971.

152 Wick Collins, ET Sept. 3. 1971.

Incident and response: ET July 29, Aug. 2, 19, 25, 1971.

153 Walter Stewart, *Strike!* p. 100.

154 Smallwood: ET Sept. 3, 1971.

Greene Commission: ET Sept. 7, 9, 1971.

Election call: ET Oct. 7, 1971.

155 Violence: ET Oct. 19, 20, 1971.

156 Moores: ET Oct. 20, 1971.

Greene report summarized: ET Oct. 21, 1971.

157 Lake, Smallwood: ET Oct. 27, 1971.

158 Burgess press conference: ET Nov. 1, 1971.

Lake, ET Nov. 2, 1971.

159 Peter Simple, DN Nov. 3, 1971.

	Harold Horwood, ET Nov. 2, 1971.
	Burgess: ET Nov. 2, 4, 10; DN Nov. 2, 1971.
	Moores rumours: ET Nov. 16, 17, 1971.
160	Sally's Cove: see Dave Butler, ET Dec. 3, 1971.
	Horwood: ET Nov. 3, 1971.
	Task force, Smallwood, Lake: ET Dec. 15, 18, 1971.
162	Burgess, St. Barbe, Smallwood: ET Jan. 12, 13, 14, 1972.
	Burgeo takeover: ET March 13, 1972.
163	Crosbie: ET June 28, 29, 1972.

CHAPTER 7

165	Marystown: Bob Benson, ET Feb. 26, 1972.
	Fermeuse: ET Feb. 7; March 4, 7; April 3, 1972.
166	Locking, abattoir: ET May 9, 11, 24, 1972.
168-169	Locking letters in NFFAWU files.
168	Trawler crews: ET Aug. 5, 1970.
172	Letter in NFFAWU files.
176	John Joy and Brian O'Neill, "Locking and Cashin: Union Power Struggle" *Alternate Press* Vol. 2, No. 4 (June 1972).
177	Abattoir workers: ET Aug. 19, 1972.
	Torbay fisherman: ET June 14, 1972.
	Bill Short: DN May 17, 1972.
	Contract: ET June 26, 1972.
178	Contract: ET July 8, 1972.
179	Bonavista Cold Storage negotiations: ET June 28, 30, 1972; background on strike: Ron Crocker, ET July 29, Aug. 12, 1972.
180	Ron Crocker: ET Aug. 12, 1972.
	Fermeuse: Aug. 18, 19, 1972.

181 Account of Cashin's speech from eyewitness reports.

183 Convention: Ron Crocker, ET Dec. 2, 1972.

185 Outport social structure: See Michael Gaffney, *Crosshanded: Work Organization and Values in a Newfoundland Fishery*, esp. ch. 8.

186 Labour relations: Maxwell Cohen, *Report of the Royal Commission on Labour Legislation in Newfoundland and Labrador.*

187 Editorial: *Sunday Herald* (St. John's) June 9, 1946.

188 Columnist: Ray Guy, "Newfoundlanders and Mainlanders" *Canadian Forum*, March, 1974.

CHAPTER 8

191 For a discussion of the offshore fishery, see NORDCO, *It Were Well to Live Mainly Off Fish*; also William Warner, *Distant Water.*

192 Redfish: Leslie Harris *et al*, *Report of Conciliation Board*, p. 7.

192-193 Landings and prices: Newfoundland and Labrador Treasury Board, *The Economy* Mid-year, 1972, p. 25; Planning and Priorities Secretariat, *The Newfoundland Economy, Outlook*, 1974, pp. 14-16.

193 Burin peninsula jobs: DN June 14, 1973.

Bonavista settlement: DN May 9, 1973

195 Contract: ET Nov. 19, 20, 1973.

197 Disaster: DN June 13, 1974.

198 Cashin: DN June 21, 1974.

199 Cashin: DN May 31, June 21; ET June 28, 1974.

200 Etchegarry: ET July 2, 1974; Cashin July 5, 1974.

General background on inshore strike: Earle McCurdy, ET July 27, 1974.

Cashin: ET July 12, 1974; Short: ET July 27, 1974.

201 Portugese: ET July 12, 1974.

202 Cashin: ET July 13, July 27, 1974.

Fishermen: e.g. ET July 16, 1974.

203 Tie-up: ET July 27, 1974.

205 Trawler statistics: Statistics Canada, quoted in Parzival Copes, *The Resettlement of Fishing Communities in Newfoundland*, p. 222.

207 Copies of collective agreements in NFFAWU files.

208 The observation about trawlers at sea was made by James R. Thoms in the *Daily News Fishermen's Annual* for 1982.

209 The terms "co-venturer" and "co-adventurer" were used interchangeably, and both appear in this account.

210 Unusable fish: NFFAWU *Message from the Trawlermen* p. 11.

211 More effort: DN July 13, 1974.

Earnings: Harris *et al*, p. 32.

Trawler crewman: DN Aug. 7, 1974.

212 Book losses: Copes, p. 60-61.

213 For a discussion of the 1974-75 strike, see David Macdonald, *Power Begins at the Cod End*.

Meeting: DN Aug. 5, 1974.

Booth trawler: DN Aug. 8, 1974.

214 McKinnon: DN Aug. 7, 1974.

Advertisement: DN Aug. 8, 1974.

Cashin: DN Aug. 9, 1974.

Rousseau: DN Aug. 19, 1974.

215 Industry spokesman; strikers, difficulties: DN Sept. 5, 1974.

Government plan: DN Sept. 9, 1974.

216 Harris, *et al*, p. 3.

Return to work, Cashin: DN Sept. 12, 1974.

CHAPTER 9

218 Harris, *et al*, *Report of Conciliation Board.*

219 Philpott: DN Nov. 27-29, 1974.

Cashin: ET Nov. 30, 1974.

Philpott: ET Dec. 2, 1974.

220 Crosbie: ET Nov. 30, 1974.

Cashin: ET Dec. 10, 1974.

Harris, *et al*, pp. 5-6.

221 Harris, *et al*, p. 15; p. 35.

222 Harris, *et al*, p. 73; p. 81

223 Company offer: ET Dec. 30, 1974.

Wells, Cashin: ET Dec. 23, 30, 1974.

223-224 Vote: ET Dec. 31, 1974.

224 Social assistance: DN Jan. 6, 7, 9, 15, 1975.

225 Wells: DN Jan. 10, 1975.

McKinnon: DN Jan. 15, 1975.

226 Editorials: DN Jan. 13, 15, 16, 17, 1975.

Advertisement: DN Jan. 15, 1975.

227 Cashin: ET Jan. 11, 1975.

228 Demonstration: ET Jan. 17; DN Jan. 20, 21, 1975.

229 Crosbie, Cashin, Hickman: DN Jan. 15, 22; Feb. 3, 1975.

230 Letter in NFFAWU files. Also reprinted in NFFAWU, *A Message from the Trawlermen*, pp. 30 a, b, c; and in David Macdonald, *Power Begins at the Cod End*, pp. 91-92.

231 *Message from the Trawlermen* p. 32.

Information centre: ET Jan. 20; DN Jan. 21, 1975.

232 Marystown meeting: DN Feb. 10, 1975.

233 Crosbie, Harris, etc.: ET Feb. 13; DN Feb. 13, 14, 1975.

234-235 The account of Cashin's remarks is largely from newspaper reports (ET Feb. 15; DN Feb. 17, 1975) with some additional material from the testimony of eyewitnesses.

236 McGrath telegram: DN Feb. 17, 1975.

Moores: ET Feb. 21, 22, 23; DN Feb. 24, 1975.

237 Callahan, Farrell: DN March 3, 1975.

Headline: DN March 20, 1975.

Earnings: ET March 29, DN March 31, 1975.

CHAPTER 10

239 For a concise review of fisheries policy, see NORDCO, *It Were Well to Live Mainly Off Fish*, pp. 43-85.

Immigration: W. Gordon Handcock, "English Migration to Newfoundland" p. 18.

240 Longliners: Statistics Canada, quoted in Parzival Copes, *The Resettlement of Fishing Communities in Newfoundland*, p. 219.

Report: David Alexander, G.M. Story, *et al*, *Report of the Committee on Federal Licensing Policy and Its Implications for the Newfoundland Fisheries*, p. 12.

No public investment: quoted in NORDCO, p. 48.

242 Markets and values: Geoff Hunt, ET Jan. 3, 1977.

243 Carter: DN Fishermen's Annual, May 2, 1977.

Jamieson: DN June 1, 1977.

244 Moores: DN *Fishermen's Annual*, May 2, 1977.

Cashin, Carter: ET March 17, 1977.

Development plan: UF Vol. 1 (n.s.), No. 3, p. 17; No. 4, p. 3.

245 For a background discussion of the northern cod debate see Stratford Canning, "The Hamilton Banks Cod Fishery: A Comment on the Politics of Balanced Development" ET April 2, 1977; and "Small Decisions, Golden Opportunities" ET April 16, 1977.

Joint ventures: ET Jan. 3, 22, 29, 1977; UF Vol. 1 (n.s.), No. 3, p. 17.

Proposal: ET Aug. 31, 1977.

Joint ventures: UF Vol. 1 (n.s.), No. 1, p. 11.

246 UF Vol. 1 (n.s.), No. 4, p. 3-4.

246-247 LeBlanc: DN May 20, 1977.

247 Carter: DN Aug. 26; ET Aug. 31, 1977.

248 Demonstration: UF Vol. 1 (n.s.), No. 4, pp. 5-6.

Marystown: ET Dec. 5, 1977; UF Vol. 1 (n.s.), No. 7, pp. 5-10.

249 LeBlanc: ET Dec. 1, 1977.

Nordzee: ET Dec. 29, 1977; UF Vol. 2 (n.s.), No. 1, pp. 3-9. See also ET March 15, 1977.

250 Carter: ET Dec. 30, 1977.

Moores: ET Jan. 4, 1978.

250-251 Controversy: ET Jan. 5, 7, 1978; DN Jan. 5, 7, 11, 1978.

Harbour Grace workers: DN Jan. 8; ET Jan. 14, 1978; UF Vol. 2 (n.s.), No. 1, p. 7.

Jamieson: ET Jan. 26, 1978.

251-252 Cashin: Copy of speech in NFFAWU files; report in ET Jan. 30, 1978.

252 Editorial: ET Jan. 31, 1978.

End of Nordzee proposal: ET Aug. 18; editorial Aug. 19, 1978.

Union joint ventures: UF Vol. 2 (n.s.), No. 7, pp. 3-4; No. 9, pp. 2-6. For academic comment on over-the-side sales, see Dennis Bartels, "Markets Without Merchants," and David Close, "Union Organized Fish Sales in Newfoundland."

253 Bulgarians: ET Aug. 11, 1978.

255 Crosbie, LeBlanc: ET Aug. 17, 19, 1978.

Cashin: ET Aug. 11, 1978.

256 Crosbie, Cashin: ET Aug. 18, 21, 22, 25, 1978.

257 Government of Newfoundland, *Setting a Course* Vol. I, pp. 5-21, and Vol. IV, p. 742.

Carter: DN Nov. 14, 1978; Newfoundland Department of Fisheries, *Fish is the Future: The Development Program for the Newfoundland and Labrador Fishing Industry to 1985.*

Conference: ET and DN Nov. 14, 15, 1978.

258 Wick Collins: ET Nov. 18, 1978.

Expansion: *Setting a Course* Vol. IV.

259 Carter: ET Dec. 15, 27, 1978.

CHAPTER 11

261 Inshore contracts: UF Vol 1 (n.s.), No. 2, p. 3.

264 Quotas, etc. see C.R. Levelton, *Toward an Atlantic Coast Commercial Fisheries Licensing Policy*, p. 35.

265 Government of Canada, Department of Fisheries and Oceans, *Annual Statistical Reviews.*

266 David Alexander, G.M. Story, *et al*, *Report of the Committee on Federal Licensing Policy*, p. 19.

Bona fide fishermen: UF Vol. 4 (n.s.), No. 2, pp. 14-15; No. 3, pp. 14-15.

Processing sector: *Setting a Course* Vol. 1, p. 23; Newfoundland and Labrador Department of Fisheries, *Annual Report*, 1980.

267 Union on northern cod: UF Vol. 1 (n.s.), No. 1, p. 11; Vol 2 (n.s.), No. 10, pp. 3-4; Vol 4 (n.s.), No. 1, pp. 5-12.

268 Voluntary recognition: UF Vol. 1 (n.s.), No. 2, pp. 3-4.

269 Negotiations: UF Vol. 3 (n.s.), No. 5, pp. 5-6; No. 6, p. 5.

The actual price structure for inshore fish includes a variety of prices for different species, different sizes of cod, and different gear types. A reviewer has pointed out that in attempting to simplify for narrative clarity, I have used as an index a price that is not quite accurate. It is close enough, however, to give the sense of the negotiations and settlements, so I have allowed the error to stand. Serious readers will undoubtedly wish to check the actual prices for themselves.

270 Cashin: UF Vol. 3 (n.s.), No. 6, p. 17.

For a summary of the 1980 strike, see Earle McCurdy, "In Solidarity, Newfoundland Fishermen Win Strike."

Company offer: ET June 13, 17, 1980.

1977 prices: UF Vol. 1 (n.s.), No. 4, p. 4.

271 Prices: ET June 17, 1980.

272 National Sea, Fishery Products: ET July 5, 9, 1980.

Fishermen: ET July 14, 1980.

273 Wells, fishermen: ET July 16, 18, 19, 21, 1980.

274 Hickey: ET July 26, Aug. 1, 2, 1980.

275 Peckford: ET July 23, 24, 1980.

276 McCurdy: ET July 26, 1980.

Advertisements: ET July 21, Aug. 2, 1980.

St. Anthony: ET Aug. 9, 11, 1980.

277 Collins: DN Aug. 13, 1980.

Wells: ET Aug. 11, 1980.

278 Parsons: ET Aug. 12, 1980.

St. Anthony: ET Aug. 15, 1980.

Royal Commission: ET Aug. 18, 20, 1980.

279 Quidi Vidi rally: ET, DN Aug. 22, 1980. Some of the description comes from eyewitness accounts.

280 Settlement: ET Aug. 23, 25, 26, 1980.

Picket signs: ET Sept. 26, 1980.

281 Cashin speech: copy in NFFAWU files.

Token increase: UF Vol. 5 (n.s.), No. 1.

282 Brose Paddock *et al*, *Report of the Royal Commission to Inquire into the Inshore Fishery of Newfoundland and Labrador* (in two volumes).

NFFAWU expansion: UF Vol. 5 (n.s.), No. 3, p. 11.

CHAPTER 12

285 Academic authority: Wallace Clement, "Unions, Cooperatives and Associations in Canada's Coastal Fisheries."

Maritime provinces: See, e.g., Sue Calhoun, *The Lockeport Lockout.*

Social movements: See Peter Sinclair, "Mobilizing the Nazi Movement."

290 Fishery in the Newfoundland economy: Parzival Copes, *Resettlement of Fishing Communities*, p. 57.

293 Cashin: ET Feb. 8, 1971.

293-294 Union in politics: UF Vol. 1, No. 2 (March 1971).

294 UF Vol. 1, No. 3 (August 1971).

295 Liberal vote: Parzival Copes, "The Fishermen's Vote in Newfoundland."

Quotation: Clinton S. Herrick *et al*, "Continuity and Change in Newfoundland Politics." See also Mark W. Graesser and Michael Wallack, "Social Mobilization and Voting in Newfoundland: An Ecological Regression Model of the 1962-72 Elections," and Ralph Matthews, "Perspectives on Recent Newfoundland Politics."

297 D. Drache and David Alexander, "Interview with Richard Cashin."

297-298 Cashin: UF Vol. 3 (n.s.), No. 1, p. 5.

299 J. Smucker, *Industrialization in Canada*, p. 213.

Bibliography

ALEXANDER, David

"Development and Dependence in Newfoundland." *Acadiensis* Vol. IV, No. 1, Autumn 1974.

"Newfoundland's Traditional Economy and Development to 1934." *Acadiensis* Vol. V, No. 2, Spring 1976.

"The Political Economy of Fishing in Newfoundland." *Journal of Canadian Studies* Vol. XI, No. 1, 1976.

The Decay of Trade: An Economic History of the Newfoundland Saltfish Trade, 1935-1965. Newfoundland Social and Economic Studies No. 19, Institute of Social and Economic Research, Memorial University of Newfoundland, St. John's, 1977.

ALEXANDER, David, G.M. Story *et al.*

Report of the Committee on Federal Licensing Policy and its Implications for the Newfoundland Fisheries. Memorial University, 1974.

AMULREE, William Warrender Mackenzie, baron (*et al.*)

Newfoundland Royal Commission Report. H.M. Stationery Office, London, 1933.

BARTELS, Dennis

"Markets Without Merchants: The Political Economy of the Newfoundland Fishermen, Food, and Allied Workers Union's Direct Sales to Bulgaria and Sweden." *Canadian Journal of Anthropology/Revue Canadienne d'Anthropologie* Vol. 2, No. 1, Spring 1981.

BRODY, David

The Butcher Workmen: A Study of Unionization. Harvard University Press, Cambridge, 1964.

BROWNE: William J.

Eighty-four Years a Newfoundlander: Memoirs Vol. I. Dicks and Co., St. John's, 1981.

Eighty-seven Years a Newfoundlander: Memoirs Vol. II. Dicks and Co., St. John's, 1984.

BROX, Ottar

Newfoundland Fishermen in the Age of Industry: A Sociology of Economic Dualism. Newfoundland Social and Economic Studies No. 9. Institute of Social and Economic Research, Memorial University, St. John's, 1972.

CALHOUN, Sue

The Lockeport Lockout. Lockeport Lockout, Halifax, 1983.

CAMERON, Silver Donald

The Education of Everett Richardson: The Nova Scotia Fishermen's Strike 1970-71. McClelland and Stewart, Toronto, 1977.

CANADA, Department of Fisheries and Oceans, Economic Policy Branch, Economics Development Directorate.

Annual Statistical Review of Canadian Fisheries.

CANNING, *Stratford*

A Policy Framework for a Licensing System in the Newfoundland Inshore Fisheries. Interim Report prepared for the Department of Fisheries and Oceans, Newfoundland Region, 1979. Ms. in author's possession.

CASANOVA, Giacomo

History of My Life. Translated by Willard R. Trask. Harcourt, Brace, New York, 1966.

CASHIN, Major Peter

My Life and Times 1890-1919. Edited by R.E. Beuhler, Breakwater, St. John's, 1976.

CHADWICK, St. John

Newfoundland: Island into Province. Cambridge, at the University Press, 1967.

CLOSE, David

"Union Organized Fish Sales in Newfoundland." *Journal of Canadian Studies* Vol. 17, No. 2, Summer, 1982.

CLEMENT, Wallace

"Unions, Cooperatives and Associations in Canada's Coastal Fisheries." Paper presented at Annual Meetings of Canadian Political Science Association, 1983. Ms. in author's possession.

COAKER, W.F.

History of the Fishermen's Protective Union of Newfoundland from 1909 to 1929. Advocate Publishing Co., St. John's, 1930.

COHEN, Maxwell

Report of the Royal Commission on Labour Legislation in Newfoundland and Labrador. The Commission, St. John's, 1972.

COPES, Parzival

"The Fishermen's Vote in Newfoundland." Department of Economics and Commerce, Simon Fraser University, Discussion Paper 70-1-1, 1970.

The Resettlement of Fishing Communities in Newfoundland. Canadian Council on Rural Development, 1972.

DOUGLAS, Fred G.

"A Brief General History of the Town of Fortune." Ms. in Centre for Newfoundland Studies, Memorial University, 1973.

DRACHE, D. and David Alexander

"Interview with Richard Cashin." *This Magazine* Vol. 9, No. 4, September, 1975.

FELTHAM, John

The Development of the FPU in Newfoundland (1908-1923). Unpublished M.A. thesis, Memorial University, 1959

GAFFNEY, Michael Edward

Crosshanded: Work Organization and Values in a Newfoundland Fishery. Unpublished Ph.D. Dissertation, Ohio State University, 1982.

GILLESPIE, William E.

A History of the Newfoundland Federation of Labour 1936-1963. Unpublished M.A. Thesis, Memorial University, 1980.

GRAESSER, Mark W., and Michael Wallack

"Social Mobilization and Voting in Newfoundland: An Ecological Regression Model of the 1962-72 Elections." Paper presented to the Annual Meeting of the Atlantic Provinces Political Studies Association, 1976. Ms. in Centre for Newfoundland Studies, Memorial University.

GRIFFIN, Harold (ed.)

A Ripple, A Wave: The Story of Union Organization in the B.C. Fishing Industry. (From a draft Manuscript by George North.) Fisherman Publishing Society, Vancouver, 1974.

GUY, Ray

"Newfoundlanders and Mainlanders." *Canadian Forum* Vol. LIII, No. 638, March 1974.

GWYN, Richard

Smallwood, The Unlikely Revolutionary. McClelland and Stewart, Toronto, 1968.

HANDCOCK, W. Gordon

"English Migration to Newfoundland." In John J. Mannion (ed.), *The Peopling of Newfoundland: Essays in Historical Geography*. Social and Economic Papers No. 8, Institute for Social and Economic Research, Memorial University, St. John's, 1977.

HANNA, Hilton E., and Joseph Belsky

The 'Pat' Gorman Story: Picket and Pen. American Institute of Social Science, Yonkers, 1960.

HARRIS, L., E. Johnson, and P. Russell

Report of the Conciliation Board Appointed in the Matter of the Fishing Industry (Collective Bargaining) Act and in the Matter of a Dispute Between the Newfoundland Fishermen, Food and Allied Workers Union, Local 465 and B.C. Packers Limited, Atlantic Fish, Division of Consolidated Foods Limited, National Sea Products Limited, Fishery Products Limited, and Booth Fisheries, 1974.

HATTENHAUER, Rolfe G.

A Brief Labour History of Newfoundland. Prepared for the Royal Commission on Labour Legislation in Newfoundland and Labrador, 1970. Ms. in Centre for Newfoundland Studies, Memorial University.

HERRICK, Clinton S., Paul S. Dinham, and Mollie O'Neill

"Continuity and Change in Newfoundland Politics: The Election of 1971." Paper presented to the annual meeting of the Association of Atlantic Sociologists and Anthropologists, 1972. Ms. in Centre for Newfoundland Studies, Memorial University.

HODDER, L.L.

A Brief History of the Society of United Fishermen, 1873-1975. SUF, St. John's, 1973.

HUTCHINGS, J.W.

Report of the Proceedings at the Fishermen's Convention Held at the Gaiety Theatre, St. John's, April 2nd-April 9, 1951. Dicks and Company, St. John's, 1951.

LAIDLAW, Alexander F. (ed.)

The Man From Margaree: Writings and Speeches of M.M. *Coady*. McClelland and Stewart, Toronto, 1971.

LODGE, T.

Dictatorship in Newfoundland. Cassell and Company, London, 1939.

LEVELTON, C.R.

Toward an Atlatic Coast Commercial Fisheries Licensing System. A Report prepared for the Department of Fisheries and Oceans, Government of Canada, 1979.

MACDONALD, David

Power Begins at the Cod End: The Newfoundland Trawlermen's Strike, 1974-75. Social and Economic Studies No. 26. Institute of Social and Economic Research, Memorial University of Newfoundland, St. John's, 1980.

MATTHEWS, Ralph

"Perspectives on Recent Newfoundland Politics." *Journal of Canadian Studies* Vol. 9, 1974, pp. 24-27.

McCURDY, Earle

"In Solidarity, Newfoundland Fishermen Win Strike." *Canadian Labour* Vol. 25, No. 14, 1980.

McDONALD, Ian

W.F. Coaker and the Fishermen's Protective Union in Newfoundland Politics 1908-1925. Unpublished Ph.D. thesis, University of London, 1971.

MOWAT, Farley

A Whale for the Killing. McClelland and Stewart, Toronto, 1977.

NEARY, Peter

"The Issue of Confederation in Newfoundland, 1864-1949," 1974. Ms. in Centre for Newfoundland Studies, Memorial University.

"Canadian Immigration Policy and the Newfoundlanders 1912-1939." *Acadiensis*, Vol. XI, No. 2, Spring, 1982.

NEARY, P.F., and S.J.R. Noel

"Continuity and Change in Newfoundland Politics," 1971. Ms. in Centre for Newfoundland Studies, Memorial University.

NEWFOUNDLAND AND LABRADOR, Department of Fisheries

Setting a Course: A Regional Strategy for Development of the Newfoundland Fishing Industry, 6 Volumes, 1978.

Fish is the Future: A Development Plan for the Newfoundland and Labrador Fishing Industry to 1985, (Brochure) 1978.

NEWFOUNDLAND AND LABRADOR, Planning and Priorities Secretariat, Economic and Resource Policy Division.

The Newfoundland Economy, Outlook 1974.

NEWFOUNDLAND AND LABRADOR, *Treasury Board, Fiscal Policy Division*

The Economy, Mid-Year, 1972.

NFFAWU

Founding Convention, Newfoundland Fishermen, Food, and Allied Workers, Hotel Newfoundland, April 26, 27, 28, 1971. Coordinated and recorded by the Extension Division of Memorial University, St. John's, 1971.

Message From the Trawlermen. Mimeographed pamphlet, 1974.

NOEL, S.J.R.

Politics in Newfoundland. University of Toronto Press, Toronto, 1971.

NORDCO

It Were Well to Live Mainly Off Fish: The Place of the Northern Cod in Newfoundland's Development. (A report prepared for the Government of Newfoundland and Labrador) Jesperson, St. John's, 1981.

NRDA

First Annual Conference of the Northern Regional Development Association (NRDA). Prepared by the Extension Service, Memorial University, 1969. Copy in possession of the author.

O'BRIEN, Janet

"Collective Bargaining in the Fishing Industry of Newfoundland." 1977. Ms. in Centre for Newfoundland Studies, Memorial University.

PADDOCK, Brose, *et al.*

Report of the Royal Commission to Inquire into the Inshore Fishery of Newfoundland and Labrador. St. John's, Phase I, 1980, Phases II and III, 1981.

SINCLAIR, Peter

"Mobilizing the Nazi Movement." Ms. 1981.

SMALLWOOD, J.R.

Coaker of Newfoundland. Labour Publishing Company, London, 1927.

SMUCKER, J.

Industrialization in Canada. Prentice Hall (Canada), Scarborough, 1980.

STEWART, Walter

Strike! McClelland and Stewart, Toronto, 1977.

WARNER, William W.

Distant Water: The Fate of the North Atlantic Fisherman. Penguin, Harmondsworth, 1984. (First published by Little, Brown, 1983.)

Index

Printed in Canada